BEHAVING BADLY

*This volume is dedicated by the editors
to their parents*

Behaving Badly

Social Panic and Moral Outrage –
Victorian and Modern Parallels

Edited by

JUDITH ROWBOTHAM and KIM STEVENSON
Nottingham Trent University, UK

Published by
Ashgate Publishing Limited
Wey Court East
Union Road
Farnham
Surrey, GU9 7PT
England

Ashgate Publishing Company
110 Cherry Street
Suite 3-1
Burlington, VT 05401-3818
USA

www.ashgate.com

British Library Cataloguing in Publication Data
Behaving badly :social panic and moral outrage
    – Victorian and modern parallels
    1.Crime - Great Britain - History - 19th century 2.Crime -
    Great Britain - History - 20th century 3.Crime - Great
    Britain - Public opinion 4.Deviant behavior - Great Britain
    - Public opinion 5. Great Britain - Public opinion
    I.Rowbotham, Judith II.Stevenson, Kim
    364.9'4109034

Library of Congress Cataloging-in-Publication Data
Behaving badly : social panic and moral outrage--Victorian and modern parallels / edited
    by Judith Rowbotham and Kim Stevenson.
        p. cm.
    Includes bibliographical references and index.
    ISBN 0-7546-0965 0 (alk. paper)
    1.Crime--Great Britain--History--19th century. 2. Crime--Great Britain--History--20th
    century. 3. Crime--Great Britain--Public opinion--History. 4. Deviant behavior--Great
    Britain--Public opinion--History. 5. Criminal law--Great Britain. I. Rowbotham, Judith.
    II. Stevenson, Kim.

HV6943.B43 2003
364.9'41'09034--dc21   2002028369

ISBN 978 0 7546 0965 0

Transferred to Digital Printing 2014

MIX
Paper from
responsible sources
FSC
www.fsc.org   FSC® C004959

Printed and bound in Great Britain
by Printondemand-worldwide.com

Contents

Contributors

Mike Ahearne is Senior Lecturer in Criminology at Nottingham Trent University where his teaching and research interests are on issues relating to drugs, corporate crime and gambling. Previous publications include 'Beccaria: A Suitable Case for Reconstruction', Occasional Paper Series 1994, Centre for Criminology, Middlesex University.

David Bentley was appointed QC in 1984. Subsequently, he was appointed Recorder of the Crown Court 1985. He has been a Circuit judge since 1988 sitting mainly in Sheffield, Hull and York trying crime; and sitting in London as a Deputy High Court judge. Designated Civil Judge for South Yorkshire since 1998. He is also a legal historian and author of three books: *Select Cases from the Twelve Judges' Notebooks*, 1997, *English Criminal Justice in the Nineteenth Century*, 1998 and *Victorian Men of Law*, 2000, as well as of various articles on legal history

Susan Edwards BA., MA., Ph.D., LLM is Associate Dean of the School of Law, University of Buckingham. A widely-respected academic and lawyer, she is currently a consultant to the Home Office Crime Reduction Unit on Domestic Violence and to the Crown Prosecution Service on Expert Witness Project. She has published widely in the field of domestic and sexual violence and is the author of *Female Sexuality and the Law*, and *Sex, Gender and the Legal Process*.

Roger Hopkins Burke is Senior Lecturer in Criminology at Nottingham Trent University, Director of the Nottingham Crime Research Unit and one of the five Faculty Co-ordinators of The SOLON Partnership. An active researcher and commentator on police and disorder, his recent publications include *Zero Tolerance Policing* (Perpetuity Press, 1998) and *An Introduction to Criminological Theory* (Willan Press, 2001).

Judith Knelman, Professor Emerita of the University of Western Ontario, taught in the Faculty of Media and Information Studies. An active researcher in the field of women and crime, most recently she is the author of *Twisting in the Wind: The Murderess and the English Press* (University of Toronto Press, 1998) and 'Can We Believe What the Newspapers Tell Us?: Missing Links in "Alias Grace"', *University of Toronto Quarterly*, 1999, 68, 2.

Tom Lewis is a solicitor and Senior Lecturer in Law at Nottingham Trent University. Publications include: 'The Human Rights Act 1998, Section 12 – Press Freedom over Privacy?' (with Jonathan Griffiths) *Entertainment Law Review*, 1999, 8; 'Rights of Passage: Highways, Demonstrations and the House of Lords', *Nottingham Law Journal*, 1999, 8; co-editor, *Healthcare Law: the Impact of the Human Rights Act* (Cavendish, London, 2001).

David Nash is Senior Lecturer in History at Oxford Brookes University. He has written extensively on aspects of secularism and republicanism in Victorian England. His interest in the interface between law, religion and class formation shapes his current research, with plans for future publications in the area. Recent publications include *Blasphemy in Britain 1789–Present* (Ashgate, 1999). He is currently writing *Blasphemy in the West* for Oxford University Press.

Kiron Reid is a Lecturer in Law at the University of Liverpool, having previously taught law at the Universities of Leeds and Kent. His legal writing has been published in leading criminal law journals. In 2001 he was a principal speaker in the Office of the High Representative Bosnia-Hercegovina Legal Workshops, speaking on peaceful protest, police powers and human rights.

M. E. Rodgers is a solicitor and Senior Lecturer in Law at Nottingham Trent University. Her areas of research cover family law, medical law and criminology. Recent publications include 'Mental Health Nursing' in *Nursing Law and Ethics* 2nd edn (forthcoming). Co-authored with Michael Gunn, 'Protection for Whom? The right to a sexual or intimate relationship', *Journal of Learning Disabilities*, 2000, 4, 3.

Judith Rowbotham is Senior Lecturer in History at Nottingham Trent University and Co-Director of The SOLON Partnership. An active researcher, using printed matter as an historical source, she has recently worked on the popular presentation of foreign missions in Britain, and is now combining her interests in colonial perspectives with the history and contemporary relevance of 'bad' behaviour and crime. As well as many conference papers, her recent publications include: '"Soldiers of Christ"? Images of Female Missionaries in the late C19. Issues of Heroism and Martyrdom', *Gender and History*, April, 2000; 'Utopian Visions? The Dream of the Code Victoria in Criminal Law', with Kim Stevenson, *Nottingham Law Journal*, Autumn 2000; 'Only When Drunk!: The Stereotyping of Violence, c1850-1900', in S. D'Cruze (ed), *Everyday Violence in Britain, c1850-1950: Class and Gender*, Longmans, 2000; 'Ministering Angels, Not Ministers: Women's Involvement in the Foreign

Missionary Movement, c.1860-1910' in S. Morgan (ed), *Women, Religion and Feminism in Britain 1750-1900* (Palgrave, 2002).

Kim Stevenson is Senior Lecturer in Law at Nottingham Trent University and Co-Director of The SOLON Partnership. Her main research areas are sexual offences and sexuality, particularly from a historical perspective. Recent publications include 'Unequivocal Victims: the Development of the Historical Mystification of the Female Complainant in Rape Cases', *Feminist Legal Studies*, 2000, 8/3; '"Ingenuities of the Female Mind": Legal and Public Perceptions of Sexual Violence in Victorian England 1850-1890' in Shani D'Cruz (ed.) *Everyday Violence in Britain c1850-1950*: (2000, Longmans). With Judith Rowbotham she is also co-editor of *Criminal Conversations: Victorians Behaving Badly – the Modern Echoes* (forthcoming Ohio State Press, 2003).

Richard Stone is a Visiting Professor at the Institute of Law, City University. A respected academic lawyer, his publications include *Textbook on Civil Liberties and Human Rights* (Blackstone Press, 2000), 3rd edition, *Entry, Search and Seizure* (Sweet and Maxwell, 1997), and 'Breach of the Peace: the Case for Abolition', *Web Journal of Current Legal Issues*, 2001, 2.

Gavin Sutter is a Research Fellow with the Information Technology Law Unit of the Centre for Commercial Law Studies at the University of London. He has published a number of papers on subjects including electronic payment systems, internet censorship and interception of electronic communications. His views on computer pornography and workplace sexual harassment have been quoted in *Shine*, a magazine marketed at women in their late twenties. He is researching a PhD thesis in cross-border enforcement of internet content regulation.

Sarah Wilson is Lecturer in Law at Keele University. Her teaching interests in Company Law and Financial Crime, the Criminal Process and Business Policy are strongly reflective of her key research interest in the historical origins of modern business crime. Most recently she has published with Gary Wilson (Senior Lecturer at Leeds University) '"Responsible risk takers": Notions of Directorial Responsibility – Past, Present and Future', *Journal of Corporate Law Studies*, 2001, 1.

Tom Williamson recently retired from the post of Deputy Chief Constable of Nottinghamshire Police. He is a chartered forensic psychologist and Senior Research Fellow at the Institute of Criminal Justice Studies, University of Portsmouth where his main research areas are policing and management, miscarriages of justice and investigative interviewing. His publications include 'From interrogation to investigative interviewing: Strategic trends in police questioning', *Journal of Community and Applied Social Psychology*, 1993, 3;

'Police investigation: the changing criminal justice context' in F. Leishman, B. Loveday and S. Savage (eds), *Core Issues in Policing*, (Longman, 1996); 'London Policing: the changing criminal justice context – twenty-five years of missed opportunities' in F. Leishman *et al* (eds), *Core Issues in Policing* (Longman, 2000), 2nd edn.

Foreword

Len Findlay

Individual acts that attract the attention of citizens, authorities, the media, are often apprehended and represented as *both* unique *and* as contributions to trends, patterns, or episodes in a familiar or unfolding story. Of course, to some extent all events are both *sui generis* and more broadly generic. It is a matter of emphasis, not essence, that distinguishes them from each other. However, the particular emphasis placed on an instance of troubling behaviour can itself be seen as apt or unwarranted, even good or bad, depending on the level of public scrutiny the act has attracted. Thus the tragic events in the United States on September 11, 2001, for example, were seen as an act of *unprecedented* evil directed against freedom and civilisation, and also as the predictable though twisted *response* of religious fanatics to American hegemony in general, and American policy in the Middle East in particular. As one of the most virulent forms of bad behaviour, if not indeed its ultimate example in the modern world, terrorism activates social panics that help mobilise the 'national insecurity state' and set it on a war footing, even if the 'war' in question is claimed to be more 'asymmetrical' than ever before and thus, perhaps, like the 'war on drugs', not really a war at all.[1]

However, such mobilisation through panic can only discourage, not permanently prohibit, searching for answers beyond the simplicities of demonisation and the placement of catastrophe outside history. And so in due course doubts are more openly voiced and increasingly heeded, causality and culpability are redistributed more complexly than on separate sides of an insuperable divide separating good from evil, 'us' from 'them'. If September 11 can be connected to all sorts of analogues and antecedents, then it can no longer mean one (American) thing. Accordingly, 'freedom itself' escapes its patriotic leash and attempts to monopolise its meanings,

---

[1] See Reg Whitaker and Gary Marcuse, *Cold War Canada: The Making of a National Insecurity State* (University of Toronto Press, Toronto, 1994). For an academic attempt to influence the Canadian government's reaction to September 11 by putting independent analysis in the hands of parliamentarians during the development of legislation, see Ronald J. Daniels, Patrick Macklem, and Kent Roach, *The Security of Freedom: Essays on Canada's Anti-Terrorism Bill* (University of Toronto Press, Toronto, 2001).

and civilisation refuses to remain monologic and megaphonic, resuming instead those forms of more equitable, less vehement exchange which permit, if indeed they do not require, disagreement and scepticism within and beyond a temporarily coercive consensus. The moment of social panic is reabsorbed in the contingent conversations that throw up less charged but no less pertinent questions than the understandably uncomprehending, 'Why do they hate us?'. After the initial denial and shock, for example, what do you decide to name the perpetrators of such acts? What do you call their hosts and supporters? How do you bring the surviving culprits to justice, and to whose justice? What use is international law if it is respected by major powers only when it suits them? Is punitive violence ever a remedy for despair? How can a loose allegation such as the 'axis of evil' (Iran, Iraq, and North Korea), become the basis of defensible foreign policy for the custodians of 'infinite justice', 'enduring freedom', and other globalising euphemisms?

In sum, the unquestionable cannot be always and only that. The incomparable will sooner or later generate comparisons as part of the uncertain but necessary process of making sense of things that matter. To be sure, comparison is neither a simple nor ever a neutral process. And this is especially true when it is part of a broader moral urging to make comparisons less invidious, separations less insuperably estranging, as in E. M. Forster's famous exhortation in the context of Britain's ongoing struggle to deal justly with diversity at home and in the empire, 'Only connect'.[2] The Victorians knew this struggle only too well. Indeed, the remarkable flourishing of historiography, comparative philology, or the comparative method in the natural and life sciences during the Victorian period attests to the need during volatile and immensely acquisitive times to connect and compare past and present, genus and species, me and you, us and them. The pointed comparisons of Chateaubriand's *Génie du christianisme* (1802) inspired the memorable architectural juxtapositions of Pugin's *Contrasts; or, a Parallel between the Noble Edifices of the Fourteenth and Fifteenth Centuries, and Similar Buildings of the Present Day; shewing the Present Decay of Taste* (1836), the more radical anti-modernism of Carlyle's *Past and Present* (1843), and so much more. This is not to say that comparisons offered or required a simple choice between alternatives. Disraeli's vision of the 'two nations' in *Sybil* (1845), the divisively gendered world of literary culture in Elizabeth Barrett Browning's proto-feminist epic poem, *Aurora Leigh* (1856), the famous 'best of times ...worst of times' declaration of Dickens' most concertedly comparative novel, *A Tale of Two Cities* (1859), were part of a collective

---

[2] E. M. Forster, *Howard's End* (Penguin, London, 1988), ch. 22.

effort to educate authors and their publics so that social mobility could constructively channel the energies of revolutionary *mobilité* that led so readily to panic and disorder. Also at issue was the need to avoid that economic and cultural backwardness, those differences apparently frozen in time and space, that Hegel termed 'the antitheses of Asia'.[3]

The Victorians, then, in all their diversity of interest and need, could have little quarrel with any effort to use them in turn as a quarry for comparisons. If the difference between a revolt and a revolution was indeed that revolutionaries had to do their history, then history would either be claimed as a revolutionary instrument or reclaimed as well by those who saw reaction or reform as the better option. Any professed return to 'Victorian values' is the beginning of an exploration and not the end of a discussion, because what those values were remains a matter of lively dispute that helps define the living disputants as well as the dead of whom they write, whether 'eminent' in the Strachey sense or otherwise. The SOLON project and the activities pursued under the rubric of Bad Behaviour offer timely and important resistance to the remorseless focus on the present moment in so much of contemporary life. But this is not the heritage industry at work in a more academic register, looking to the past with a decidedly escapist gaze. It is instead an engagement with the present through a re-appropriation of the past, and in terms of the crucial intersections of law and culture where justice can seem as imposing and palpable a presence as the buildings dedicated to it, or as elusive and unsettlingly self-satisfied as the Cheshire Cat. Investigation is rarely free of invention, upon the bench or beyond it, whether the matter at hand is *visible* or not, and this is especially true in politically uncertain times, as John Barrell has reminded us so compellingly recently.[4]

If one looks, as I have been doing recently, at the policing and media representation of activities coinciding with meetings of the World Trade Organisation, G8, and Free Trade Association of the Americas, it is easy to make comparisons between jurisdictions and across the international media. One can see how readily bad behaviour is assimilated to anti-youth stereotypes, how virtually any coalition involving organised labour raises venerable fears and rancour among the wealthy, and how some interests pursued in the public domain are dismissed as 'special' while others are perceived as universal, and even universally beneficial. Violence is understood largely as property damage, threatened trespass, and challenging

---

[3] Georg Wilhelm Friedrich Hegel, *Lectures on the Philosophy of World History*, trans. H. B. Nisbet, Duncan Forbes, Introduction (Cambridge University Press, Cambridge, 1975), p. 195.

[4] John Barrell, *Imagining the King's Death: Figurative Treason, Fantasies of Regicide 1793-1796* (Oxford University Press, Oxford, 2000).

the police, a reductive interpretation designed to criminalise dissent in the public mind. Behaviour that hovers between illegality and civic activism in order to make certain concerns and values more broadly visible, remains an intriguing index of democratic freedoms and the powers of government, the judiciary, and the mass media to frame or spin them in alarmist or dismissive ways. But we need to follow that index in time as well as across national borders. While writing about events at the Quebec City Summit of the Americas which took place in Spring of 2001, for example, I found myself thinking, not about, say, the treatment of the Gordon Riots in Dickens' *Barnaby Rudge* or about rick-burning in George Eliot's *Felix Holt the Radical*, but about smaller scale staging of dissent in chapter 22 of Thomas Hardy's *The Mayor of Casterbridge*, a novel whose many versions of public humiliation and disgrace are attentive to the influence of the big battalions − particularly the power of industrial capital and modern accounting to transform agriculture and the face and faces of the British countryside − but attentive also to the nourishing or punitive cultural particulars that help define, sustain, and disfigure one or another way of life.

It might seem more than a stretch to connect fiction and fact, the 'skimmington ride' in a late Victorian English novel undertaken to expose the moral turpitude of prominent citizens, and the use of a catapult that pretended to fire contaminated teddy bears to protest the hidden agenda of those meetings inside the Wall of Shame in Quebec city under the elite aegis of The Free Trade Association of the Americas.[5] But class, gender, and regional politics of food production are at the heart of both incidents, as is the endless ingenuity and resolve evinced by those who behave badly on principle. Like the resentful 'miserables' in a fictional Victorian slum, the youthful protestors in a World Heritage city internally divided by a successor to the Berlin Wall were not fully aware of the significance of their own mischief, far less in control of how that mischief would be interpreted by others as reason for panic. Such analogies point to the virtues, vulnerabilities, and complexities of behaving badly within increasingly regulated public spaces where technologies of surveillance and enforcement lay open the insecurities at the heart of security, and detect the social toxins accumulating behind even the most pristine public facade. Casterbridge, and Quebec City may stand here as undeveloped, preliminary signage for the carefully considered and highly suggestive comparisons and historical convergences in this book, where scholars accept the risks and reap the rewards of a topic as important but tricky as Behaving Badly.

---

[5] See L. M. Findlay, 'Desperately Seeking Sanctuary: Learning from APEC, or Not', forthcoming, *Review of Education/Pedagogy Cultural Studies*, 24, 1&2 (2002).

Preface and Acknowledgements

This is an interdisciplinary volume, with chapters from a range of disciplinary perspectives, focusing upon the ways in which anti-social behaviour, including crime, is stereotyped, presented and managed. As such it is a reflection of the strategies of the SOLON project. Preliminary airings of the chapters were given as papers at the 'Behaving Badly conference' held in Nottingham in September 2001, and the final versions were honed by the debates promoted by the conference and the resources of the SOLON Partnership. The conference was organised by SOLON, an interdisciplinary project based around a Partnership between Nottingham Trent University and the Museum of Law in Nottingham, which brings together academics, professionals and practitioners concerned with Bad Behaviour, and promotes its agenda through mechanisms such as the ESRC-funded SOLON database pilot scheme. An ESRC small grant has supported development of a pilot qualitative database of newspaper references to bad behaviour and crime, from the Victorian and modern periods. The database has supported the development of several of the chapters in this volume, and may be freely accessed through *http://solon.ntu.ac.uk*.

To maintain disciplinary integrity and, consequently, the useful accessibility of this volume to a range of disciplines and professions, it has been decided to use the approved legal systems of citation of cases and statutes, thus providing tables of cases and of statutes, as well as a thematic index. This means an amount of overlap, and the use of certain thematic entries in the index which are not usual for lawyers, but which less specialist readers in the area of law will find useful as pointers to topics of interest to them. A guide to legal citations is also provided with the list of abbreviations.

The editors acknowledge, with gratitude, the help and support of the Museum of Law and its personnel, including the CEO, Peter Armstrong, the Archivist, Bev Baker, and the Education Officer, Tim Desmond; and also the Department of Academic Legal Studies and the Economic and Social Sciences Department at Nottingham Trent University, including Professors Peter Jones, Michael Gunn, and David Webb, in forwarding the SOLON project and consequently, this volume. The Library staff at Nottingham Trent University, notably Terry Hanstock, have also been a constant support and necessary resource, in the development of the database as well as this volume. On behalf of all the contributors, we thank the staff at the Public

Records Office and British Library staff at St Pancras for their help. The editors also owe a particular debt of gratitude to the staff at the British Library Staff at Colindale for their unflagging kindness to us when we were researching material for the newspaper database. As well as the chapter contributors, whom the editors thank warmly for their efforts and insights, the members of the SOLON membership network, including Professor Len Findlay who has kindly provided our Foreword, have provided an intellectually stimulating context for the evolution of these chapters – they are too numerous to mention individually, but our gratitude to them is no less. We thank, also, our typesetter, Dr. Robert Preston of Westfield Typesetting for his kind advice and attention to detail, above and beyond the normal, and Rosemary Rix, who so nobly gave her time to checking the proofs for us and to making suitably trenchant comments on the contents! Finally, the SOLON Research Assistant, Paul Baker, has been a central figure in development of the database, has helped to keep the editors sane (no easy task) and acted as an important point of contact for all those involved in the production of the volume – mere thanks are an inadequate recompense for all he has done but we offer them gratefully none the less.

Abbreviations, Conventions and Notes on Legal Terminology

In an interdisciplinary text of this nature, it has been decided to avoid abbreviations as far as possible, since well-known acronyms to one discipline may not always be more widely familiar. However, the following should be noted:

ACPO   Association of Chief Police Officers
AG   Attorney General
ASBO   Anti-Social Behaviour Order
BBFC   British Board of Film Classification
BCS   British Crime Survey(s)
DPP   Director of Public Prosecutions
CPS   Crown Prosecution Service
ECHR   European Convention on Human Rights
ECtHR   European Court of Human Rights
EU   European Union
ISP   Internet Service Provider
MP   Member of Parliament
J   Justice
LCJ   Lord Chief Justice
LJ   Lord Justice
OAPA   Offences Against the Person Act
OPA   Obscene Publications Act
PACE   Police and Criminal Evidence Act
PRO   Public Records Office
QBD   Queen's Bench Division
SFO   Serious Fraud Office

Notes on Sources Used

Various series of *Hansard* are referred to. The overall reference however, is simply to *Hansard*, and to the year and relevant volume number and either column or page numbers.

Much use of newspapers has been made. Nineteenth century references in particular are available via the SOLON database, at http://solon.ntu.ac.uk.

Notes on Legal Terminology

Actus reus refers to the physical elements of an offence i.e. criminal conduct; *mens rea* refers to the mental elements of an offence i.e. criminal intention.

Deciphering Case Citations for Non-Lawyers

Annually, some 2,500 English court cases are fully reported in a variety of law report series, usually where a particular point of law is clarified or interpreted. Every law report has its own mode of citation which includes the abbreviation of the law report series, the year the case was reported, the volume number where appropriate and the number of the page where the report starts. Hence [1995] 1 All ER 513 refers to the case of *R v Somerset County Council, ex parte Fewings* which can be found in **volume 1** of **The All England Reports** for **1995** starting at page **513**. The citation will not, however, identify which court the case was heard in. Official reports such as **QB – Queen's Bench Division** do, but equally **AC – Appeal Cases** do not!

From 2001 a form of neutral citation has been used by the House of Lords, the Court of Appeal and the Administrative Court with a unique number being allocated to each judgment of these courts as in *R v A* [2001] UKHL 25 – the **25th** numbered judgment of the year **2001** in the **House of Lords**.

Pre-1865 citations can be particularly disconcerting as there was a proliferation of law reports series during that period. Most of the major series have been gathered together and reprinted to form the **The English Reports** and **The Revised Reports**, for example, **(1853) 1 EL & BL 435** refers to the case of *R v Dugdale* reported in the report series of **Ellis & Blackburn 1851-1858**. Many Victorian criminal cases can also be found in **Cox C C – Cox's Criminal Cases**. An index for all the abbreviations used can be found in Donald Raistrick, Index to Legal Citations and Abbreviations, 2nd ed. (Bowker-Saur, London, 1993).

Table of Statutes

Table of Cases

Introduction: Behaving Badly

Judith Rowbotham and Kim Stevenson

Bad Behaviour

Bad behaviour, including crime, is an ever-present element in society, across time and location. It is, of course, the crime element in bad behaviour that receives the most serious and sustained attention, because it goes beyond the merely offensive to establish itself as an offence against a canon of laws, not just rules of conduct. Yet one problem with a single focus on crime and criminality, particularly when the spotlight is centred on just one type of serious crime, is that crime can seem immutable as well as ever-present. After all, it could be said that murder is murder is murder – or is it? A very complex set of issues is now, as it has always been, involved in deciding what constitutes murder for any society at any time. Understanding the essentially fluid boundary between the criminal and the anti-social is made further convoluted in British history by the complexities of the interaction between the gaze of the legal professionals, and of popular understanding. Despite ready assumptions of a coincidence of view across these gazepoints, such a unity of comprehension has not, in British experience, been a distinguishing factor of the last two centuries. There has not even been a unity of perspective between disciplines, since the parameters of different disciplines are based on individual agendas of research leading to end analysis and conclusions appropriate to those disciplines.

Yet where the same material is used to different ends, it is not always plain to even fellow academics that work done in one discipline makes significantly different assumptions to that of another. This is important, because crime has provided a focus of interest both to those intellectually concerned with the behaviour of society, and to those practically involved in or affected by the expressions of crime. A failure to invoke the historical dimensions to these issues is a major weakness, but so, too, is a habit of historical reference which implicitly assumes a logical 'progression' of events. This volume has brought together a range of disciplinary and practitioner perspectives on the issue of 'Bad Behaviour' (a label chosen because it enables a movement outside the stricter limits of what is actually an offence in legal terms) which have resulted from genuine interchange of ideas and an exploration of different assumptions.

We believe that a consideration of crime alone is inadequate when seeking to understand the defining factors of what constitutes an offence, and what is simply bad behaviour, let alone when seeking comprehension of the wider legal processes associated with dealing with crime and punishment. Scholars, professionals and practitioners debating these concepts, whether intellectually or as part of practical daily strategies, become participants in a set of wide-ranging discourses on the nature of society and societal behaviour, past and present. These discourses are self-evidently interdisciplinary in their intellectual remit, multi-agency in their practical applicability. They have the capacity to influence popular understandings of the ways in which society should react to the badly behaved and the actual 'criminal', according to the law, as well as to influence government policy and legal practice in this area. But where does the boundary lie between bad behaviour and crime? Any examination of crime across even a short period of time shows how fluid, within a single society, that boundary is, raising questions about how and why such boundaries shift.

This volume sets out to explore the dimensions of bad behaviour and its mutation into crime through a series of chapters examining aspects of crime and offensive conduct, and the ways in which aspects of this anti-social behaviour is presented for popular consumption, both reflecting and feeding popular understandings of how to identify it. In itself, this is no new thing, but where this volume differs is in its desire not just to explore the wider socio-cultural contexts which promote offending and the offensive, including issues of visibility, but also to challenge present complacencies by linking together two periods – the Victorian and the present. These have been chosen because there are a number of important resonances in areas relevant to the 'bad behaviour' focus of this volume. Both are perceived contemporaneously as periods of very significant socio-cultural, economic and political change. Developments, especially those associated with the impact of new technology, not only promoted fears which also linked (though with different nuances) to concerns about demographic growth and shifts in demographic patterns, but also related to alterations in many aspects of British social organisation, cultural attitudes, and economic performance.

For the Victorian period, especially the years 1848 to 1885, fluctuating economic fortunes combined with both pride and concern over new developments to produce what may be called an atmosphere of equally fluctuating *social panic*, which in turn produced a range of expressions of *moral outrage* manifested in both the outpourings of that elusive beast 'public opinion', and the diatribes of professionals and officialdom. Similarly, the last 25 years (approximately) of the twentieth century, up to the present time, are characterised by a correspondingly fuelled and expressed form of social panic. Both eras also feature heightened levels of morally-expressed concern about bad behaviour and crime, based on a belief that there is something fundamentally different, or 'new', about the shapes and forms with which these afflict society. It is on these themes that this volume concentrates.

Victorian and Modern Echoes

The chapters share a determination to compare and contrast the Victorian and the present in ways which not only highlight the continuities and discontinuities, but seek to comprehend the reasons for these. For this reason, what may be termed a 'snapshot' approach has been adopted. Contributors have, on the whole, omitted the linking historical details between the periods to concentrate on the most direct comparative focus. Apart from the impossibilities of giving adequate weight to the intervening years within the constraints of a volume of this nature, such an approach avoids the impression of an inevitability about the continuities and discontinuities conveyed through the 'explanation' of chronological narratives which do not reveal the viable alternative scenarios which were equally possible at various key points. Instead, the focus is on the intrinsic dimensions of the comparison across time.

For both periods, uncertainties and insecurities relating to novel forms of, for example, communications, including transport, have taken a high profile in contemporary commentaries. The impact on the Victorian age of the railways and the information they physically conveyed should not be underestimated. Similarly, the impact on modern society of the arrival of the digital age, with the information 'superhighway', has been equally profound, as Gavin Sutter emphasises. Changes not just in manufacturing patterns but in socio-political concerns about the roles of companies and corporations are features of both periods. Now, as in the past, such developments lay a renewed stress on the perennial concerns about 'fault' and responsibility when, in the perceptions of society, 'things go wrong': a stress which demands corresponding legal shifts in the process of officially apportioning liability.

This is especially the case given the legacy of a range of legislation and legislative responses produced by a Victorian climate of social panic which still has relevance to late twentieth century society. David Bentley's wide-ranging chapter traces a number of continuities in both legislation and practice, while highlighting crucial differences in attitudes towards both the court system and the policing of bad behaviour. Thus, though recommendations have been made for the repeal of the Offences Against the Person Act 1861, this remains a substantial presence defining many of the expressions of bad behaviour encountered today, as Kiron Reid points out in his discussion of the political resort to legislation in both periods. In terms of the operation of the criminal law, codification of legislation undertaken in the Victorian period also has a contemporary impact, as do the comments of the leading Victorian jurist Sir James Fitzjames Stephen. Debates about how, in legislative responses, to achieve a balance between 'offences' against persons and against property also feature prominently in both periods, as do the distinctions and regulatory objectives of the public law/private law divide. Just as the Victorian period was one that saw considerable activity relating to socio-legal developments, so too is the late twentieth century, though this does not, as David Bentley points out, automatically ensure progression in the area of legal reform, say. Kiron Reid, by contrast, does identify a genuine development in the last decades in at least some areas of legislative reform.

Both periods have been affected by a sense of change in the global role of the British nation and a consequent desire to regulate such change through aspects of the legal system – a wider dimension that provides the context for David Nash's discussion of the use of the Blasphemy Statute. But also, different perspectives on the role of the police in the process of producing a case can, for instance, be compared in ways that throw unflattering lights on both periods under scrutiny, as both Roger Hopkins Burke and Tom Williamson illuminate respectively in their discussions on the policing of 'incivilities' and the abuse of crime statistics. Understandably, the pace of social, legal and parliamentary debate is, as Kiron Reid notes, swifter in the latter age, hence the respective focus on the periods c1850 to c1900, and c1975 to c2001 when seeking to draw parallels between the climates of 'Victorianism' and 'modernism'.

One important echo between the two periods is provided by considerations of crime statistics. It has long been argued, for example, that crime in the Victorian period was stabilised at low levels. Yet, as Tom Williamson points out in his examination of the misleading nature of these statistics and their effects on public perceptions of 'good' policing, recent research has suggested that the 'real' crime figures for both periods were higher than officially agreed. Authority had and still has a vested interest (partly for economic reasons) in ensuring that prosecution of crime remained at low levels, with the focus being upon particular types of crimes and criminals, or upon individual cases which achieved notoriety.[1] Such research provides grounds for taking more seriously popular anxieties, expressed in the press and various other media forms including fiction, than has often hitherto been the case in academic studies. It is something dealt with from various perspectives in chapters by Susan Edwards, Gavin Sutter and Tom Lewis. Current debates, especially in the media, over themes like pornography supply an interesting commentary which, as these chapters underline, provokes a reconsideration for both periods of popular, as opposed to official, perceptions of the actual levels of criminality, since it is in these popular perspectives that the roots of social panic lie.[2] However, further interesting light on the partial nature of social panic is provided by Richard Stone's chapter, which concludes the volume. Rather than crime *per se*, Stone examines two public order issues linked to two apparently acceptable social groups: the Salvation Army 'riots' of the 1880s, and the anti-hunt protests of the 1990s, both leading to significant legal cases and to government initiatives. However, what is noticeable is that the wider public, as reflected, certainly, in newspaper reporting, was less stirred to panic over their activities than was the government or legal profession over these expressions of anti-social behaviour.

By contrast, dealing with issues relating to new technology and the impact of morally 'dubious' material on vulnerable audiences, Sutter and Lewis, dealing with clearly discernable social panics and outbursts of moral outrage, survey the continuing failure of official legislation to deal adequately with 'problems' surrounding the production and dissemination of pornography in various formats. Both also suggest the insubstantial nature of so much of popular concern about the content of such material, contrasting interestingly with the far less mythic disturbances examined by Stone. Susan Edwards, with a focus on children, raises a number of still controversial issues about pornographisation across print, art and photography. The whole amounts to a cross-disciplinary discussion of this aspect of bad behaviour which challenges accepted beliefs about the nature and substance of morally 'dubious' material, as well as its audience, circulation and the ways in which the legal process regards this.

---

[1] Howard Taylor, 'Rationing Crime: the political economy of criminal statistics since the 1850s', *The Economic History Review*, LI, 3, 1998, pp. 569–90.

[2] See, for example, J. Holt Schooling, 'Crime', *Pall Mall Magazine*, 1898, XV pp. 239–244; M. Hough and J. Roberts, *Research, Development and Statistics Directorate. Attitudes to Punishment Findings from the British Crime Survey* (HMSO Home Office Research Study 179, 1998).

This volume does not claim that there is a complete echo between the two periods, though it is easy to find resonances in issues and themes of common concern to both, such as juvenile delinquency, social exclusion, sexual abuse and property crime, as well as the levels of visibility (especially on the streets) of much misconduct. However, the ways in which society actually reacted to these issues is often the area where there is the clearest divergence, not so much in terms of results as in terms of identified purpose behind the underlying strategies. The greater moral certainties, along with the imperial demands, of the Victorian period, for instance, can be said to have encouraged a greater liberalism of attitude in areas such as male bad behaviour, and a lesser sympathy towards anything that might be described as feminine transgression, as Judith Knelman points out. As a result of such divergences, the chapter themes concentrate on areas where there is, broadly, a common interest issue whether the focus is actually criminal or not, while also exploring the ways in which reactions to the issues differ, and why.

The growth in interest in defining and examining crime in both contemporary and historical contexts, encourages a re-examination of the past in ways which promote a re-writing of history and its modern relevance. However, a number of prominent 'crime' and bad behaviour themes which echo across the chronological divide are not included here, either because work which explores the dimensions of these resonances has not yet been undertaken by SOLON, or because they are so familiar to the debates that to deal with them adequately, in terms of reference to the differing subject methodologies involved, was impossible within the space allowed. Thus while there are no chapters solely on drink and drugs or on prostitution as issues of crucial concern to both periods, key assumptions linked to these, especially those relating to gender and class, are covered in the wider discussions on social panics and moral outrage which form part of every chapter.

'Social Panics'

Both the Victorian age and the late twentieth century are characterised by contemporary consciousness of apparent economic affluence but also by a widespread conviction that the stability of society as a whole, including that affluence, is threatened by the activities of social deviants.[3] There

---

[3] Judith Rowbotham, 'Introduction to Gendered Perspectives on the Golden Age', in I. Inkster *et al* (eds), *The Golden Age. Essays in British Economic and Social History 1850-1870* (Ashgate, Aldershot, 2000).

was, and is, an identifiable concern about the impact of new developments, intellectual and technological, and the extent to which those developments have the power to inflict radical change on a scale or to a degree which may not be positive in its impact on both individuals and society. In other words, both are ages of 'social panic' and resultant 'moral outrage'. We have preferred to use this extended terminology, partly to avoid the assumptions made by different disciplines in association with the term 'moral panic', and partly because we feel that it is more descriptive of what is actually being identified in these chapters.

One of the most acknowledged and widely-cited definitions of 'moral' panic is provided by Cohen:

> Societies appear to be subject, every now and then, to periods of moral panic. A condition, episode, person or group of persons emerges to become defined as a threat to societal values and interests; its nature is presented in a stylised and stereotypical fashion by the mass media; the moral barricades are manned by editors, bishops, politicians and other-right thinking people; socially accredited experts pronounce their diagnoses and solutions, ways of coping are evolved or (more often) resorted to; the condition then disappears, submerges or deteriorates and becomes more visible. Sometimes the object of the panic is quite novel and at other times it is something which has been in existence long enough, but suddenly appears in the limelight. Sometimes the panic passes over and is forgotten, except in folklore and collective memory; at other times it has more serious and long lasting repercussions and might produce such changes as those in legal and social policy or even in the way the society conceives itself.[4]

In line with this, as Gavin Sutter discusses, the major elements of a moral panic are:

- identification of a (perceived) threat to the established order, leading to
- 'a spiralling escalation of the perceived threat through the media and censorship lobbying'.[5]
- resulting public outcry influences perceptions of the legal process, and may even result in legal reform of some nature, however,
- the moral panic will diminish as public interest in the threat fades, or in the face of a new perceived threat.

---

[4] Stanley Cohen, *Folk Devils & Moral Panics* (Paladin, St Albans, 1973), p. 9.
[5] John Springhall, *Youth, Popular Culture and Moral Panics* (Macmillan Press, London, 1998), p. 146.

This volume seeks a less disjointed approach to understanding social fears and the public expressions associated with them, insisting that while it is always possible to distinguish some form of individual threat to the established order, a period of social panic is one which sees a succession of such threats which are, in popular understanding, frequently muddled up together, particularly in the ways in which they are represented in popular public discourse, such as media productions. This requires an insight into the links between media presentations of bad behaviour and the legal world, something which forms the core of the editors' joint chapter and its discussion of the 'hidden' agendas involved. Based on work associated with the ESRC-supported database, the chapter examines not just the reporting of crime and bad behaviour in the press, but also what lay behind its production, in terms of the interest groups involved.

SOLON identifies 'social panic' setting in over challenges to a range of socio-cultural traditions, held to act as the cohesive bonds providing social stability, with the effects of the sense of panic manifesting themselves in the form of concerns expressed through a moral dimension. Some general statements can be made which are common to any social or moral panic. At such times, certain 'classes', or 'types', of people are, individually and communally, identified as particularly threatening when/if they turn to behaviour identified as socially 'offensive'. Feminist scholars from a range of disciplines have explored the gendered nature of the labels associated with offending and offensive behaviour – and chapters in this volume explore aspects of this in ways which take such explorations further. Female offenders can be argued to be particularly susceptible to creating climates of social panic, with the consequent sense of moral outrage in society producing both new legislative enactments and new interpretations of existing law, something featuring strongly in Judith Knelman's chapter on 'murderesses'.[6] As Knelman demonstrates, disturbing echoes still remain today from the Victorian period, between public and legal attitudes towards women accused of murder, based on stereotypes about appropriate femininity.

The chapter from Liz Rogers, with its focus on essentially professional 'panic' about sanity, women and childbirth, illuminates that the reality of a social panic is not the convenient coherence that such comments imply. A sense of social panic is generally widespread, but capable of affecting different social groups within the nation at different times, and in reaction to different themes of immediate relevance to them, as with the ongoing

---

[6] D. Eastwood, *Governing Rural England: Tradition and Transformation in Local Government 1780-1840* (Clarendon Press, Oxford, 1994); see also Shani D'Cruze (ed.), *Everyday Violence in Britain, c1850-1950: Gender and Class* (Longman, London, 2000).

reluctance of the medical profession to accept women's mental competence when 'disturbed' by childbirth. The chapters thus provide a focus on a range of themes which do not automatically coincide completely chronologically, even though they are characteristic of the overarching Victorian and present panics, being founded in the shared fears about the opportunities to bad behaviour offered by technology and 'modernism'.

There existed in the Victorian period a presumption that 'crime', certainly habitual and visible crime of a type to offend social sensibilities, was a predominantly lower class affair. This perception has continued into the modern period. Fraud and other essentially financial 'offences', carried out by apparently 'respectable' members of society became identified as issues of moral outrage in the Victorian period, something which has also been suggested as having major implications for 'modern perceptions of white collar crime and the white collar criminal' Sarah Wilson suggests that the perception that financial crimes actually amounted to a fraud on society was articulated strongly throughout the latter half of the nineteenth century, with the modern parallel being the identification of white collar crime as a cancer in modern society. Both are stark positions, inflating the damage perpetrated by the guilty parties beyond the immediate impact of their crimes and making them threats to the health of society as a whole. This is something which has important implications for understanding the presentations of such 'criminals' by the legal system and the popular media. Certainly modern attitudes towards 'respectable' crime reflect Victorian condemnations (as the current attitudes towards previously socially prominent figures like Jeffrey Archer and Jonathan Aitken underline). Essentially, the sentences such 'offenders' receive reflect society's outrage at their behaviour quite as much as the severity of the actual 'crime'. This also relates to fears about the roles of companies and corporations, where power largely lies in the hands of the respectable elements, but with such elements acting 'immorally' and apparently 'above' the law, as Gavin Sutter also comments. The result is the negative portrayal of certain companies and corporate bodies because they are portrayed as offending against society's popularly displayed sensibilities about a range of issues, including environmental ones.

In both the periods, in reaction to what are (rather incorrectly) identified as 'radical' challenges to society, the role of family and 'family values' have become matters of concern. These are inextricably linked to the role played by religion. In the Victorian period, the rise of atheism provided an alarming challenge. Today, it is the context of a 'multi-faith' society in Britain, where decline in Christian worship is contrasted with the strength of non-Western religions like Islam, and with the rise of alternative religious forms. Fears about the religiously-generated threat to social stability have included a popular belief in the rise of satanism and satanic abuse, and most recently, popular reaction to the events of 11 September 2001 and the launching of the 'war' on terrorism, with its strong anti-Islamic connotations.[7] Blasphemy provides, as David Nash argues, an important focus through which to understand such challenges to a cultural *status quo*, especially through the expectation of official sanction against 'blasphemers' and invocations of the legal system to underpin established positions.

This evokes the broader question of why social panics are such a regular feature of societies, particularly when they are in a state of flux, or perceive themselves so to be. Is it because a high profile social panic provides a convenient explanation for society's ills, providing an excuse to avoid acknowledgement of the actual causal factors underlying contemporary social problems? Is it diversionary 'scapegoating', pointing the finger at individuals or groups of individuals in society who are accused of deviating from 'normality' by behaving 'badly'? These chapters suggest that this perspective has considerable substance to it. A problem facing Victorian society, for example, was that ambition for social and material betterment on the part of individuals was central not only to capitalism as an economic consideration, as pointed out by Sarah Wilson, but also, as Rowbotham and Stevenson reiterate, to the Smilesean cultural concept of 'Self-Help', much admired and required by respectable elements. Yet it was acknowledged that such aspirations could lead respectable members of society into temptation to indulge in bad behaviour and even commit crime, where gambling led to speculation and fraud. Mike Ahearne's chapter echoes the writings of commentators such as Mayhew, and novelists such as Dickens and Mrs. Henry Wood, in demonstrating that there was an uncomfortable similarity between these twisted aspirations for material betterment and the entirely admirable impulses driving figures like George Stephenson to financial and economic success.[8] How was it possible to distinguish morally between the entrepreneur and the criminal, especially given the complication of those expressions of 'deviant' behaviour by members of the working classes that were fuelled by economic desperation? Arguably it was the very success of enterprises such as the development of the railway

---

[7] Jean La Fontaine, *The Extent and Nature of Organised and Ritual Abuse. Research Findings* (Department of Health, 1994); Jean La Fontaine, *Speak of the Devil: Tales of Satanic Abuse in Contemporary England* (Cambridge University Press, Cambridge, 1998).

[8] J. Rowbotham, '"All Our Past Proclaims Our Future": Popular Biography and Masculine Identity during the Golden Age, 1850–1870', in Inkster *et al* (eds), *The Golden Age*.

network which encouraged the proliferation of dishonesty – something which has uncomfortable parallels with the opportunities for dishonesty now being appreciated by elements among the equally respectable (or at least reasonably educated) computer literate, as is explored by several of the chapters, including those from Wilson, Sutter and Williamson.

There is also the issue of 'professionalism', something stressed and prized by both Victorian and late twentieth century society. Professionalism not only sets high standards, but also provides (through the emphasis on self-regulation) opportunities for fraud and deceit through misuse of those standards, by individuals, institutions and corporations.[9] Much of the apparent confusion and hypocrisy of Victorian society over moral values may well relate to the difficulties of reconciling similarities of motivation behind the performance of certain activities labelled socially constructive and desirable and the performance of others labelled socially dysfunctional. Similar confusions are apparent today, as with the changing media positions taken towards modern entrepreneurial figures such as Mohammed Al Fayed. Thus it can be said that in terms of social attitudes, as well as the exercise of legal discretion in areas such as sentencing, there can be a similarity of response based on the social position of the person on trial, despite the context of very different crimes. Such a perspective could provide interesting insights into similarities between attitudes towards property crimes and crimes against the person during periods of social panic.

Consciousness of this has been a major factor in the fears surrounding the development of new technologies and the spread of information, as their disseminators and practitioners have rapidly associated themselves with the concept. Middle class Victorians could, and did, as the editors and Gavin Sutter point out, blame unwholesome fiction for juvenile delinquency, instead of taking a clear-sighted perspective on the causes of social injustice and its results. Today, additives and junk food are blamed for some forms of juvenile delinquency, avoiding a focus on equally uncomfortable questions about parenting and home environments. It cannot be denied that the contemporary rhetoric surrounding social panics distance questions about the real roots of discontent and disorder in society, and conclusions about the need for uncomfortable remedies. The implications of this are that a society falls back on a collective set of fears at points in time when the scale of the adverse effects of bad behaviour is perceived to have reached levels unacceptable to a majority of people

---

[9] For a discussion of the nature of professionalism in society, see, for example, Harold Perkin, *The Rise of Professional Society, England since 1880* (Routledge, London, 1989).

because dealing with the most logical causes of the bad behaviour is equally unacceptable and uncomfortable to that majority. In other words, a social panic provides a set of scapegoats, comfortably identified and distanced from the mainstream by the rhetoric of the moral outrage which defines the panic and its supposed causes.

Legal Responses

During periods of social panic, when 'society' seeks to adjust to new practical demands placed on it, rapid and apparently all-embracing legal responses or 'solutions' to perceived crises are demanded. The intensity of the demands can lead to ill-considered changes, which, as Kiron Reid discusses, often prove to have unexpected long-term consequences for both individuals in society and society as a whole. Whether in the form of the passage of new legislation, or the establishment of new legal precedents, or by utilising established legislation in different ways such adjustments were, and are, often undertaken when legislators and judicial figures are pressurised into swift, and 'appropriate' retributive public action without time being taken to reflect on the full scope of the legislation. Yet little attempt has been made to provide scholarly assessments of the consequences of such change on the standing of the legal process, underlining the importance of David Bentley's review of this area. In seeking to remedy the neglect of certain areas of offending by examining them, in concert with others, in the wider social context as well as the actual legal system, the project aims to look beyond the traditional resources of research into the area of criminality and law. The objective is to place an emphasis on intertexuality between the more established sources for legal research and newspaper reporting, along with parliamentary debates, biographies and memoirs, articles in periodicals (both elite and popular), humour, fiction and drama from various genres including pornography and also illustrative sources including cartoons. Obvious Victorian sources include Dickens, Mayhew and Wilkie Collins, but in addition, authors (of both fictional and non-fictional texts) who, like Mrs Henry Wood, are currently less well-known but who were considered to have an authoritative voice by Victorian contemporaries are invoked by contributors, along with reference to modern echoes.

This examination of the discourse of 'offending' has the merit of drawing out the similarities of attitude towards types of crime and criminal behaviour and resulting stereotypification of both offenders and victims, and the practical impact of such attitudes on the legal system and the participants therein, as the editors highlight in their chapter. Further it illuminates the hierarchies of offences that developed, including modifications in these over time — with all the implications this has for assessments of the practical effectiveness of both statute law and legal practice when responding to social concerns about levels of crime and bad behaviour. The chapters from Roger Hopkins Burke, Tom Williamson and Richard Stone in particular focus on aspects of this relationship in their surveys of policing and bad behaviour. This encourages a greater understanding of the nature of the essentially cultural relationship between 'law' and 'society', and the ways in which shifts in societal attitudes in particular affect that relationship.

Beyond a shared agreement that there are resonances between these two periods which are worth exploring through a focus on issues of considerable topical interest which also have important links to the past, and significant implications for any legal reform or reinterpretation, it has not been thought necessary to enjoin the same perspectives on all the contributors. The objective has not been a bland commonality — indeed a range of perspectives and emphases is present across, for example, the chapters by Lewis, Sutter and Edwards — but rather, to provide a stimulating debate across the topics within the volume, and, we hope, outside it as a result of reading the opinions voiced within these chapters.

The questions that interest enquirers when investigating past periods are generally dominated by those that have a current resonance for them, with a linkage also to their levels of visibility to the public gaze, especially through their reportage. A sense of the relation of history to the present is thus at least implicitly central to modern comprehensions of what Britain is today. As a result, the past has been interrogated in this volume from perspectives which produce answers relevant to the late twentieth and early twenty-first century, but presented in ways that seek to encourage readers to question an even wider range of 'certainties' about automatic human progress. It is habitual to characterise the sense of pride in a present age primarily by reference to a less glorious past, something which may even be achieved by an apparent rejection of the importance of history, a stance apparently taken by some of today's politicians. The complacencies engendered by such a position are best challenged by attempts to marry assessments of the present with an honest revisiting of both the demerits and the merits of the past, achieving this through marrying a range of disciplinary and practitioner perspectives, and so throwing up an array of responses which still reflect on each other. This, in the crucial arena of debates on bad behaviour and the successful management of state and society, lies at the core of this volume. It is not intended as a final answer, but rather, as a contribution to a debate which is in urgent need of further stimulus.

Chapter 1

Acquitting the Innocent. Convicting the Guilty. Delivering Justice?

David Bentley

In Victorian England public confidence in the criminal trial system was high. That wrong convictions occurred but rarely, and wrongful executions never, was an article of faith amongst judges and politicians alike and would remain so until at least the 1960s. In April 1948, during a debate on the death penalty, Sir David Maxwell-Fyfe (soon to achieve notoriety as the Home Secretary who refused to reprieve Derek Bentley) told the Commons:

> There is no practical possibility [of an innocent man being put to death]. Of course a jury might go wrong, the Court of Criminal Appeal might go wrong as might the House of Lords and the Home Secretary: they might all be stricken mad and go wrong. But that is not a possibility which anyone can consider likely ... it is impossible for anyone who views and examines fairly the facts of any murder cases of which he has knowledge to say that such a miscarriage has taken place.[1]

Such affirmations of faith in the system were routine in nineteenth century debates in the Commons as confirmed by Thomas Denman MP – 'it [is] the practice to indulge very much in commonplace eulogies on the tenderness and humanity of the law of England towards prisoners'.[2] Nor did the general public (or at least that section of it which had had no dealings with the courts) need any persuading as to the superiority of English criminal justice: to most Victorians it was a self-evident truth.

Today public perceptions are very different.[3] When the *Solicitors' Journal* carried out a survey in the wake of the Report of the Royal

---

[1] *Hansard*, 1947-48, 449, col. 1077. Bentley's conviction was quashed by the Court of Appeal in July 1998 and a posthumous pardon granted, see *The Times* 31 July 1998.

[2] *Hansard*, 1824, 11, p. 217.

[3] The phrase 'This has destroyed my faith in British justice' which comes so readily to the lips of today's disappointed litigant, looks back to a time when the British regarded their justice system as the best in the world.

Commission on Criminal Justice 1993, it found that only 21 per cent of those questioned considered British justice was the best in the world.[4] It is not hard to understand why. The rot started with the grant of a posthumous pardon to Timothy Evans in 1968; what had so long been claimed could never happen, had happened: Britain had hanged an innocent man.[5] But the real damage was done by the seemingly endless series of high-profile miscarriages of justice which came to light in the 1980s and 1990s. The best-known are listed in the introduction to the report of the Royal Commission set up to investigate them and include the cases of the Birmingham Six, The Guildford Four, the Maguires, Judith Ward, the Broadwater Farm Three, Stefan Kiszko, the Cardiff Three, a number of 'cases based on evidence gathered by members of the West Midlands Police Serious Crime Squad ... [and] cases where the convictions ... [arose] out of ... malpractice by officers based at Stoke Newington police station'.[6]

The Victorian and Present Day Trial Systems Compared

Although the nineteenth century criminal trial system scored well in terms of public approval, and certainly better than does the present day system, there is no escaping the fact that it had serious deficiencies, particularly in regard to the legal representation of defendants, and appeals. Anyone reading a report of a nineteenth century criminal trial will have little difficulty in following what is happening, and this may lead him to suppose that trial procedure has changed relatively little since Victoria's day. Nothing could be further from the truth. Palmerston's claim in 1853 that English law afforded to the innocent 'every possible security which human institutions can [do] for freedom from unjust punishment' is one which present day politicians would doubtless echo, but the means by which the law today seeks to safeguard accused persons are very different to the securities to which he was referring.[7]

In Victorian England the principal safeguards, so far as those accused of indictable offences were concerned, were pre-trial scrutiny by examining magistrate and grand jury, the accused's right of peremptory challenge, the requirement that the verdict of a trial jury be unanimous and the rules of

---

[4] *Solicitors' Journal* 1993, 137, p. 650.

[5] Granted on 18 October 1966; see Ludovic Kennedy, *10 Rillington Place* (Grafton, London, 1971) pp. 10-11.

[6] Report of Royal Commission on Criminal Justice 1993, Cmnd 2263, paras. 1, 3 and 22. The appointment of the Royal Commission was announced on the same day as the Court of Appeal quashed the convictions for murder of the Birmingham Six.

[7] *Hansard*, 1852-53, cxxvii, p. 980.

criminal evidence, not least those protecting the accused against self-incrimination.[8] On the other hand the accused had no right to free legal representation nor had he any right of appeal against either conviction or sentence. Today the most significant safeguards, besides evidential protections, are the right to legal aid and the right of appeal. Further, although evidential protections are still considerable, they are fewer than a century ago. The law still requires the Crown to prove guilt and prove it beyond reasonable doubt, excludes unreliable and improperly obtained confessions and excludes hearsay and evidence of the accused's bad character and criminal convictions. But the old protections against self-incrimination have been reduced to vanishing point and rules as to corroboration swept away. Of the triple safeguard of preliminary examination, grand jury scrutiny and trial jury unanimity nothing now remains.[9] Likewise with the peremptory challenge. The key changes in the last 160 years have undoubtedly been those relating to the accused's police interrogation, legal aid, the accused's competency as a witness and criminal appeal. The impact upon the trial system has been enormous.

Police Interrogation

A question which quickly arose in the wake of the establishment of paid professional police forces in London and elsewhere in the mid-nineteenth century was whether it was permissible for a police officer, who had arrested a man upon suspicion of having committed a crime, to question him about the offence.[10] The judicial answer was emphatic. While there could be no objection to an officer listening to and recording any explanation or account which the prisoner might choose to give, it was quite improper to question him. To do so would be a usurpation of the function of an examining magistrate without any of the safeguards which attended magisterial examinations.[11] When the Jervis Act 1848 deprived magistrates of the power to examine prisoners, this was seen as providing further justification of the prohibition: if judges and magistrates were forbidden to question prisoners, it was unthinkable that inferior officers of justice, such

---

[8] Indictable offences are those triable by jury; the right of peremptory challenge was the right of an accused to challenge a juror without showing cause.

[9] The grand jury and the requirement of jury unanimity were abolished in 1933 and 1967 respectively; as to the preliminary investigation see in particular s.51, Crime and Disorder Act 1998.

[10] Clive Emsley, *Crime and Society in England 1750-1900* (Longman, London, 1996).

[11] See e.g. Denman LCJ in *R v Anon* (1839) Times Law Reports, 1 August; *R v Glennon Toole and McGrath* (1840) 1 Craw & D 359.

as policemen, should be permitted to do so.[12] This would remain the stance of the courts until well into the twentieth century.

Today interrogation is one of the main investigative tools used by the police, and the law sanctions it. A police officer is entitled to question any person whom he arrests about the offence for which he has been arrested. In carrying out such questioning he is obliged to follow a code of practice which includes such protections for the suspect as a right to free legal advice and the tape recording of his answers.[13] Further, although suspects still remain free to answer or not questions put to them, since 1995 an accused who fails to mention, when questioned by the police, a matter relied upon by him in his defence at trial, runs the risk of an adverse inference being drawn from such failure.[14]

That a right of police interrogation needs to be hedged about by the most stringent safeguards seems obvious. But, astonishingly, when in the course of the last century the judges stood by and sanctioned first the undermining and finally the complete abandonment of the prohibition on police questioning, they took no steps to protect those in custody against the risk of their answers to police questions being misreported or, worse still, fabricated.[15] Nineteenth century judges, in voicing their objections to police interrogation, had spelt out clearly the dangers but their warnings were ignored. This was a mistake which was to have dire consequences for the reputation of English criminal justice.

By the 1970s the lack of safeguards for suspects interviewed by the police was beginning to cause public unease. Claims by accused that they had been 'verballed' by interviewing police officers were now being regularly heard and it was hard to believe that all of them were false. In 1974 the Court of Appeal called for reform: 'Something should be done',

---

[12] See for example *R v Mick* (1863) 3 F & F 822.

[13] Police and Criminal Evidence Act 1984 Code of Practice C.

[14] Criminal Justice and Public Order Act 1994, s.34.

[15] The process whereby the prohibition upon police questioning came to be overturned was both long and tortuous. Throughout the nineteenth century the judges had stressed the impropriety of police officers questioning persons whom they had arrested but, despite the prohibition being repeated in police handbooks, some officers just as regularly ignored it. Had the courts ruled that answers obtained by improper questioning were inadmissible, the practice would no doubt have quickly died out. Unfortunately, opinion upon the point was badly split as per Lord Sumner in *Ibrahim v R* [1914] AC 599. The position was rendered still more confusing when in response to requests from the police for clarification of the law, the judges formulated between 1912-1918 nine rules for the guidance of police officers. These Judges' Rules, revised in 1964, went a long way to undermining the old bar on police questioning, forbidding the questioning of those in custody without the caution being first administered.

said Lord Justice Lawton 'and as quickly as possible, to make evidence about oral statements [to police officers] difficult either to challenge or concoct'.[16] Ten years later the Police and Criminal Evidence Act (PACE) was enacted, obliging police officers to conduct interviews in accordance with the Codes of Practice issued thereunder, something discussed at greater length by Kiron Reid.[17] This was a major advance so far as defendants were concerned and one which has made the evil of 'verballing' largely a thing of the past. But, unfortunately for the reputation of 'British' (actually English) justice, its past would catch up with it in the years ahead. When the miscarriage of justice cases began to hit the headlines how urgent had been the need for the PACE reforms immediately became clear.

Legal Representation

To modern eyes the greatest weakness of the trial system at the end of the nineteenth century was the absence of legal aid for poor prisoners. Although all accused had enjoyed, since 1836, the full right to be defended by counsel, lawyers cost money and those who could not pay had to conduct their own defence.[18] Trials of unrepresented prisoners were likely to be hopelessly one-sided. Unable to defend themselves effectively, many did not even make the attempt, for them the trial 'passed before [their] eyes and mind ... like a dream which [they could not] grasp'.[19] In the eighteenth century when, more often than not, there was no prosecuting counsel (in such cases the Crown witnesses would be taken through their evidence by the judge), that the accused was unrepresented did not appear unfair: if the Crown had no counsel how was it to his disadvantage that he had none? When, in the 1830s, the judges had begun to insist that counsel be instructed to prosecute cases tried at the Old Bailey and at the assizes this 'inequality of arms' became patent. Yet what could be done? The cost to the state of providing counsel for poor prisoners would be horrendous. What could not be changed must be borne and, in any event, what legal skill was required to make an honest defence?

Had the will been there, the problem could in fact have been solved. In Scotland the legal profession had since the sixteenth century provided free representation for those who could not afford to pay, and it would have been

---

[16] *R v Turner* (1975) 1 Cr App R 67 at p. 77.

[17] PACE Code of Practice C.

[18] See generally David Bentley, *English Criminal Justice in the Nineteenth Century* (Hambledon, London, 1998), ch. 23.

[19] James Fitzjames Stephen, *A History of the Criminal Law of England*, 3 vols (Macmillan and Co, London, 1883), I, p. 442.

perfectly simple to have adopted a similar scheme south of the border. By 1850 there had evolved in England a practice of assigning counsel to undefended prisoners in capital cases (counsel were by etiquette obliged to accept such assignment and to give their services free) but that was the limit of the law's assistance.[20] Where the charge was not capital and the vast majority were not (by 1864 only four offences remained punishable by death), the prisoner, if he could not afford a lawyer, was obliged to shift for himself. Throughout the century most defendants in magistrates' courts and many of those appearing in the higher courts charged with indictable offences were tried undefended. The numbers were high. Where the trial was in one of the higher courts, the unrepresented accused had to take what comfort he could from the maxim that the judge was his counsel. All the maxim in fact meant was that it was the duty of the judge to ensure that the accused had the benefit of any legal point which told in his favour. The fact that the judge had no communication with the prisoner meant that, except where the latter had made a statement to the police or before the examining magistrate, he would be unable to defend him effectively, even if he were so inclined, since he would have no idea what his answer was to the evidence against him.

Today defendants in criminal cases unable to afford legal representation have the right to be represented by a lawyer of their choice paid for out of public funds.[21] The impact which this has had on the fairness of criminal trials has been enormous. When in 1902 the Dorset Quarter Sessions Bar set up a *pro bono* scheme for the defence of poor prisoners the result was an immediate increase in the acquittal rate. The impact of state-funded criminal legal aid has been the same. Accused persons with a good answer to the charge against them no longer stand the risk of being convicted for want of a lawyer to put their case.

---

[20] Bentley, *Criminal Justice*, ch. 12.

[21] Progress in the twentieth century towards the establishment of a system of criminal legal aid was slow. Following the implementation of the Criminal Evidence Act 1898 opinion at the bar had begun increasingly to favour free representation for poor prisoners. In 1903 four barrister MPs introduced a Poor Prisoners Defence Bill which, to universal surprise, reached the statute book. Under the Act free representation was only available to those facing trial on indictment. To qualify for a defence certificate the accused had to satisfy the committing magistrates that he was without means and that the grant of a defence certificate was desirable having regard to the defence disclosed by him. Because of the limited scope of this Act (and its successors) and the restrictive way in which its provisions were applied by many courts, the evil of prisoners charged with serious offences taking their trials undefended persisted until well after the Second World War. Only in 1960 was the nettle finally grasped and a comprehensive scheme of criminal legal aid established.

Allowing Prisoners to Testify

The common law doctrine of incompetency through interest barred from the witness box, in both civil and criminal cases alike, any person regarded as having an interest in the outcome of the proceedings before the court. This included, in civil cases, the parties and their spouses, and, in criminal cases, the accused and his spouse. After Brougham's Acts 1851-1853 rendering the parties and their spouses competent to give evidence in civil suits, the only substantial remnant of the rule was the prohibition upon an accused and his spouse giving evidence in his defence. Attempts were made in the 1850s to bring the criminal law into line with civil law but they were fiercely resisted. The same justification for the rule was espoused irrespective of whether it was a civil or criminal case, namely that an interested person would inevitably be biased and therefore worthless, but the two cases were not in fact the same. In the first place, an accused was permitted to do something which the parties to a civil suit could not do, namely make an unsworn statement in his own defence giving his answer to the charge. Secondly, there was a compelling reason for refusing to allow accused persons to testify. This was the need to protect them against the risk of self-incrimination. To abolish the incompetency rule would, so it was argued, lead to the establishment in England of something akin to the disliked French form of procedure, where accused persons were compelled by rigorous cross-examination to convict themselves out of their own mouths. England had had experience of such a system in the days of Scroggs and Jeffreys and since the Glorious Revolution of 1688 the law had set its face firmly against prisoners being subjected to such 'moral torture'. Prosecutions should succeed on their own merits and not by extracting admissions from the accused. Given that most prisoners were poorly educated and took their trials unrepresented, permitting them to give their answer to the charge in the form of an unsworn statement, upon which they could not be cross-examined, was the only fair way of placing their cases before the jury. The argument carried the day and continued to do so for the next two decades.

By the 1880s however, opinion both within parliament and the legal profession was changing. In 1864 the state of Maine had passed a statute permitting prisoners to testify. By 1878 its lead had been followed by no fewer than 27 other American states, with the reform hailed as an unqualified success by judges and lawyers alike. Also, since 1860, a number of *ad hoc* exceptions to the rule had been created by English statutes, such as the Master and Servant Act 1867 and the Merchant Shipping Acts 1871-76, starting a trend which would continue right down until 1898. A major turning point was the inclusion in the Criminal Law Amendment Act 1885, of a section permitting prisoners charged with rape and other serious sexual offences to give evidence in their own defence.[22] This was a huge exception and its creation meant that the days of the bar on prisoners' evidence were numbered. A Prisoners' Evidence Act would have appeared on the statute book by 1890 had it not been for the obstruction of the Irish Nationalist MPs who were adamant that 'Ireland was not in a suitable condition for the application of such a reform... the administration of public justice there [being such as to inspire] little confidence'.[23] In the event the reform was not finally carried until the enactment of the Criminal Evidence Act 1898.

One of the problems which the draftsmen of the Prisoners' Evidence Bills had to grapple with was the position of prisoners who had previous convictions. If accused who gave evidence were left unprotected against cross-examination as to credit, those with convictions would be put in an impossible position. If they gave evidence the jury would inevitably learn of their unattractive pasts; if they declined to enter the witness box, the Crown would tell the jury that this was because they had no answer to the charge. The solution adopted in the 1898 Act was twofold. First, it forbade comment by prosecuting counsel upon the accused's failure to give evidence.[24] Secondly, it prohibited cross-examination of an accused as to his character or convictions save in three cases: (i) where he had attacked the character of a prosecution witness; (ii) where he had put himself forward as of good character and (iii) where his previous convictions were relevant to an issue in the case.[25] A snare inherent in the solution, which would become more obvious as the police acquired powers of interrogation, was that an accused against whom the police had fabricated evidence could only raise such a defence at the risk of being cross-examined as to his record if he went into the witness box.

The 1898 Act marked a turning point in English criminal procedure. With its passage the criminal trial moved closer to its present-day model. Its most important effects were to strip the accused of his old immunity from cross-examination. If he wished to offer an explanation of the evidence against him he would have to give it from the witness box or run the risk of the jury drawing an inference to his discredit. Secondly, anyone accused who attacked the character of the Crown witnesses was exposed to a new peril:

---

[22] Criminal Law Amendment Act 1885, s.20.

[23] C. Jackson, 'Opposition to the Passage of the Criminal Evidence Reform', in J. McEldowney and P. O'Higgins (eds), *The Common Law Tradition* (Irish Academic Press, Dublin, 1990), p. 186.

[24] s.1(b).

[25] s.1(f).

retaliation in kind should he venture into the witness box. Its coming into force made a scheme of criminal legal aid daily more urgent.

Although the Act incorporated safeguards for those accused there was always the danger that once it was in force these would sooner or later be stripped away or whittled down. So it has proved. In 1994 parliament repealed section 1(b) Criminal Evidence Act 1898 which prohibited comment by the prosecution upon the accused's failure to give evidence. Section 35 Criminal Justice and Public Order Act 1994 provided that henceforth such failure would be a matter from which negative inferences might be drawn. Thus, the position of an accused who fails to give evidence is worse today than it was at the time of the 1898 Act. Twentieth century experience of the operation of this Act has demonstrated that it is capable of putting an accused with a criminal record, against whom the police have fabricated evidence, in a near impossible position. If he goes into the witness box and accuses them of fabrication, he renders himself liable to cross-examination upon his record. If he stays out of the witness box, the penalty he will pay is to hear the judge instruct the jury that there is no evidence from him to contradict the evidence of the police. Therefore if the jury considers that the Crown evidence is such as to call for an answer, it is open to them to draw from his failure to testify the inference that he has no answer to it.

Appeals

In the nineteenth century a prisoner had no right of appeal against a jury's verdict or a judge's sentence. If his case involved a doubtful point of law, there was always the hope that the trial judge would reserve it for the consideration by the whole bench of common law judges. Reserving, which was a review procedure of considerable antiquity, was, in 1848, put on a statutory footing. A Court for Crown Cases was established to hear reserved cases and the power to reserve, which until then had been limited to Assize and Old Bailey judges, extended to courts of Quarter Sessions. Whether a case was reserved or not was entirely in the judge's discretion. The accused had no right to require him to so reserve and, if he refused, the prisoner's only means of redress was to petition the Home Office for a pardon or revision of sentence. Until statutes of 1859 and 1879 gave to those summarily convicted a limited right of appeal against conviction and sentence, their position was broadly no different to that of a defendant convicted on indictment: if they were aggrieved they must take their complaint to the Home Office, the law affording no other means of redress. During Victoria's reign no fewer than 30 bills for the establishment of a

Court of Criminal Appeal were introduced. All failed to pass. Wrong convictions were, claimed the anti-reform lobby, extremely rare and such as did occur could be and were effectively dealt with by the Home Office, petitioning the Crown being a remedy available to rich and poor alike. Allowing defendants to appeal their convictions would result in the courts being swamped with work, and would introduce such delays into the administration of criminal justice as would make it impossible to maintain a system of capital punishment. Although the reformers came close to success on a couple of occasions, criminal appeal was destined to remain the century's 'standing lost cause' [26] The lack of adequate appellate remedies had consequences which went far beyond the misfortunes of individual prisoners, wrongly convicted or over-harshly sentenced, who could get no redress therefrom. Lack of an appeal remedy meant that judicial misconduct went largely unchecked, with adverse press publicity the only sanction. It also meant that judges in the lower courts (of whom many were laymen) were almost wholly without authoritative guidance (of the kind now given by the Court of Appeal) as to how the duty of summing up should be discharged. The result was that many prisoners were convicted after summings-up which by twentieth century standards were wholly deficient.

Today the position is entirely changed. A defendant convicted by the magistrates' court has a right of appeal to the Crown Court against either conviction or sentence, or both, and both prosecution and defendant have a right of appeal to the High Court on a point of law. Those convicted on indictment have a right of appeal to the Court of Appeal against either conviction or sentence, although one which is conditional on the court granting leave to appeal – a mechanism intended to filter out unmeritorious cases. The Attorney General also has the right to appeal to the Court of Appeal against any Crown Court sentence which he considers unduly lenient.[27] Appeals in the Crown Court are by way of rehearing: the court retries the case. In the Court of Appeal the appeal proceeds by way of review. The court reconsiders the appellant's conviction or sentence in the light of the material available to the court below and any new evidence permitted to be called. In conviction appeals, the test the court is required to apply is to ask itself whether the accused's conviction is safe. If it concludes

---

[26] In 1858 when the New Trials in Criminal Cases Bill passed its Commons second reading and was referred to committee, and in 1883 when the government introduced its Criminal Code and Court of Criminal Appeal Bills.

[27] The Council of Judges in its annual statutory report for 1892 had recommended that the Crown should have the right to appeal over lenient sentences but it was not until 1988 that it was given the right to do so, Criminal Justice Act 1988, ss.35 and 36.

that it is, it must quash the conviction, with power, if it thinks fit, to order a retrial. The Home Office, which ever since the establishment of the Court of Criminal Appeal in 1907, had the power to refer cases of possible miscarriage of justice to the court, has lost the right to do so, such references now being the preserve of the Criminal Cases Review Commission established in 1995 in the wake of the Royal Commission report.[28]

Public Dissatisfaction with the Trial System

The twentieth century saw remedied the two most serious shortcomings of the Victorian trial system, namely the lack of representation for poor prisoners and of adequate appellate remedies. There have also been other respects in which the lot of accused persons has been improved. The Criminal Procedure and Investigation Act 1996 places upon the Crown a duty to disclose to an accused any material in its possession which may assist him in his defence.[29] In the last 30 years guidelines and a code of practice have been put in place which have gone a long way to reduce the risk of persons being convicted as a result of mistaken identification evidence.[30] One can also point to the emergence of a doctrine of abuse of process and the introduction of custody time limits, the combined effect of which is to give accused persons a measure of protection against undue delay and other unfair conduct on the part of the prosecution. But, for all this, there is still considerable dissatisfaction with the trial process, far more than in Victoria's day. Inevitably one asks why should this be.

Distrust of the police is certainly one factor. By the end of Victoria's reign the reputation of the police stood high, the hostility which Peel's Metropolitan Police had initially aroused having long since subsided. Certainly, few doubted the integrity of the British bobby (a familiar term for the police). What the public picked up in the 1980s from high-profile cases like those of the Birmingham Six and the Guildford Four was something which criminal defence lawyers had long known, namely how little compunction some police officers had about fabricating evidence against suspects whom they considered guilty. 'Noble cause corruption' was the police euphemism but, to a generation brought up to believe that British policemen were the best in the world, the revelation was horrifying. Trust was lost and has yet to be won back, particularly amongst the black

---

[28] Criminal Appeal Act 1995.

[29] See ss.3, 4, 7 and 9.

[30] See *R v Turnbull* [1977] 63 Cr App R 132 and PACE Code of Practice D.

Behaving Badly

community who regard the report of the Stephen Lawrence Inquiry as vindicating long-standing complaints of police racism.[31]

But politicians, too, must take their share of the blame. While, as Tom Williamson's chapter underlines, criminal statistics are far from trustworthy overall, it is generally agreed that in the latter half of the nineteenth century crime was in decline. Since the end of the Second World War the picture has been very different, crime has risen relentlessly and detection and conviction rates have correspondingly declined. Following the enactment of PACE the police, who had long been critics of the trial system blaming it for their inability to bring known criminals to book, began to demand its reform. The balance, they argued, had swung too far in favour of the criminal. Now that the state provided the poor prisoner with free legal representation and protection against the risk of fabricated evidence, as a *quid pro quo* ancient safeguards such as the right to refuse to answer police questions and to decline to go into the witness box should go. With the crime rates continuing to rise and the conviction rate in Crown Court trials standing at just over 50 per cent, politicians took little convincing and legislation soon followed.[32] In 1988 the accused was stripped of his right of peremptory jury challenge and the need for corroboration of the evidence of children was abolished.[33] In 1995 the accomplice and rape corroboration rules were dispensed with.[34] It was also enacted that a jury might draw an adverse inference from the failure of the accused to disclose, when questioned by the police, matters later relied upon by him at trial or to give evidence at trial.[35] In 1996 a duty was placed on a Crown Court defendant contesting guilt to furnish a defence statement to the prosecution and the court setting out his answer to the charge.[36] With the passage of time the appetite of politicians for reforms, which it is believed will improve the conviction and prevent the guilty escaping justice, has steadily grown. Now the two major political parties vie with each other to convince the electorate that it is they who are tough on crime, and each year

---

[31] *Report of an Inquiry by Sir William Macpherson of Cluny*, Home Office, February 1999.

[32] Not only were conviction rates low but numbers of defendants pleading guilty were steadily rising: in the last ten years the percentage of defendants pleading guilty in the Crown Court has fallen steadily year on year; in 1991-92 it was 87.2; in 1999/2000 it was 82.7 (CPS *Annual Reports*, 1991-92 to 1999-2000).

[33] By ss.54 and 118, Criminal Justice Act 1988 respectively.

[34] By the Criminal Justice and Public Order Act 1994, s.32.

[35] Criminal Justice and Public Order Act 1994, ss.34 and 35. A survey commissioned by the *Solicitors' Journal* in 1993 found that 61 per cent favoured maintenance of the accused's right to refuse to answer police questions: *Solicitors' Journal*, 1993, 137, p. 650.

[36] Imposed by s.5(5) Criminal Procedure and Investigation Act 1996, the duty is in practice easy to evade and the requirement almost wholly ineffective as a means of informing either the court or the prosecution of the nature of the defence.

sees the enactment of some fresh statute on criminal evidence procedure or sentencing. This appetite for stripping away protections from accused is all the more curious given the high-profile miscarriages of justice above referred to which, in the 1990s, dragged the reputation of English justice through the mud. One might have hoped that the report of the resulting Royal Commission would have served to check the trend but it has made hardly any difference. The cases which gave rise to the Commission's appointment have been comfortingly explained away as due to evils which PACE has done away with and the clamour for further illiberal reform remains unabated.[37] The latest batch of proposed reforms includes curtailment of the right of jury trial.[38] In addition, the abolition of the double jeopardy rule in murder cases (and presumably in due course in rape, drug dealing and so on), granting the prosecution the right to appeal perverse jury verdicts, relaxation of the prohibition upon the Crown adducing evidence of a defendant's criminal convictions and the introduction of a public defender system are under threat.[39] It is almost as though the establishment is no longer interested in the fairness of the criminal justice system, but merely in getting the conviction rate up and doing so at least cost to the public purse. Nineteenth century judges and politicians had no compunction in stopping up loopholes, as the reforms effected by Campbell's Criminal Evidence Act 1851,[40] section 4 of the Criminal Law Amendment Act 1885[41] and the judgment of the Court for

---

[37] 'Most horrific cases of alleged miscarriage of justice related to activities in the 1970s and 1980s before PACE and the rigid controls that now exist' (David Maclean MP, Minister of State at the Home Office, *Hansard*, 1995, 258, col 1889). But compare with the Royal Commission report para. 22 '[the case of] the Cardiff Three ... occurred after the implementation of PACE'

[38] To defenders of civil liberties one of the merits of juries is that they acquit a higher percentage of accused than do magistrates.

[39] See G. Bindman and J. Bennathon, 'Civil Liberties Surrendered', *The Times*, 16 October, 2001.

[40] Prior to Campbell's Act every year a number of accused, as to whose guilt there could be no doubt went free because of trifling defects in the indictment or variances between the indictment and the evidence called to support it. In 1818-19 Frances Clarke, tried three times for a horrific child murder, escaped on each occasion, twice because the indictment was bad and the third time on a plea of *autrefois acquit* (see *The Times*, 30 March 1818, 3 August 3 1818 and 6 August 1819). In 1841 Lord Cardigan was acquitted of attempted murder because the Crown failed to prove that his victim bore one of the Christian names ascribed to him in the indictment (see *A Century of Law Reform* (Macmillan and Co, London, 1901), p. 61). The 1851 Act closed such avenues of escape.

[41] At common law a child who did not understand the nature of an oath was not competent to give evidence against her attacker with the result that if hers was the only testimony, he went free. Section 4 put an end to this patent injustice by permitting child complainants in sexual cases to give evidence unsworn. In 1894 the exception was extended to cases of child cruelty and neglect.

Crown Cases Reserved in *Baldry* (1852) well demonstrate.[42] But they were always concerned to ensure that accused persons were treated fairly.[43] Today, by contrast, improving protections for the accused appears to rank very low on the political agenda, with the result that when even modest additional safeguards are proposed, such as the introduction of a requirement that confession evidence be inadmissible unless corroborated, they are seldom taken up. Worse still, protestations that, by tilting the balance ever further in favour of the prosecution, one increases the risk of wrong convictions are simply ignored. It is this which causes disquiet amongst judges, lawyers and others concerned with civil liberties. If it could be shown that the in-roads which have been made upon the rights of accused persons over the last twenty years had resulted in a substantial and sustained improvement in the conviction rate, that would afford a modicum of justification for the course that has been taken. But this is not how things have turned out, for, although the percentage of defendants convicted in Crown Court trials rose between 1993 and 1998 to around 58 per cent, by 1999/2000 it was back down to 55 per cent (which is where it had been in 1987/1988).[44]

Conclusion

Although in many respects the present-day trial system is immeasurably better than its Victorian counterpart, critics are quick to point out that it compares badly in terms of evidential protection. But the European Convention of Human Rights and the jurisprudence which has grown up around it may yet serve to redress the balance and to check the illiberal tendencies of 'law and order' politicians. Britain, although an early signatory to the Convention, for years steadfastly refused to incorporate it into English law. However, by the Human Rights Act 1998 the courts are now enjoined to construe legislation in a way which is compatible with the rights guaranteed under the Convention and, where this proves impossible, to make a declaration of incompatibility. Convention rights include the right to a fair trial and, as the recent case of *R v A (No 2)* has shown, the House of Lords is quite prepared to rewrite legislation which offends against that

[42] *R v Baldry* (1852) 5 Cox 523. The case signalled the adoption by the courts of a much more robust approach to the question of voluntariness of confessions. Campbell LCJ memorably observing that in this area of law 'justice and common sense seem to have been sacrificed on the altar of mercy'.

[43] Would any modern-day 'law and order' politician subscribe, as Holroyd J did in *R v Hobson* (1823) 1 Lew CC 261, to the view that it was 'better ten guilty men ... escape rather than one innocent man suffer'?

[44] CPS *Annual Reports*, 1991-92 to 1999-2000.

right, even if it flies in the face of the expressed will of parliament.[45] That is the most encouraging sign seen for some time.

---

[45] [2001] 2 WLR 1546.

Chapter 2

Causing a Sensation: Media and Legal Representations of Bad Behaviour

Judith Rowbotham and Kim Stevenson

Introduction

Political spin aside, public perceptions of certain crimes and behaviour, offensive or otherwise, can be strongly influenced and shaped by two major factors: the ways in which the media portray such behaviour in its reporting, and legal commentary in the form of statements made in and out of the courts, primarily by judges and other legal professionals. The media's role in promoting the high profile of bad behaviour, including the legal processes surrounding it, is something which seems particularly apparent in the late twentieth century but is by no means exclusive to it. The Victorian media can also be justifiably described as obsessed with depicting offensive conduct and legal intervention. Both periods demonstrate deep concern over the wider social effects of bad behaviour and crime, justifying this media emphasis by the need to give publicity to crime and criminal conduct in order to keep the public informed, or warned. In times of social panic such as these, resultant expressions of moral outrage stemming from public or 'popular' reactions to that information can provide a two-way channel, 'feeding' a type of media 'frenzy' concentrating on certain cases or individuals. While it is not always easy to identify and comprehend the precise causal factors behind such media expressions, it is evident that predominantly cultural perspectives inform a range of essentially subjective and qualitative judgments about the dimensions of particular social panics. Either to focus simply on media effusions, or to avoid such populism and concentrate solely on the legal dimension, is to misrepresent the realities underlying these media representations. It omits the need to take account of an active legal input in media definitions of bad behaviour.

This chapter highlights the collaboration between the print media and the legal establishment in the Victorian period and uses this to question the extent of its continuation in the present, albeit in a different format. Such a co-operation, drawing together the authority of two powerful forces, has the potential to influence significantly the determination and presentation of those types of conduct which ultimately may become publicly constituted as the dimensions of 'bad' behaviour. If this collaboration is not acknowledged, a distorted picture of where the responsibility lies for such depictions is formed. The readiness of past and present commentators to blame the media alone for popularising these narratives of offence, while leaving legal figures largely positioned above such criticisms, is challenged through the examination not just of newspaper presentations but also the dimensions of the legal contribution. It is possible to do this in considerable detail for the Victorian period; the minutiae for the modern period is less accessible. However, this process of comparison still provides a range of questions through which legal involvement can be interrogated for the present age.

This has important implications because for either period, an unfounded belief in the independence of the views of the media can insulate these opinion-forming institutions from balanced assessment and useful criticism. As Jane Soames percipiently pointed out in 1938:

> How far the character of our public life influences the Press and determines its tone, how far public indifference is responsible, to what extent the ownership of the Press accounts for what it says or does not say, and whatever other factors there may be, the salient fact is that we are spoon-fed, though the public as a whole does not realise it.[1]

These two establishment pillars, the law and the media, were and still are, highly influential in promulgating a unity in popular and legal perceptions of the existence of social panics, and the subsequent morally-expressed justifications of actions presented as resulting from the panic. They can be shown to have collaborated to a considerable extent in promoting a substantially shared Victorian vision of 'bad' behaviour, including strategies to punish its perpetrators. In adopting tones of moral righteousness, the media still displays this longstanding preoccupation with the 'ethical' dimension of news stories. This demonstrates how public attention can be focussed onto a topic rousing popular indignation, generally over some form of 'bad behaviour' which is 'revealed' by the media. The danger is, it can lure the individual consumer into an uncritical acceptance not just of a moral stance echoing their personal opinion but also of the linkage often implicit in such reporting between the subjectivities of moral opinion and the actions and

---

[1] Jane Soames, *The English Press. Newspaper and News* (Lindsay Drummond Ltd, London, 1938) p. 31.

agenda of state authority and its agents. The severe scrutiny on politicians and government, however, means that the relationship between media and politics has entered popular consciousness. The same is true to a considerable extent for the police. However, the modern press reflects the Victorian in obscuring the relationship between the media and the legal world.

While comparative analysis of the Victorian and modern press is both illuminating and justifiable, it is not claimed that there is a complete echo between the two periods. There are some obvious differences of perspective, such as the ways of depicting individuals in positions of prominence or power. The Victorian period looked to 'heroes' to provide models for good behaviour. In line with this general cultural acceptance of heroes as helpful factors in society, the Victorian newspaper press adopted a generally positive attitude towards leading legal figures in society, practically enhancing their reputations both during their lifetimes and after their death. A much more complex, and cumulatively negative, position is now taken towards prominent public figures, including legal professionals. Cultural shifts have produced, today, a distrust of uncomplicated heroism, certainly in terms of promoting prominent figures as models of 'good' behaviour for the rest of society to emulate. Instead, as the constant flood of personal 'exposures' underline, this less heroic age prefers to use the personal to *undermine* the individual professional.[2] The modern willingness to expose 'bad' behaviour amongst prominent professionals indicates also a different approach to the most effective way to deal with social panics and popular moral outrage. Victorians did, on the whole, trust their political and legal leaders to produce workable solutions in times of crisis. This confidence in the good behaviour of leading figures is markedly absent from the anticipations of the modern age, where prominent individuals associated with a failure to control or eradicate 'bad' behaviour of some kind are regularly pilloried and their 'professionalism' questioned.

These prominent differences should not, however, divert attention from the underlying commonalities, including the shared obsession with the moral dimensions of 'bad' behaviour because of the assumptions about its negative effects on both individual 'victims' and society as a whole. In particular, such diversities of perspective and practice should not be used to obscure the extent to which the media and legal worlds have continued to look to each other to provide backing and credibility where their respective agendas overlap. Certainly the modern relationship between the press, and the legal world is different to the more practically inter-dependent

---

[2] See, for example, *Daily Mail* serialisation of the son's autobiography of George Carman QC, in February 2002.

one that existed in the nineteenth century where lawyers themselves (especially barristers) provided the bulk of actual crime writing in newspapers. Many media reports, especially of high profile crimes, are self-evidently informed by expert knowledge providing depth and conviction, underlining the continuing input of legal professionals into the reportage of bad behaviour and crime. They draw, it would seem, on the long-established, if rarely openly acknowledged, tradition of co-operation between the two worlds.

'Moral Guardians'?

The tradition was established when relationships between the legal and media worlds took on new dimensions in the Victorian age, with considerable implications for the present. Both institutions were seeking to establish themselves as 'professions' in a modern sense and considered themselves entrusted with responsibility for the well-being and morality of society, ready to exploit the new opportunities offered by technological innovation to convey their message.[3] As Gavin Sutter also notes, the speed of communication permitted by innovation, notably in printing technology, plus its communication ally, the railway, gave the wider public the perception of a revolution in information and understanding – but one accompanied by 'new' dangers in terms of the behaviour this encouraged. The parallels with the modern age, with the development of the internet and 'on-line' newspaper updates providing immediate communication with their audience linked to panic over the implications of the electronic medium, are powerful. In the resulting atmosphere of fluctuating social panic experienced by both eras, types of offensive behaviour which, in their core essence, are neither new nor unexpected, assume a freshly threatening aspect.

The consequence for both periods is the development of fears about the negative aspects of technological innovation, that it provides opportunities to expand and twist the impact of offensive behaviour on society as a whole, not just on the victims of a particular expression of bad behaviour. The focus in such panics on forms of offensive conduct as the spark for mass outbursts of public moral outrage is a link between the periods. Another common reality is the apparently almost insatiable (certainly according to the media) public fascination with information about all dimensions of 'crime' and the legal world in general – including the 'real people' who play out their 'sensational' stories on the legal stage. But this

---

[3] Harold Perkin, *The Rise of Professional Society: England since 1880* (Routledge, London, 1989).

relates to the genuine need that the public has for insights into a highly complex, even arcane, world which they may encounter at times of misfortune, quite as much as to their love of an exciting narrative. Then, as now, the chances of an enforced encounter with the law, whether as victim or defender in any action, were high.[4] Similar opportunities present themselves where members of the public are called upon to act, albeit often reluctantly, as jury members in a wide range of criminal and civil trials.[5] Insecurities about the actual expectations of participants in the legal process can be allayed by regular exposure in the media to real examples of all the mechanisms surrounding the system. Today, such exposure promotes the acquisition of 'knowledge' about the elements of the legal world, just as it did for the Victorians, serving as the major source of information for the mass of the non-professional community. However, there is a long-standing concern that by dwelling on the details of crime or bad behaviour, these reports can also operate in a more negative sense.

Today, as Kidd-Hewitt and Osborn comment, there is a large body of opinion that accepts that the mass media are responsible for encouraging, and even creating crime, but theoretical debates about the relationship between crime and the media remain locked in paradigms of effects and quantification.[6] The fairness of this perspective remains open to question – newspapers *react* to public mood quite as much as they create it, despite their claims to the contrary, Victorian and modern.[7] Newspapers act as a channel through which established authority, including the law, can influence public mood by the presentation of information. It is worth remembering that government, for example, is rarely critical of the media when it is apparently effective in purveying its agendas to the public, reserving its hostility for occasions where the media obstinately reflects an oppositional stance, clearly in tune with public mood as in the controversies over the MMR triple vaccine between 2001 and 2002.[8]

---

4 David Taylor, *Crime, Policing and Punishment in England 1750-1914* (Macmillan: Basingstoke, 1998) ch. 4; Clive Emsley, *Crime and Society in England 1750-1900* (London: Longman 1996).

5 Recent proposals to extend jury service to all professionals including legal professionals mean that virtually no-one would be excused. See Lord Justice Auld, *A Review of the Criminal Courts of England and Wales*, Lord Chancellor's Department, September 2001.

6 David Kidd-Hewitt and Richard Osborn (eds), *Crime and the Media: the Post-modern Spectacle* (Pluto Press, London, 1995) p. x.

7 A. Fiest, *The Effective Use of the Media in Serious Crime Investigation* (Home Office, London, 1999).

8 MMR represents Mumps Measles and Rubella vaccines. See *Daily Mail*, 27 February 2002, for example.

The print media has also remained particularly effective at establishing a series of stereotypes where bad behaviour and crime are presented within the legal context, if only because the legal input into such representations has remained more hidden than political input. Such stereotypes, while possessing a more unforgiving edge to their definitions, are clearly linked to broader social classifications. This may be disguised to an extent today by a willingness to explain the effects of a disadvantaged background on an individual offender, yet closer examination shows how stereotyped these surveys are in terms of the ways in which they depict both the person and the offence and link them to certain kinds of disadvantage. By contrast, contemporary texts, including newspaper editorials and fiction, underline the greater faith held by the Victorians in the ability of the individual to avoid temptation and rise to goodness despite unequivocally adverse circumstances.[9] Possessed of the 'right' instincts, and an 'in-born purity of nature', Oliver Twist resisted all the blandishments Fagin and the Artful Dodger could offer to lure him into bad behaviour. However, with a greater belief in the negative impact of adverse environments on instincts towards 'right' conduct, his modern counterpart (had he the initiative and verve Oliver showed) might be more likely to be expected (at least by more left-liberal elements) to replace the Artful Dodger as Fagin's right-hand adjutant with a due measure of accompanying sympathy for the disadvantages that drove him to such a course.

At times of crisis, the presentation of crime in the mass media can, because of the stereotypification of the individuals involved, operate as a metaphor for a perceived disorder and decline in society generally, reflecting a feeling of social panic in the community and generating outbursts of morally-justified concern expressed in terms of a desire for more order and security to curb bad behaviour. The media often is identified as both villain and vital tool of communication. As Ericson concludes, it can become associated with the low culture and low life of crime and deviance, in contradistinction to an imagined high culture and better life — respectable fears about crime are coupled with respectable fears about the negative effects of mass media.[10] Newspaper reportage of bad behaviour is particularly vulnerable to such complicated expectations — its readership demands a sustained diet of the very information which causes it most concern, and in order to maintain sales levels, and so

---

[9] See J. Rowbotham, '"All Our Past Proclaims Our Future": Popular Biography and Masculine Identity during the Golden Age, 1850–1870', in I. Inkster (ed.), *The Golden Age. Essays in British Economic and Social History, 1850-1870* (Ashgate Publishing, Aldershot, 2000), especially p. 282.

[10] See Richard Ericson (ed.), *Crime and the Media* (Dartmouth, Aldershot, 1995) pp. xi-xiv.

profitability, newspapers respond with the desired material. The demand by audiences for 'topicality', 'relevance' and 'reality' means that the pressure to focus on particularly high profile types of bad behaviour and ways of dealing with it is powerful, demanding 'authenticity' and 'accuracy'.

Fact-based reporting acquired a new, popular dimension in the Victorian age when, for the first time, a substantial amount of information about real events could be conveyed to a mass audience more or less simultaneously. Newspaper reporting therefore exerted a considerable impact upon perspectives on the administration of justice at a time of major legal reforms with real impact on the population because of the expansion of summary justice.[11] The greater availability of affordable print for an already highly literate population spawned a new importance for newspaper writers − though not everyone recognised this:

> Very few persons have any idea of the important role played by the reporter in modern social life... He is, as a rule so unobtrusive that he seldom comes under the eye of the public [but without him] there would be no interesting 'police news', opening up a hundred strange phases of life, and putting us upon our guard against a thousand modes of imposition.[12]

Printed comment was then held to convey a veracity that endowed it with a real moral authority just as, arguably, television or radio do today. As early as 1839, an anonymous 'Student at Law' recognised the potential educational powers of the news media in a pamphlet *The Fourth Estate: or the Moral Influence of the Press*.[13] The author exhorted the public to respect the press and to feel indebted to the newspapers for the knowledge and sense of moral duty they promote. In its new mass guise, the Victorian press aimed to act as a popular parliament, testing and informing public opinion on legislative proposals, and as a popular court of justice, commenting upon all issues of public conduct and private and public morals.[14] The press took upon itself the cudgel of 'public interest'. It became *their responsibility* not only to warn and inform the public of crimes committed in the community and to reassure it that the culprits were in custody, but also to educate that public in how they were to react to

---

[11] The Jervis Act 1848 and Criminal Justice Act 1855 are crucial here.

[12] Henry S. King, *Two Idle Apprentices, Briefs and Papers, Sketches of the Bar and the Press* (King, London, 1872) pp. 186-8.

[13] A Student at Law, *The Fourth Estate: or the Moral Influence of the Press* (Ridgeway, London, 1839), pp. 9-12.

[14] Charles Pebody, *English Journalism and the Men who have Made It* (Cassell Petter Galpin and Co., London, 1882) pp. 177-178.

criminals and how they might identify them.[15] The question is, how far their reportage was driven by factors other than an objective desire to report 'facts'.

Through its reporting, the Victorian press established a range of stereotypes associated with criminal behaviour which echoed those operating more broadly at the time, but which possessed much less flexibility, just as the law itself possessed less flexibility than the operation of social sanctions. In reflecting the perspectives of those participants in the legal process who provided information and opinion, individuality and the contribution of a single personality had less effect than assumptions linked to class, age, gender and the over-arching concept of 'respectability'.[16] Hints on appropriate demeanour and dress, as well as forms of address, have been established since the Victorian period as staple features of crime reporting. Victorian newspaper reports regularly included references as to the respectability (or unrespectability) of witnesses and defendants, in terms of dress, conduct and reputation.[17] Even today smart dress, a sharp hair-cut, or an apparently deferential manner are still thought by many participants in the legal process to hide a multitude of sins. Conversely a more careless person supposedly demonstrates the exact opposite.

Gender and class assumptions feature strongly in the formation of both media and legal opinion. For instance, women in the Victorian period often found their evidence less valued than that of men, especially where it was the uncorroborated testimony of a woman from the lower classes, as shown in the following comment of a police court magistrate:

> Such indeed is the partisanship and such is the amount of personal feeling infused into the evidence of this class of witnesses, so great is the exaggeration to which they will resort, and so extravagant are their assertions,... that to ascertain the real truth of any complaint amounts, in the great majority of cases in which this class of woman alone are witnesses, to a moral impossibility.[18]

[15] Marjorie Jones, *The Relationship Between the Criminal Courts and the Mass Media* (Barry Rose, Chichester, 1974) p. 45.

[16] Kim Stevenson, '"Taking Indecent Liberties"; The Victorian Encryption of Sexual Violence', unpublished paper, History of Violence conference, Liverpool, July 2001; F. M. L. Thompson, *The Rise of Respectable Society: A Social History of Victorian Britain 1830-1900* (Fontana, London, 1988).

[17] See Kim Stevenson, 'The Respectability Imperative: A Golden Rule in Cases of Sexual Assault?' in Inkster *et al* (eds), *The Golden Age*, pp. 237-48.

[18] Horace Cox, *Metropolitan Police Court Jottings* (London, 1882) p. 7.

Equally a woman was not competent to testify against her husband and it is only recently that the mandatory common law requirements as to corroboration in the case of young children and females alleging sexual assaults have been relaxed.[19] Where a man gave single testimony this was an entirely different matter as, 'however low their condition, a certain stratum of truth is usually visible... they rarely resort to the unblushing falsehoods which form of the staple of the evidence of this rank of the gentler sex'.[20] Essentially, those who, for reasons of class, age or gender, had less authority associated with their persona than did the 'normal' respectable adult male could expect that their evidence for or against a prosecution case would assume less value in both its legal determination and its reporting. Similarly, the highly-coloured rhetoric of newspaper coverage has always been notorious for its reliance on essentially hierarchical and gendered assumptions.

Attention-Grabbing Sensationalism

Press headlines, front-page stories, dedicated crime pages, and pictorial images convey messages intended to have an immediate impact on the public. Often labelled 'sensationalist', carrying with this disapproving overtones implying an undesirable exaggeration, critics blame the media for grabbing the reader's attention with headlines that stress the disreputable nature of the crimes reported. Sensationalist phraseology such as 'shocking violent outrage', 'unspeakable violence', 'murderous assaults', and 'crime of dreadful depravity', were commonplace in most Victorian national and local papers, just as their counterparts are today. An editorial in the *Daily Telegraph* provides a justification which remains current in newspaper thinking:

> So far as the public is concerned the newspapers must report the proceedings. If one paper abstained, twenty others would take its place and nothing would be gained by the public. Moreover, on the broadest grounds of common interest, it is better that society should be occasionally shocked with the report of the most detestable charges than that judicial proceedings should at any time take place in secret, or that crime itself should derive a fatal safety in continuity from the secrecy accorded to it by an abuse of decorum.[21]

---

[19] See s.80 Police and Criminal Evidence Act; s.34 Criminal Justice Act 1988.

[20] Cox, *Jottings*.

[21] *Daily Telegraph*, 23 May 1870. The Victorian title at this date was a very different beast to today's *Daily Telegraph*, being a newspaper aimed at the lower classes, and having a left radical aspect.

The press has long been unstinting in editorials declaring abhorrence and intolerance of certain types of conduct while publicising that conduct in news reports, always of course in the interests of 'public information'. A typical Victorian example from the *Pall Mall Gazette* comments on the case of William John Bainton, aged 28, sentenced to 18 months imprisonment at Middlesex Sessions for having stripped and beaten his stepdaughter and another young girl with a cat-o' nine-tails of thick rope. The paper asserted that:

> Every now and then occurs in our criminal reports a story of filthy brutality so fantastic in outrage, and so cruel, too, that one is tempted to think the sober-minded Paley was, at least, excusable.... To suggest that some such punishment as being pitched into a den of wild beast... sought to be reserved... for exceptionably abominable crimes.[22]

The editor, that noted legal figure James Fitzjames Stephen, concluded that even 18 years imprisonment with occasional cat-o' nine-tails 'would not satisfy the indignation which such a tale arouses'.[23] Today, tabloid newspapers still provide details of 'horrid' cases linked to editorial moral disapproval of the behaviour resulting in the cases.

Any serious assessment of the role of the print media in depicting bad behaviour means that the usefulness of the media to the legal world, in seeking to control and diminish crime and offensive conduct needs to be taken into account. In theory, that relationship might be expected to be rather distant. After all, journalism has remained based on the market economy whereas law claims to be rooted in the artificially constructed principles of a fair trial.[24] In practice the pressures for a closer collaborative relationship are powerful. The high profile of crime reporting in newspapers, including descriptions of the parts played by police and lawyers, was extremely useful advertising, as well as serving to establish the heroic nature of the denizens of the legal world (or most of them!). The press was seen as a real adjunct to the police and the legal profession in the process of identifying and punishing bad behaviour. In a parallel to the modern use of encouraging the public to come forward in television programmes such as 'Crimewatch', Victorian newspapers were used to appeal, overtly or implicitly, for information from their readership. A survey of the correspondence and editorial columns from papers such as the *Daily Telegraph* reveals that they frequently received it. For example,

[22] *Pall Mall Gazette*, 9 February 1865, p. 5.
[23] *Ibid*.
[24] J. Edward Gerald, *News of Crime: Courts and Press in Conflict* (Greenwood Press, Connecticut, 1983) p. 5.

in 1870 a letter from a landlord in Stoke Newington warned of a gang whose *modus operandi* was not only to fail to pay any rent due for premises leased but to clear those premises of 'everything capable of being taken away or turned into money'. He exhorted the readership to help in tracking down 'these thieves and swindlers', trusting that 'the publicity thus given may lead to the apprehension and conviction of the gang'. It was later reported, with satisfaction, that due to the 'vigilance' of the readership, this had indeed happened.[25]

The reality is that, underlying the attention-grabbing sensationalism, newspapers past and present combine with the denizens of the legal world to convey a substance of belief that profoundly affects popular understandings of the legal world and its operations. Together, they create real expectations about the operation of the justice system for 'ordinary' folk. Through appeals for information and support to their wider public, they involve members of the community in sustaining those realities. What can be attributed to the media is the ability to make choate the incoherent fears existing more widely in society. Television programmes like 'Crimewatch' or the fictional 'Cracker', which spawned interest in the 'real' forensic psychiatrist, together with fly-on-the-wall documentaries and docu-dramas continue a process started in the Victorian period, of blurring the fact-fiction boundaries on a grand scale. This highlights a very basic truth: that the certainty of sizeable audiences for anything that can be labelled either 'real' or 'realistic' narratives of crime and punishment ensures those boundaries will remain fluid. This in turn guarantees that the media will continue to feature such narratives as a staple, if only in the interests of the profit margin, and that the legal world will continue with practical support for this through provision of information and authority.

Collaboration and Collusion

Such far-reaching statements require illustration. An investigation of the networks behind the public faces of both the publishing and the legal worlds confirms the existence of a long-standing and very close connection. From a professional perspective lawyers have long relied, and indeed still do, on 'the efficient rendering of *The Times* Law Reports and for special legal points on the *Solicitors' Journal*, first published in the mid-nineteenth century.[26] But from the point of view of the ordinary

---

[25] Letter, *Daily Telegraph*, 5 September 1870; *Daily Telegraph*, 15 September 1870.

[26] G. Binney Dibblee, *The Newspaper* (Williams and Norgate, London, 1913), p. 196.

Victorian reader, it was generally agreed that 'In order to intelligibly report a case in one of the higher courts of justice, considerable legal knowledge is necessary, and only men who are duly qualified should undertake such work'.[27] Victorian reportage of actual trials and legal events was controlled largely by legal professionals, not journalists or reporters. For instance, between 1850-1900, the majority of the crime reporters for *The Times* were barristers doubling as reporters in the interests of expanding their income such as Alfred Plowden:

> by a piece of good fortune I had been appointed Law Reporter for *The Times* on [Oxford] Circuit; an appointment which was followed later on by my being made Chief Reporter for the Common Pleas Division at Westminster. Both of these appointments I continued to hold until I was appointed a Police Magistrate in 1888.[28]

Using professionals in this way undoubtedly gave an authority and credibility to *The Times* reports that it has never lost (also suggesting the continuation of its powerful links with the legal community). While *The Times*, due to its resources and reputation, made the greatest use of barrister reporters, it was not alone.

A number of high-profile lawyers, such as Lord Brougham and James Fitzjames Stephen, were known at the time as active and prolific reporters and commentators, though the full extent of their contributions was not then recognised, due to the anonymity of much of their output.[29] Then as now, the extent to which other Victorian legal figures were similarly employed, expanding their income through collaboration with the media, has been largely ignored, partly due to the enthusiasm with which these legal figures embraced the tradition of journalistic anonymity.[30] The reality that numbers of Victorian lawyers were owners or editors of prominent newspapers and periodicals has also been little touched on. Mr. Serjeant Cox, chairman of the Middlesex Sessions, 'made an enormous fortune by his marvellous newspaper ventures, but he diligently discharged the duties of Chairman of the second court for many years'.[31]

---

[27] John Dawson, *Practical Journalism. How to Enter Thereon and Succeed* (Upcott Gill, London, 1885), p. 23.

[28] Alfred Chicele Plowden, *Grain or Chaff, The Autobiography of a Police Magistrate* (T. Fisher Unwin, London, 1903), pp. 107-8.

[29] Detailed work by scholars hints at their full outputs, see *Wellesley Index for Victorian Periodicals*, vols 1-5, for instance.

[30] Diblee, *The Newspaper*, pp. 102-4.

[31] Edmund Purcell, *Forty Years at the Criminal Bar. Experiences and Impressions* (T. Fisher Unwin, London), 1916, p. 172.

This helps to explain the degree of collaboration between these two overtly disparate Victorian worlds. Behind-the-scenes-knowledge and experience enhanced the private mutual respect that each held for the other, as well as the extent of their practical dependence on the assets of the other side. Thus, while an amount of humour could be, and was, poked at prominent legal figures including Serjeant Ballantine and Lord Justice Cockburn, their professional merits were never seriously questioned and their personal probity and good behaviour enhanced in public perspective by laudatory biographical articles and summaries.[32] This reflects the Victorian reality that 'no real opposition Press exists in England' Differences between papers was, according to Jane Soames, 'chiefly due to the different classes of society to which they address themselves', for 'neither oversteps the boundary which divides tepid comment from real criticism; and neither reports facts of importance which are not mentioned by the other'.[33] A comparison of the reportage of bad behaviour and crime in the Victorian press confirms this – few incidents reported in either the *Daily Telegraph* or *Reynolds Newspaper*, radical, working-class orientated papers, were not also reported in *The Times* or the *Morning Post*. How different is it today?

Aided by the anonymity of contributions when desired, relationships between the Victorian media and bar were very cosy – almost dangerously incestuous in fact. The press was controlled by a very small ring and the comment of the time was: 'If you know who owns the Press, you will know what to expect of it'.[34] Yet that reality was not part of wider popular knowledge. This is not to say there were not concerns and tensions within that relationship. Conflict between law and press was and is most obviously likely to occur over decisions about when to publish crime news, and how much detail to include: raising the cry of trial by media rather than trial by jury. In 1861 the *Law Times* warned the profession about the proclivity of newspapers to intervene in, and so undermine, the judicial process:

> Perhaps the most remarkable case of late occurrence in which this publicity of investigation baffled inquiry was the mysterious Road case, in which every step of the investigation was clearly indicated

---

[32] For example see, 'Serjeant Ballantine at Home', *Town Talk*, 2 August 1879, pp. 5-6; 'Baron Brampton of Brampton' by 'E', *The Strand Magazine*, 1899, xv, pp. 318-26; 'Who's Who in the Legal World', *The Harmsworth London Magazine*, 1903, pp. 179-81; Harold Spender, 'Mr. Rufus Isaacs MP KC, A Character Sketch', *The Pall Mall Magazine*, 1907, pp. 577-83.

[33] Jones, *Justice and Journalism*, p. 29.

[34] Soames, *English Press*, p. 53.

by the local and metropolitan papers before it was taken... Directly
these notorious cases occur, the reporters set to work, to obtain all
the information they can obtain, good bad and indifferent... collected
from all manner of sources, for the most part quite unreliable... by
men very frequently not of very sound judgment and quite ignorant
of the laws of evidence. Day after day, the public mind is besieged
with this unreliable information. It is digested into public opinion
and enters into every conversation which takes place about the
matter... This is as much to assert that an utterly irresponsible and
anonymous journalist, a man of no special legal training, has right
not only to comment upon the preliminary investigation, but even to
assess and review the decision of the Queen's judges.[35]

What the *Law Times* was advocating, however, was the use of proper legal
professionals as reporters, who would understand the responsibilities of
crime reporting!

A similar problem can be identified today. Defence lawyers, for instance,
have claimed several times recently that unsubstantiated and reckless
journalistic speculation, unfuelled by legal expertise, has damaged chances
of a fair trial for their clients. In April 2001 the trial of Leeds United football
players Jonathan Woodgate and Lee Bowyer, charged with serious assault of
an Asian student collapsed, because of the publication, by the *Sunday
Mirror*, of an interview with the victim's father. That disclosure forced the
resignation of that paper's editor.[36] Concerns over media payment to
witnesses *before* a trial has caused tensions between the law and newspapers,
with claims about inappropriate media intervention in legal affairs, as,
notoriously, in the 1996 Rosemary West trial, when 19 witnesses received
payments for their stories.[37] More recently, Gary Glitter's accuser received
£10,000 from the *News of the World*, with, if he was convicted of seducing
her at 14, a further promise of a 'win bonus' of £25,000. A jury, informed of
this, convicted Glitter, but not for *her* seduction. It was, instead, for his
possession of pornography on his computer.[38] Conversely, too close a liaison
between crime journalist and law officer has been seen as counter-
productive, as leading to situations where the journalist might be tempted
to 'ignore' a story that should be made public.[39] Either way, the issue is

---

[35] *County Courts Chronicle*, 1 August 1861, pp. 210-11.

[36] *The Financial Times*, 16 May 2001; *The Guardian*, 16 May 2001.

[37] *Daily Mail*, 30 November 1995; *The Guardian*, 30 November 1995.

[38] *The Times*, 26 November 1999; *Bristol Evening Post*, 1 December 1999. See also chapters
by Edwards, Sutter and Lewis in this volume.

[39] Peter Burden, 'The Business of Crime Reporting: Problems and Dilemmas', in Colin
Summer (ed.), *Crime Justice and the Mass Media. Papers presented to the 14th
Cropwood Round Table Conference* (University of Cambridge, Cambridge, 1982), p. 6.

journalistic objectivity in relation to law reporting. Victorian concerns over crime reporting therefore has familiar resonances for any survey of modern newspaper reporters seeking out evidence and publishing details of cases *sub judice*.

Yet the voiced resentment of modern legal professionals in such cases should not divert attention from the indications of the continuation of an actively collaborative relationship between the legal world and the media. Newspaper articles by John Mortimer, barrister and creator of Rumpole of the Bailey, underline the dependence each has on the other.[40] While research has begun to demonstrate the collaboration of the Victorian period, the shape and extent of modern co-operation remains as obscure to most external observers as the nineteenth century collusion was to commentators then. How satisfactory is this? The key question remains how far this relationship was and is simply one of intrinsic mutual benefit working for the good of the popular audience, or whether it is part of a more complex and less beneficial macro-dynamic. Does collaboration between the media and the legal world operate simply to provide a mass audience with expertly judged information as a basis for their own independent process of forming opinion? Or is it part of a collusion which, operating within the overall political establishment, possesses the intention to 'educate' subliminally by moulding public opinion in ways that *obscure* rather than promote the process of independent opinion-forming by a mass audience?

Conclusion

The relationship between the legal world and the media has, for reasons of self-interest, necessarily been one of reciprocity. Each relies upon the other as a means of communicating to the public various perspectives and understandings that seek to avoid independent criticism of the operations of the legal system and its processes. For reasons of a more direct comparison, this chapter has focused on the print media, where a significant proportion of the Victorian legal profession were actively engaged in the public presentation and representation of the law. As such legal professionals formed a largely unacknowledged element in influencing and shaping the reportage of the criminal process and determination of what constitutes bad behaviour, individually and generally. Lawyers are no longer crime writers in the same way, but how far are they still involved in news production? Has the

---

[40] John Mortimer, 'The Trials and Tribulations that Helped to Make Rumpole. The Truth About Britain's Most Celebrated Barrister', *The Mail on Sunday*, 7 May 2000, p. 61.

relationship changed in terms of the underlying common agenda? There are powerful indicators that it remains substantially the same. Given that most people's understanding of how the legal world operates *still* comes through the media, including newspapers, it is important that the potential for manipulation be openly acknowledged. There is nothing intrinsically wrong or undesirable with close links between the media and the legal world, focused through the input of legal professionals. But such relationships should be subject to the sort of scrutiny that is commonplace for the relationships between media and the police and media and politicians.

Chapter 3

Policing a Myth, Managing an Illusion: Victorian and Contemporary Crime Recording

Tom Williamson

Introduction

A major reform of the police in England and Wales has just been announced by Home Secretary David Blunkett, in a government White Paper, *Policing A New Century: A Blueprint For Reform*.[1] The reform of the police is part of the government's modernising agenda for the public sector. One of the principles of public sector reform is to raise performance through a national framework of standards and accountability. The need for police reform according to the White Paper is due to increase in the fear of crime; to perceptions of poor police performance relating to detection and conviction rates, leading to low public confidence in the police.[2] Upon further examination, each of these criteria provides weak grounds for establishing the need for reform. For example, according to the 2001 British Crime Survey 26 per cent of respondents considered that crime had risen, 'a lot', despite the fact that the survey had shown a fall of 12 per cent in the overall level of crime. There is therefore a gap between public perception and the real position. This is not new and was also a feature of the Victorian period, although public confidence was rather the opposite — that crime was falling![3]

Another present concern appears to be the need for improved performance in detection and conviction rates benchmarking against European and international standards, despite the acknowledgement that

---

[1] David Blunkett, *Policing A New Century: A Blueprint For Reform*, White Paper, 2001.

[2] Blunkett, *Policing A New Century*, paras 1.25; 1.34; 1.46.

[3] J. Holt Schooling, 'Crime', *Pall Mall Magazine*, 1898, XV, p. 241; Howard Taylor, 'Rationing crime: the political economy of criminal statistics since the 1850s', *Economic History Review*, LI 3 (1998), pp. 569-90.

'European and international comparisons are unreliable because of different definitions'. Like may not, therefore be being compared with like. Current statistics also indicate the impact of such figures on public perceptions of those bodies entrusted with the task of crime prevention and law enforcement. Thus, for instance, public satisfaction with the police in England and Wales was 66 per cènt in the British Crime Survey (BCS) compared to around 70 per cent for international comparators. Yet such snapshot statistics provide no indication of trend, or whether the comparison reached the level of being statistically significantly different. Measures of confidence showed no comparison with other professional groups. Whereas confidence in the police has fallen from 83 per cent of those responding in 1983 as having 'a lot or fair amount of confidence', down to 54 per cent in 1999, during the same period, confidence in parliament has dropped from 54 per cent to 15 per cent.[4] The White Paper hardly seems to provide incontrovertible evidence of the need for radical reform of the police. Rather, the main thrust of the reforms is to improve performance by managing detection and conviction rates with published league tables of individual police force performance.

It is the reliance on this data and the way it is intended to be used which is the most worrying aspect of the White Paper. However, it is not the first time that statistics have been misapplied by authority. By providing a snapshot comparison of two different periods, this chapter will show that for around two centuries, the major policing philosophies of prevention and detection have largely failed, but that the true extent of that failure has been masked by the way crime statistics have been manipulated, and society has then reacted to them. The social problems that contemporary society is endeavouring to address through policing are very similar to those affecting Victorian society. This underlines an often overlooked reality – that a focus on official criminal statistics without addressing their social context inevitably leads to a description of crime that is illusory, as shown by the gap between reality and perception consistently revealed by respondents to successive BCS since the first in 1982, showing that nearly three-quarters of all crime experienced by those surveyed never enter the official criminal statistics.

As Shadow Home Secretary, Tony Blair campaigned on being, 'Tough on Crime, tough on the causes of crime'.[5] Not for the first time, the popularity and apparent success of 'tough-on-crime' policies such as Zero Tolerance Policing that ignore the real causes of crime rely on crime

---

[4] *Planning for Social Change 1983* (Henley Centre, 2000).

[5] *The Independent*, 4 December 1993.

statistics that do not stand up to scrutiny — an interesting reflection which amplifies the conclusions reached by Roger Hopkins Burke's chapter. The current Home Secretary has said, 'We do not in this White Paper deal with the broader economic and social issues relating to the causes of crime'.[6] This is a fundamental error that inevitably leads to over-dependence on official criminal statistics and to a situation where the police are *policing a myth* not reality and those concerned with managing police performance will discover that they are managing an illusion. Tough crime policies will only succeed if they are balanced by policies that are equally tough on the causes of crime. Were the Victorians *actually* tougher on crime? They can appear so in certain areas, such as vagrancy or begging, which are now effectively de-criminalised for the most part — yet there is currently pressure for this to change.

What IS a Crime?

A problem for any attempt at measuring crime is that what is tolerated, even if considered anti-social, and what is considered an actual *crime* changes over time. Not only has there been a difference in the crimes which are enforced, but also, different behaviours have at various times been both criminalised and decriminalised. For example, enforcement of betting and gaming legislation, which preoccupied Victorian police officers, has been decriminalised since the Betting, Gaming and Lotteries Act 1963 and the Gaming Act 1968, the implications of which are discussed in Mike Ahearne's chapter. Currently there is an active campaign for decriminalisation of possession and use of certain drugs, which would be a practical return to the Victorian *status quo*, operating on moral disapproval such as, for example, the fictional Watson's disapproval of Sherlock Holmes' opium habit. Male homosexual behaviour has been considered worthy of being criminalised, yet lesbianism never has been a crime — an interestingly gendered reflection. According to the Royal Commission on Criminal Procedure 1981, there were 469 behaviours prior to 1901 defined in law as separate criminal offences. This had grown to 1,396 by 1960 and to 7,500 by 1975, half of which did not require proof of criminal intent on behalf of the offender.

Despite the elasticity inherent in the definition of what is a crime, the totally unrealistic goal of the first police force was to produce the absence of crime. The primary objectives of the Metropolitan Police were set out

---

[6] Blunkett, *Policing*, para. 3.64.

when it was formed in 1829 by the first Commissioners, Rowan and Mayne as follows:

> The principal object to be attained is the prevention of crime. To this great end every effort of the police is to be directed. The security of the person and property, the preservation of public tranquillity and all the other objects of a Police Establishment will thus be better effected than by the detection and punishment of the offender after he has succeeded in committing crime.[7]

The purpose of the police was to ensure that there was no crime. The police were there to stamp out crime. They did this by concentrating their efforts on the areas of greatest deprivation, the worst slums, known to Victorians as 'urban rookeries', which were the abode of the 'dangerous classes' and the habitual criminal class. The dangerous classes were those who drifted in and out of criminality for largely social reasons, but could, if imprisoned, become members of the habitual criminal class. This cohort was a long-standing worry to society, because this habitual criminal class was considered at the time completely irredeemable, and also hereditary – hence the use of transportation, in the belief that this action would actually cut the canker of criminality out from the healthy body of the state.[8]

Victorian discourse about crime tends to focus on crimes committed by the poor. In this, Victorians largely sought to ignore the enormous cost and scale of business and financial fraud, for example, a form of crime generally committed by those with both income and education, unless forced to take notice as a result of some particularly high profile scandal such as the Overend Gurney scandal, 1865-8.[9] Statistically, this was made easier because such offences only accounted for a tiny proportion of the Official Crime Statistics. Indeed, crime was considered to be largely a working class phenomenon, and the impression given by attendance at the magistrates courts and assize courts (a popular pastime) reinforced this.

According to Robb, financial fraud was widespread in the nineteenth century with up to one-sixth of company promotions being fraudulent, a reality which is the focus of Sarah Wilson's chapter. The sentences handed out to those members of the respectable middle classes who were convicted of major fraud were lenient in comparison to those for the 'criminal classes'.[10] The same was true for members of the middle classes

---

[7] P Rawlings, *Policing. A Short History* (Willan Publishing, Cullompton, 2002), p. 118.

[8] See G. Himmelfarb, *The Idea of Poverty. England in the Early Industrial Age* (Faber and Faber, London, 1984), pp. 371-400 for a discussion of the dangerous classes.

[9] Though in her chapter, Sarah Wilson would not entirely endorse this position.

[10] G. Robb, *White-collar Crime in Modern England: Financial Fraud and Business Morality 1845–1929* (Cambridge University Press, Cambridge, 1992), ch. 7.

who committed minor crimes of a more generic type, something which was commented on at the time by the liberal or radical press at least, from that aimed at a working class readership such as the *News of the World*, to more elite publications, like the *Pall Mall Gazette*. In 1875, for instance, Mrs. Louisa Smith appeared at Worship Street magistrates court charged with stealing a chop. Her friends pleaded she was not larcenous, but weak-minded, and 'the magistrate, moved by their apparent respectability and grief, replied that he had no doubt of the culprit's guilt; but that as these interesting mourners wished him to convert the sentence of imprisonment into a slight fine, he would oblige them'.[11] The *Pall Mall Gazette* added that: 'had she been a poor ragged creature without a friend or a sixpence, driven by hunger to theft, we cannot help suspecting that the magistrate would have been inexorable, and that she would have been employed in oakum-picking for the next fortnight at least'.[12]

The 'criminal classes' have always been considered to be a threat, to persons as well as property. Yet crimes of violence have generally represented a small proportion of the total crime recorded in the Official Criminal Statistics, currently standing at about seven per cent. From the beginning of the process of crime recording there has been a bias in favour of counting crimes committed by the poor, while either downplaying or ignoring fraudulent activity. Historians of the Victorian period have also argued that since we cannot be sure why particular crimes were reported and prosecuted, and because of variations in recording practices across police jurisdictions, the figures are worthless.[13] What the statistics do reveal is that the kinds of crime the police concentrated on have been thefts (generally of property of very low monetary value) and to a much lesser extent violence, which provides a range of important insights into the values and expectations, hardening into stereotypes, of that age. Subsequent historians of the later twentieth century are likely to make the same kind of comment, albeit from the advantageous perspective of a 100 years or so hence.

Crime Control

The enabling legislation for the new London police force and in those in the newly-emerging boroughs and counties provided powers for detecting

[11] *Pall Mall Gazette*, 31 May 1875.

[12] *Ibid.*

[13] R. Sindall, *Street Violence in the Nineteenth Century: Media Panic or Real Danger?* (Leicester University Press, Leicester, 1990), pp. 16-28.

crime, such as the power under section 66 of the Metropolitan Police Act
1839. This allowed constables to 'stop, search and detain' persons on
whom a constable suspected stolen property might be found. However, the
most striking feature to twenty-first century observers of this nineteenth
century type of legislation is the very prosaic level of behaviour that
required the attention of parliament, and enforcement by constables.
Examination of the extant court records shows that police work mainly
consisted of enforcement of petty offences committed in the streets –
drunkenness, assaults, kite-flying, gambling and even shaking carpets
between certain times. Rawlings estimates that between the 1850s and
1880s, indictable offences never amounted to more than five per cent of
the total.[14]

The so-called 'feckless' poor as a community has remained a steady
focus for crime control, from the Victorian period to the present. The
labelling of the theme has modified, with present labels reflecting recent
concerns about social exclusion, but a constant for both eras is that the true
extent of the activity of offenders has never been properly reflected in the
various government crime statistics. These have always been kept
artificially low in order to manage public perceptions. An example of
the manipulated and misleading nature of criminal statistics is the fact that
there were 91,671 indictable offences known to the police in 1857. Fifty
years later in 1906, despite a trebling of police numbers, a doubling of the
population, major changes to criminal law and procedure, rapid
urbanisation and industrialisation, along with other enormous social
upheavals, this had fallen by just *six* crimes to 91,665.

From the very beginnings of the modern police service, police
managers, bureaucrats and politicians have taken credit for police
efficiency by keeping down crime statistics. The substance of these
statistics was not challenged in the Victorian period, and is still rarely
publicly challenged today except by sceptical scholars. Part of the recent
police reform programme has been the creation, within the Home Office,
of a Police Standards Unit, which is expected to produce significant and
measurable improvements over a range of areas. The first of these has
addressed variations in tackling crime across forces, including clear-up
and detection rates and has trumpeted recent success in reducing different
categories of crime. This, of course, begs the question of how reliable any
subsequent crime data quantifying these improvements in performance
will be. The evidence from successive BCS since 1982 shows that the
masking of the true crime rate in official criminal statistics is not confined

---

[14] *Ibid.*

to the Victorians. The habit engrained by nearly two hundred years, preoccupation with bogus numbers has also militated against identifying and addressing the true causes of crime and diverted resources away from successful intervention.

How Reliable is Crime Data?

In the 1898 *Pall Mall Magazine*, J. Holt Schooling acknowledged that when measuring crime 'opinion varies from time to time' as society's disapproval of certain acts ameliorates or vice versa.[15] It was for this reason that he concentrated on acts unequivocally considered crimes to base his arguments for the decline of crime in Victorian society. According to Schooling, 'During the last five years for which the facts are available, there have been 876 deaths ascribed to murder in England and Wales'.[16] In his 1998 article, however, Howard Taylor was less than complimentary to such interpretational complacency about such statistics. The 'English miracle' of a declining crime rate at a time of rising population is, he argues, a hollow sham. There was a need for prosecutions for crime to be kept within bounds because of the expense of prosecutions. For many more minor crimes, the unwillingness of the various private individuals to go to the expense of undertaking prosecutions could be relied on to act as a constraint. But for crimes such as murder, the full burden of the cost of detection, arrest, trial and imprisonment (whether until execution or for life) fell upon the state, local and national. There was consequently little impetus for the police to discover murder unless it was particularly blatant.[17] Even then, the murder statistics do not always match up to apparent newspaper reporting. There is a reasonable willingness among commentators to accept that the Victorians were incapable or unwilling to record crime accurately – but it is not so readily accepted that current crime statistics are equally open to accusations of misrecording and of misinterpretation. It is believed that modern statistical methods are 'scientific', and so by and large, beyond reproach. However, this raises a number of questions.

British Crime Surveys have been conducted since 1982. For the 2000 survey, face-to-face interviews were conducted with a nationally-representative sample of just under 20,000 people aged 16 and above,

---

[15] J. Holt Schooling, 'Crime', *Pall Mall Magazine*, 1898, XV, p. 241.

[16] *Ibid.*

[17] Howard Taylor, '"Forging the Job". A Crisis of 'Modernization' or Redundancy for the Police in England and Wales, 1900–39', *British Journal of Criminology*, 39, 1, Special Issue 1999.

together with a further ethnic sample of 3,874. From 2001 the survey is to
be conducted annually and the sample size will be increased to 40,000.
According to the BCS there were 11,297,000 crimes in 1999 as against
2,573,000 for a comparable sub-set of crimes recorded by the police
nationally. This means that only about a quarter of crimes against private
individuals and their households were formally recorded as crimes by the
police. Despite this, the public debate on the prevalence of crime
invariably takes place on the basis of statistics published by the relevant
departments including the Home Office or Audit Commission, based on
figures which have been supplied by the police themselves. The knowledge
that police crime statistics are a very distorted data set has been in the
public domain for nearly two decades yet it rarely informs public debate,
the media or policy formulation. The 2001 BCS shows that there has been
a 21 per cent fall in overall crime since 1977 and a 12 per cent reduction in
the year from 1999 to 2000. According to the BCS the chance of becoming
a victim of crime has fallen to its lowest level since the introduction of the
BCS 20 years ago.[18]

The official criminal statistics fail to take into account the numbers of
people or premises within a particular area *not* victimised, which would be
a better measure of success. Nor do they take into account how many
people or premises have been victimised more than once. This inflates the
number of apparent victims, and masks the fact that the majority of crime
is concentrated in particular geographic areas and that a proportion of
victims are offended against repeatedly.[19] The 2000 BCS survey found
that only 41 per cent of volume crimes were reported to the police. This
varied with the type of crime. Theft of a vehicle was reported on 95 per
cent of occasions, whereas theft of property from a motor vehicle was only
reported on 47 per cent of instances. In 46 per cent of incidents
respondents said that they did not report to the police because they did not
consider the offence to be serious enough or they considered the loss to be
too trivial and 30 per cent considered the police could not do much about
it.

There is a similar pattern with serious offences. Those crimes
considered to be serious were more likely to get reported. Nevertheless
the 2000 survey found that nearly 6.5 million crimes went unreported to

---

[18] C. Kershaw, N. Chivite-Mathews, R. Thomas, and R. Aust, *The British Crime Survey, first
results, England and Wales*. Home Office Statistical Bulletin 18/01 (Home Office,
London, 2001).

[19] S. Everson and K. Pease, 'Crime against the same person and place: detection opportunity
and offender targeting' in R. V. Clarke *et al* (eds) *Repeat Victimisation*, Crime Prevention
Studies, vol. 12 (Criminal Justice Press, New York, 2001).

the police, of which nearly three million were considered to be serious. The BCS surveys have consistently shown that there is a shortfall between those crimes that respondents consider they have reported to the police and what actually enters the official criminal statistics. In attempted burglaries and those with no loss, there is a shortfall of 67 per cent.

Attrition of Reported Crime: Police Discretion

The police have considerable discretion in determining whether a complaint of a crime is recorded. Burrows *et al* assessed the recording policies and practices in ten police forces.[20] In some forces they found that the police officer is able to assign a crime classification and in others this is restricted to a small number of people in a crime management unit. The Home Office Guidance on the criteria to be applied to recording incidents as crimes is contained in arcane documents known as the 'Counting Rules'.[21] Police officers receive little, if any, training in crime recording and classification. Burrows *et al* found two models of crime recording that they described as '*prima facie*' and 'evidential'. Forces adopting the *prima facie* model recorded details of the allegation without further scrutiny. Forces adopting the evidential model require the details to be substantiated before a crime is accepted and recorded in their statistics. One consequence of the latter model is that it creates a spurious impression of improvements in such a force's clear-up rates compared to what it would have been had they adhered to the *prima facie* model.

When Her Majesty's Inspector of Constabulary examined crime recording in 1996 and again in 2000 an average non-recording rate in forces of 24 per cent was found.[22] They found that most forces were employing a test of 'beyond reasonable doubt' to determine whether to record a crime or not, but that some officers went beyond challenging and validating a crime. Factors such as whether the victim had been co-operative, whether the victim could be contacted and if the offence could be detected would the Crown Prosecution Service be likely to

---

[20] J. M. Burrows, R. Tarling, A. Mackie, and G. Taylor, *Review of Police Forces' Crime Recording Practices*, Home Office Research Study No. 204 (Home Office, London, 2000).

[21] *Counting Rules for Recorded Crime*. Vol. 1, Counting Rules for Recordable Offences (Home Office, London, 1998).

[22] Her Majesty's Inspectorate of Constabulary, *A Review of Crime Recording Practices* (Home Office, London, 1996); Her Majesty's Inspectorate of Constabulary '*On the Record': Thematic Inspection on Police Crime Recording, The Police National Computer and Phoenix Intelligence System Data Quality* (Home Office, London, 2000).

prosecute, were taken into consideration. Obviously, such factors are irrelevancies when deciding whether a crime should have been recorded or not. In order to provide a national standard, guidance, issued by the Association of Chief Police Officers (ACPO) in 2001, states that the test in future for determining whether an incident is recorded as a crime will be based on the 'balance of probabilities' that a crime occurred.[23] It is difficult to see how this guidance will change a culture where performance information is routinely manipulated.

As illustrated by the objectives set for the Police Standards Unit, success within a crime control performance culture will be demonstrated by showing falling levels of recorded crime and improved clear-up rates. Both measures are easily manipulated as described above. These are not robust and standardised measurements, and cannot be an accurate proxy for comparing performance through league tables of recorded crime or clear-up rates. What they do is to perpetuate the myth of police activity controlling crime. The data sets have little to say about the reality of crime or the contribution of the police in suppressing it.

'*Caveat emptor*' on the Use of Crime Data for Historical Research

Emsley argues that until recently crime has been viewed uncritically by historians as 'something perpetrated by 'criminals' on the law-abiding majority of the population'. It is clear that the phenomena of crime is far more wide-ranging. He also points out that the first historians of Victorian institutions such as the 'new police' shared a same world-view of the progress achieved through these institutions. He concludes, 'A more cynical, more permissive age is also more critical of its institutions, and the contemporary historians of crime and crime control cannot so readily share an explanation for the changes they explore'.[24] What would be misleading is for historians to continue to use the official criminal statistics of the period they are studying as evidence for their theorising. The unreliability of these figures should encourage good historians to consign them to the rubbish bin or assign them for study in their own right fully cognisant of their blemishes.

Why have such unreliable statistics remained so influential for nearly 200 years? Why are they still taken seriously? Why has the mythology of crime control philosophies not been challenged by drawing attention to the misleading and often fraudulent nature of crime statistics? If previous

---

[23] Association of Chief Police Officers, *Guidance on Crime Recording* (ACPO, London, 2001).

[24] C. Emsley, 'Crime and Crime Control, c.1770–c.1945', in M. Maguire *et al* (eds), *The Oxford Handbook of Criminology* (Clarendon Press, Oxford, 1994).

generations had the excuse that this data represented, 'the best that was available', that excuse is no longer valid. Perhaps the most damaging effect of maintaining the illusion of crime control by reference to crime statistics is that it has obscured for too long the true causes of crime. Two case studies demonstrate the competition that continues over crime control philosophies, namely zero tolerance and social capital regeneration.

Environmental Factors

As Roger Hopkins Burke also discusses, Victorians sought to introduce their own versions of what may be called 'zero tolerance policing', though there was a greater expectation of involvement in this exercise by the community as a whole. It was far from unusual, for instance, for members of the public to identify a 'crime', and to hold onto the offender until a policeman or two appeared on the scene. Sir Robert Carden, a well-known police court magistrate in London, frequently had individuals brought before him where he had been the prime mover in their arrest, detaining beggars and other undesirables until he knew a policeman would appear.[25] The expectation of social punishment *after* conviction was also considerably higher. Baron Bramwell, for instance, regretting the law prevented him handing out a sterner punishment to a violent woman, commented that it pleased him to think that her punishment would continue after her release, at the hands of the community, which would not be slow in demonstrating its disapproval.[26]

Zero tolerance policing received a boost towards the end of the twentieth century. Criminologists studying police behaviour identified aggressive law enforcement as a recurring theme that could be summed up in their respective classifications of police officer types. Reiner characterised the aggressive law enforcer as the 'new centurion', Muir, as the 'enforcer'.[27] Brown described a patrol officer who believed in the rigid and unrelenting enforcement of the law.[28] Crime control is achieved through aggressive enforcement of minor violations and through stopping and interrogating suspicious individuals. Wilson and Kelling, and Kelling and Coles have been at the forefront of articulating a criminological theory, which became known as 'broken windows' in which they postulate

---

[25] Take the month of January 1861, for instance: *News of the World*, 6 January 1861; *News of the World*, 27 January 1861; *The Times*, 3 January 1861; *The Times*, 26 January 1861.

[26] *The Times*, 6 May 1870.

[27] R. Reiner, *The Politics of the Police* (Wheatsheaf, Brighton, 1992), revised edition; W. K. Muir, *The Police: Streetcorner Politicians* (Chicago University Press, Chicago, 1977).

[28] M. Brown, *Working the Street* (Russell Sage, New York, 1981).

a developmental link between quality of life issues such as minor crime and disorder and serious crime.[29] This has contributed to a style of policing which has become known as Zero Tolerance Policing, the most well publicised exemplar of which has been the policing of New York during the 1990s where the major indicator of the success of this policy has been the remarkable reduction in the amount of murders between 1991 and 1997. In the year 1990-91 homicides in New York had reached a peak of 2,262. By 1997 this had reduced to 767. All due to 'zero tolerance' policing? 'Not so', say the analysts who have examined this issue.

Bowling has pointed out that the decline started the following year before any dramatic changes in policing policy had been introduced.[30] From a statistical perspective there was always going to be a regression towards the mean so that when an exceptionally high or low observation is made it becomes increasingly probable that the next observation will be closer to the average. Bowling explained that the murder 'spike' between 1985-91 is attributable to the expansion and subsequent contraction of the crack cocaine markets in the 1990s. The influence of environment as a cause of homicide where the murder weapon was a firearm can be seen from a regression analysis of 1991 data. This showed that three variables could explain 80 per cent of the variation in murder rates among New York's police precincts. Homicide occurred overwhelmingly where there was multiple deprivation, exceptionally high unemployment and a proportion of the population living in poverty, leading to low social mobility and a high proportion of 16-19 year olds in the community.

It is argued that the transformation of these marginalised neighbourhoods to ones where serious violence was routine was due to a lucrative illicit drug economy and freely available guns. New York had long established distribution networks for cocaine and other hard drugs, but the sudden arrival of crack cocaine created an opportunity for new distribution networks which were based around young people in the most deprived neighbourhoods and the decline in the murder rate has been tracked as being in parallel with the decline of crack cocaine as a drug of preference. It is true that 'stop and search' initiatives were widely used by the New York Police Department (NYPD) against anyone suspected of carrying a weapon or drugs. The Commissioner also introduced greater public accountability of his Precinct Commanders. The decline in homicide was

---

[29] J. Q. Wilson, and G. Kelling, 'Broken Windows', *The Atlantic Monthly*, March 1992, pp. 29-38; G. L. Kelling, and C. M. Coles, *Fixing Broken Windows* (Touchstone, New York, 1997).

[30] B. Bowling, 'The Rise and Fall of New York Murder, Zero Tolerance or Crack's decline?' *British Journal of Criminology*, 1999, 39, 4.

also part of a national phenomenon. In nine cities with a population of more than a million inhabitants the decrease in violent crime averaged eight per cent. Homicide in Seattle dropped by 32 per cent and San Antonio by 28 per cent.

This environmental aspect to crime is not new. Again, it was part of the Victorian concern. As Sir James Fitzjames Stephen commented in 1865 in the *Pall Mall Gazette*, 'One reason why so much gross cruelty goes on among our lower orders is that they are huddled together in dens scarcely fit for a dog to die in'.[31] By the 1870s, Victorian confidence that there were genuine improvements in the working class environment helped to underpin their faith in the improving crime statistics. But the environmental concerns continued throughout, underpinning the work of philanthropists such as Octavia Hill and later, Ebeneezer Howard of Garden Cities fame. How different is modern reasoning? Kelling's 'broken windows' theory was predicated on improving the built environment. During its translation into Zero Tolerance Policing it has become synonymous with aggressive policing of disreputable people summed up in the expression 'kick ass' It is difficult to see how aggressive policing of this kind holds out the prospect for rebuilding the social capital in areas ravaged by poverty, drug abuse and violence.

An example of what can happen occurred in Brixton on 10-12 April 1981 when the police had been conducting a zero-tolerance-style stop and search exercise called 'Operation Swamp' which resulted in large scale rioting. The operation had commenced on Monday 6 April with 112 officers in ten squads under the command of two inspectors. The instructions for the operation were to flood the area: success would depend on a concerted effort of stop and search in the street and persistent street questioning. Before the operation was abandoned the squads had made 943 recorded 'stops' and 118 people had been arrested. Slightly more than half of the people stopped were black. More than two-thirds were under 21. Only one person was arrested for robbery and one for attempted burglary. The price of this zero tolerance operation was a riot in which millions of pounds worth of damage was caused, 279 police officers and 45 members of the public were injured, many buildings and vehicles were damaged or destroyed by fire. Copycat riots followed shortly afterwards in other parts of England.

The Home Secretary ordered an inquiry into the disorder to be conducted by a senior judge, the Right Honourable Lord Scarman who looked not only at policing policy and methods but also the social situation

---

[31] *The Pall Mall Gazette*, 11 May 1865.

and considered that the one cannot be understood or resolved save in the context of the other. He considered the social problems to be the difficulties that beset ethnically diverse communities who live and work in inner cities. He concluded:

> These are difficulties for which the police bear no responsibility, save as citizens, like the rest of us. But, unless the police adjust their policies and operations so as to handle these difficulties with imagination as well as firmness, they will fail: and disorder will become a disease endemic in our society.

Although Scarman made recommendations for changes in the law relating to 'stop and search' he argued that 'The failure of the many attempts over the last three decades to tackle the problem of inner city decline successfully is striking'. He drew attention to three particular areas of need: housing, education and employment. If effective policing is so inextricably linked to the social and economic conditions experienced in inner cities, why has Zero Tolerance Policing, which does nothing to ameliorate these conditions, proved to be so attractive? Innes, a sociologist, argues that it 'can only be explained as part of this movement towards an increasing degree of punitiveness amongst the electorate'.[32]

The influence of Zero Tolerance Policing is evident in the Police Reform White Paper. The causes of crime are not the focus of correctional effort. Instead it is 'the actions and behaviours of the already morally corrupted'.[33] An example of how this is translated into political action is that Zero Tolerance Policing in New York has been supported by the injection of an additional 7,000 extra officers financed through reductions in welfare and education spending. The White Paper proposes extra resources in the form of a second tier of law enforcement, community wardens, who are to provide support for the police. The backlash from the community policed by NYPD may be evident in rising complaints from citizens, increased damages paid out as a result of officers' behaviour and in criticism from human rights groups. This should not be unexpected as zero tolerance policing is simply the triumph of a crime control model of policing over due process. As certain areas become associated with the failure of social policy manifested in increased incidence of destitution, poor physical and mental health, homelessness and crime, the attraction of zero tolerance policing as a solution can be understood. Crime 'control'

---

[32] Martin Innes, '"An Iron Fist in an Iron Glove?" The Zero Tolerance Policing Debate', *Howard Journal*, 1999, 38, 4, pp. 397-410.

[33] *Ibid.*

efforts are focussed on the 'dangerous classes', popularly defined as suffering from destitution etc.

This discourse of control being achieved through moral classification rather than amelioration of social or economic conditions is one that would have been familiar to the Victorians. But whole communities cannot be kept in 'lock down' like prisoners in a high security prison. Due process models of policing contain a respect for the law, human rights and fairness in the execution of powers granted by legislation that is more likely to achieve respect for law and order. The policing objective is not 'lock down' but emancipation of communities and *self-discipline* as opposed to *enforced* discipline. It avoids the stigmatising of moral classification and recognises the importance of psychological, social and economic causes of crime. Such approaches are consistent with notions of developing 'social capital' which is being increasingly used in health research.[34] Health promoters are wrestling with the challenge of developing policies and interventions that will create 'health enabling communities' which are social environments that will support the development of health-enhancing behaviours. The Prime Minister's Social Exclusion Unit, established in 1997 and now disbanded similarly looked for ways in which community strengthening and deepening of democracy enables communities to reduce crime and the fear of crime.

Conclusion

The Crime and Disorder Act 1998 provided a legislative framework for neighbourhood renewal by requiring every district authority to form a partnership to work with all 'relevant authorities' to create and action a Crime and Disorder Plan. These plans are to be measured by independent auditors to assess success in achieving a reduction in the level of crime according to a series of key crime performance indicators. Performance league tables of best and worst performing authorities are published. The need for immediate performance improvements is likely to result in the adoption of short-term policing solutions of the zero tolerance policing kind at the expense of developing social capital. This is exacerbated by the fact that many of the crime performance indicators are not outcome measures and as shown can be easily manipulated. These short-term models of policing the 'dangerous classes' perpetuate the two-hundred-

[34] R. Putnam, *Making Democracy Work* (Princeton University Press, Princeton, 1993); R. Putnam, 'Bowling Alone: America's Declining Social Capital', *Journal of Democracy*, 1995, 6, 1, pp. 65-79.

year-old tradition of endeavouring to provide public reassurance through keeping recorded crime levels artificially low and creates the conditions in which zero tolerance policing can flourish. Its populist 'tough on crime' appeal will always be in contention with the much more long-term 'tough on the causes of crime' approaches. Instead of maintaining a balance the emphasis in the White Paper is clearly on being 'tough on crime' Government policy is currently ambiguous because it appears to be vacillating between both approaches. Commenting on the proposals in the White Paper on police reform to measure police performance, the President of ACPO, Sir David Phillips, the Chief Constable of Kent County Constabulary said 'What gets measured gets done but I've always taken the view that what gets measured gets screwed', adding, 'Statistics are so manipulable that frequently you distort a problem rather than solve it'.[35] It appears that the time-honoured tradition of policing a myth and managing an illusion is set to continue unless there is a return to the balance identified by Tony Blair in 1994.

---

[35] Sir David Phillips, President of Association of Chief Police Officers, Interview, 4 January 2002, *Police Review*, 2002, 110, 5654, pp. 16-17.

Chapter 4

Policing Bad Behaviour – Interrogating the Dilemmas

Roger Hopkins Burke

Introduction

There has been much publicity since the mid-1990s about the introduction in both the USA and Britain of get-tough policing strategies targeting, among others, drunks, vagrants and beggars 'behaving badly' on the streets. It is an approach to the policing of what criminologists now term 'incivilities'. Perpetrators are usually identified as members of a socially-excluded underclass that closely parallels similar interventions against their Victorian equivalent the 'dangerous classes'.[1] The focus of much academic study of these activities – in both periods – has been on the targeting of the weak and powerless in the interests of the rich and powerful. Certainly, such policing interventions have served the disciplinary and tutelary instincts of those motivated to ensure the efficient maintenance of capitalism. The focus of this chapter nonetheless goes beyond that recognition and considers the much wider public enthusiasm that has and does exist among all social groups for this style of policing.

The chapter has the following structure. The first section discusses academic debates about recently introduced 'get-tough' policing initiatives and their antecedents in Victorian Britain. It is followed by two case studies of the policing of begging and vagrancy in first, the Victorian era, and second, the contemporary era.

'Get-Tough' Policing Strategies

The final decade of the twentieth century witnessed the introduction in both Britain and the USA of what this author has previously termed 'proactive,

---

[1] D. Garland, *Punishment and Welfare* (Gower, Aldershot, 1985); Gertrude Himmelfarb, *The Idea of Poverty, England in the Early Industrial Age* (Faber and Faber, London, 1984), pp. 371-400.

confident, assertive' policing strategies.[2] These initiatives are termed 'zero tolerance' by some of their proponents (though increasingly, this term is less used by them), much of the media and many populist politicians, and have rigorously targeted those involved in begging, public drunkenness and vandalism.[3] These various and different policing strategies have been inspired by the 'broken windows' thesis developed in the USA in the early 1980s by two criminologists widely associated with the political right, James Q. Wilson and George Kelling. This thesis has influentially proposed that, left unchecked and uncontrolled, the existence of minor incivilities in a neighbourhood sends out a message that no one cares.[4] Legitimate business and respectable residents increasingly take heed, become discouraged and take flight to more welcoming climes leaving the locality in the hands of the weak, poor and powerless. This respectable abandonment of public spaces provides a welcoming environment for the non-respectable and criminals. Broken windows theorists thus propose that in the interests of the wider community such a spiral of decline should be arrested and reversed at the first available opportunity.

It was in New York City that the then Police Commissioner, Bill Bratton, strongly supported by the Mayor, Rudolph Giuliani, first introduced a zero tolerance-style policing strategy in 1993.[5] They argued that a positive police presence targeting petty offenders on the streets could help reverse the spiral of decline that existed in many parts of the city and lead to substantial reductions in crime. Official crime statistics show that during the following two years the crime rate fell by 37 per cent.[6] Mayor Giuliani had been originally elected after a campaign strongly focused on the issue of crime and disorder in a previously and indeed subsequently virtually impenetrable Democratic electoral stronghold. He was re-elected in November 1997 with a greatly increased majority, and electoral analysis suggests his tough stance on crime was responsible for his success.[7] Subsequently, there has been increasing

---

[2] R. Hopkins Burke, 'The Contextualisation of Zero Tolerance Policing Strategies' in R. Hopkins Burke (ed.), *Zero Tolerance Policing* (Perpetuity Press, Leicester, 1998).

[3] R. Hopkins Burke 'Introduction', *Ibid.*

[4] J. Q. Wilson and G. L. Kelling, 'Broken Windows', *Atlantic Monthly*, March 1982, pp. 29-38.

[5] G. Kelling and C. Coles, *Fixing Broken Windows: Restoring Order and Reducing Crime in Our Communities* (The Free Press, New York City, 1996); W. J. Bratton 'Crime is Down in New York City: Blame the Police', in N. Dennis (ed.) *Zero Tolerance: Policing a Free Society* (Institute for Economic Affairs, 1997).

[6] W. J. Bratton, 'Crime', p. 29.

[7] NY1 Internet Service, 4 November 1997.

criticisms of police brutality and a steady reduction in support for the policing initiative. Analysis suggests, however, a continuing demand for such police strategies if implemented in a fair and professional manner.[8]

This demand for 'proactive, confident, assertive' policing was widespread throughout New York City, even in those ethnic minority communities which were the major focus of police intervention.[9] In responding to the suggestion that the police only targeted the more affluent areas frequented by tourists, Professor Eli Silverman of John Jay College of Criminal Justice significantly observed:

> The New York City communities with the most persistent decline in crime... are scarcely visited by tourists. The beneficiaries reside in the boroughs of Brooklyn and the Bronx and are among the poorest and least skilled citizens. These areas are now experiencing an economic revival. While one may choose not to believe that the police have contributed to this, I believe that they have.[10]

The implication of this observation is clear. The poorest citizens – of whom there are many – had a rational motive for supporting the Bratton policing initiative. New York had the most extreme income distribution in the USA with unemployment levels among the highest in the country at a time of large-scale reductions in welfare provision. In the aftermath of the policing initiative, there was a large increase in employment opportunities particularly in the burgeoning service industries related to tourism. The unemployment rate plummeted to a level not known since the 1960s. Thus, the reduction in the crime statistics came to be readily associated in the public mind with increased job prospects and an improved quality of life.[11] Support for the police appears to have been a very rational choice for many poor people with upwardly mobile aspirations.

Similar zero tolerance-style initiatives were later introduced in very different, but usually metropolitan, high crime locations in the UK. In November 1996 the Metropolitan Police, London, implemented an experiment 'Operation Zero Tolerance', in collaboration with the City of London Police and the British Transport Police, in King's Cross with the intention of targeting minor crimes such as dropping litter, graffiti, aggressive begging, and

---

[8] See R. Hopkins Burke, 'Zero Tolerance Policing: New Authoritarianism or New Liberalism?' *The Nottingham Law Journal* (forthcoming, 2002).

[9] R. Hopkins Burke, 'The Socio-Political Context of Zero Tolerance Policing Strategies', *Policing: An International Journal of Police Strategies & Management*, 1999, 21, 4, pp. 666-82.

[10] E. B. Silverman, 'Below Zero Tolerance: The New York Experience' in Hopkins Burke (ed.) *Zero Tolerance*, pp. 74-5.

[11] NY1 Internet Service, 18 December 1997.

low-level disorder. Independent evaluations show some successes in reducing crime and significantly, there was an apparent improvement in the quality of life of residents and workers in the targeted areas.[12]

Hartlepool and Middlesbrough in Cleveland are two of the few places outside London where a police force has explicitly used zero tolerance-style policing.[13] Following the adoption of the strategy in Hartlepool the number of recorded offences was halved, while in Middlesbrough reported crime was reduced by one-fifth within six weeks.[14] In October 1996, the Strathclyde Constabulary introduced a similar scheme, the 'Spotlight Initiative', in Glasgow.[15] In partnership with Customs and Excise and local authorities, they devoted a significant proportion of their operational resources to target all crimes. Overall, the number of recorded offences fell by nine per cent.[16]

Although there were substantial variations in each of these UK-based, zero tolerance-style policing initiatives, there were also crucial commonalities. All involved some form of intensive targeting of street incivilities on the New York model, while significantly each received considerable public support, in particular from the working class localities in which these initiatives took place.[17] However, support has not been forthcoming from liberal academics. 'Get tough' policing strategies are observed to be invariably targeted at the poor and socially-excluded members of society, with all the implications such a focus has for arousing sympathy from such a group.[18]

The debates about the policing of the contemporary 'underclass' closely mirror those about the policing of the 'dangerous classes' of Victorian Britain. The 'teeming hordes living in unimaginable squalor... in chaotic alleys, courts and hovels, just off the main thoroughfares', with regular involvement in criminal activities and public disorder, were widely perceived to be a 'social residuum [that] would overrun the Victorians' newly built citadel of moral virtue and economic rationality'.[19]

---

[12] Paul Johnston, 'Mean Streets Where They Test the Zero Option', *Daily Telegraph*, 8 January 1997.

[13] 'Zero Tolerance: There Should be No Blind Eye to Crime', Leader, *The Times*, 19 November 1996.

[14] R. Chesshyre, 'Enough is Enough', *Telegraph Magazine*, 1 March 1997, pp. 20-26.

[15] J. Orr, 'Strathclyde's Spotlight Initiative' in Dennis (ed.), *Zero Tolerance* pp. 104-23.

[16] W. Ellis, 'Justice of the First Resort', *The Sunday Times*, 24 November 1996.

[17] Hopkins Burke, 'Contextualisation of Zero Tolerance'

[18] See P Scraton, *The State of the Police* (Pluto, London, 1985).

[19] J. Walkowitz, *City of Dreadful Delight: Narratives of Sexual Danger in Late Victorian London* (Virago Press London, 1992), p. 82; H. Mayhew, *London Labour and the London Poor* (Cass, London, 1851-62, reprinted 1967), p. 145; G. Stedman Jones, *Outcast London* (Oxford University Press, Oxford, 1971), p. 93.

The dangerous classes were a perceived threat to public health, moral and legal order and thus the city was to become the focus of efforts to incorporate and domesticate the working class.[20] Street life became subjected to greater legal control and policing.[21] 'Rational' forms of recreation and temperance movements were promoted to provide a more 'ordered' use of free time among the poor. The intention was to impose a physical, social and cultural order in the image of respectability by repressing the dangerousness of the city and making it a place where the law-abiding could go about their normal business in safety and comfort. To this end planning laws and slum clearance initiatives were gradually introduced.[22]

It is, however, quite wrong to view this disciplinary project undertaken by the affluent and prosperous Victorians to rescue the labouring poor from the clutches of criminality as simply being in the interests of the gentry and capitalist classes. The emerging respectable and potentially upwardly mobile artisan classes had as much of a material interest in the suppression of criminality, vice and disorder as their successors in the late twentieth century. The following two sections explore that proposition by examining the policing of begging and vagrancy in, first, the Victorian period and, secondly, more contemporary times.

Policing Begging and Vagrancy in Victorian Times

Begging and vagrancy have always been most common at times of economic recession and social upheaval. At such times − of actual or potential unrest − the authorities have always tended to favour some form of 'zero tolerance' intervention with the intention of protecting the interests of the status quo.[23] Thus, in the fourteenth century, the Statute of Labourers 1349 had prescribed the death penalty for anyone who gave money to a beggar deemed fit to work, a legislative initiative instigated by landlords unable to find plentiful cheap labour in the aftermath of the

---

[20] G. Pearson, *The Deviant Imagination* (Macmillan, London, 1975); G. Stedman Jones, *Languages of Class* (Cambridge University Press, 1983).

[21] R. Storch, 'The Plague of the Blue Locusts: Police Reform and Popular Resistance in Northern England 1840-57', *International Review of Social History*, 20, 1975, pp. 61-90; M. Brogden, *The Police: Autonomy and Consent* (Academic Press, London, 1982).

[22] P. Graham and J. Clarke, 'Dangerous Places: Crime and the City' in J. Muncie and E. McLaughlin (eds), *The Problem of Crime* (Sage/The Open University, London, 2001).

[23] R. Hopkins Burke, 'Tolerance or Intolerance: The Policing of Begging in Contemporary Society', in H. Dean (ed.), *Begging and Street Level Economic Activity* (The Social Policy Press, Bristol, 1999).

Black Death.[24] In the sixteenth century, the   Punishment of Rogues, Vagabonds and Sturdy Beggars Act 1597 allowed convicted beggars to be transported to the new colonies as manual workers and servants.[25] Passed at a time of mass unemployment it was widely perceived as an effective way of dealing with a dangerous class of desperate men.[26]

A further major increase in begging occurred with the great industrial revolution of the late eighteenth and early nineteenth centuries. With large numbers of people leaving the rural areas to seek employment in the new industrial towns and cities, periodical shortages of work arose with a consequential unemployed army of hungry job seekers becoming beggars in order to survive.[27] This was a situation exacerbated by regular downturns in the trade cycle throughout the nineteenth century. Some form of zero tolerance-style intervention continued to be the response to begging and vagrancy at times of economic recession throughout the Victorian period. In the depression year of 1869, for example, there were 17,541 prosecutions for begging, which compares with an average of 9,000 a year during the prosperous period between 1870 and 1875.[28] It would be fundamentally wrong however to suggest that only the wealthy propertied classes favoured a 'get-tough' approach to such activities.

The police certainly focused their attention on the lower social classes and officers could behave in a less than professional fashion. In a case reported in the *Daily Telegraph* of 1870, a constable, George Woolgar, was brought to trial for extorting money from a woman under threat of taking her into custody on a fictitious charge. The report observed that:

> The woman belonged to a class eminently liable to police oppression; while at the same time, the evidence of any woman belonging to it, leading as she must, a vicious life, and living for the most part among disreputable associates, is always and justly received with suspicion in court. Thus, a girl who walks the streets has but little chance of being patiently heard when any charge is brought on the evidence of apparently trustworthy witnesses.[29]

---

[24] M. Postan, *The Medieval Economy and Society* (Penguin, Harmondsworth, 1972).

[25] P. Coldham, *Emigrants in Chains* (Genealogical Publishing, Maryland, 1992).

[26] See P. Slack, 'Vagrants and Vagrancy in England, 1598–1664', *Economic History Review*, 27, 1974, pp. 360-79; A. L. Beier, *Masterless Men: the Vagrancy Problem in England 1560–1640* (Methuen, London, 1985).

[27] N. Rogers, 'Policing the Poor in Eighteenth-Century London: The Vagrancy Laws and their Administration', *Histoire Sociale – Social History*, 24, 1991, pp. 127-47.

[28] *Ibid.*

[29] *Daily Telegraph*, 13 January 1870, p. 5.

The point to consider here is that the *Daily Telegraph*, which enthusiastically supported the conviction of Woolgar, was a newspaper then aimed at a working class readership, rather than being an echo of the modern publication. While considering it understandable that the police might not always behave appropriately when dealing with such people, the report applauded the Recorder's decision to pay no heed to the jury's recommendation of mercy for the police officer because of his youth.

Policing the less salubrious parts of the city was essentially fraught with difficulty and opposition from the rougher elements of the community but support was nonetheless available from the more respectable elements. In the following example, Timothy McCarthy, a miscreant well known to the police and regularly subject to their attention and surveillance appeared in the magistrate's court charged with assaulting a police officer and rescuing a prisoner from the constable's custody. The officer, who was in plain clothes at the time of the incident, had reportedly said, 'Don't do that, McCarthy; you know I am a constable'. The defendant had allegedly declared that he did not care about that, and had struck the officer several times with 'great violence'. However, in court the defendant denied knowing that the complainant was a constable. A passer-by had witnessed the incident but stated that he had not interfered because he was not aware that the man assaulted was a constable. The newspaper report of the case observed that: 'such scenes were of daily occurrence and were not noticed. Several persons who saw the scuffle would have interfered had they known it was a policeman. To act in that locality in private clothes was a very precarious duty'.[30]

Active support for the police came from all classes particularly when the targets of criminals were women or children. A letter written to the *Daily Telegraph* by an apparently more affluent reader sought to warn families about allowing 'young girls' to walk alone in Kensington Gardens less they become the victims of 'beastly and brutal assaults' upon them by vagrants. He described such an attack upon his daughter and asked that the police be deployed to patrol the area.[31] Vigorous support for police intervention against such characters from the respectable elements among the lower classes is widely evident among newspaper reports of the time and is typified by the following example. Two young girls had been witnesses at an inquest giving evidence against a woman accused of murdering her child. After the case, a mob gathered with the intention of seeking revenge against the children. Several persons however begged

---

[30] *Daily Telegraph*, 18 February 1856, p. 4.
[31] *Daily Telegraph*, 17 June 1870, p. 5.

assistance of a Sergeant Townsend to go to the aid of the girls who were
being molested on their way home:

> The sergeant [in the company of two concerned citizens]
> immediately hastened to the North Road Bridge. There they found
> a mob of about 200 persons surrounding the house of Mr Hurd, a
> publican, at the corner of Arlington Street, into whose premises it
> was ascertained they had been received to avoid the inexplicable
> fury of their assailants.[32]

The constable and the two concerned members of the public duly rescued
the children. The reporter was nonetheless disturbed at the threat of
violence to two such young witnesses seeking to pervert the course of
criminal justice in such a serious case as murder.

It is clear that there were serious divisions of interest among the
emerging respectable and residual non-respectable working classes. The
latter were clearly coming to be seen as a predatory criminal class
plundering the weak and respectable elements in their midst. Beggars and
vagrants were essentially identified in the respectable mind with that class
of person. Worthy of particular disdain were those apprehended who had
actively involved their children in their nefarious activities. Charlotte
Gagett, ten years of age, and Bridget Smith, aged eleven, were reported as
appearing before the magistrates charged with begging. The mothers of the
defendants were called to give evidence and found to be making a living
out of their unfortunate children. The latter were sent to the poor-house for
a week with the instruction given that every effort should be made to get
them into an industrial school. The magistrate told the mothers they were
undeserving of any sympathy, and that others of their social class were in
greater economic plight but did not resort to such behaviour.[33] In the next
example, John Thompson and his daughter, aged six, were brought before
the magistrate at Marlborough Street charged with begging in Pall Mall. A
passer-by had drawn the attention of a nearby constable, stating that he had
seen Thompson — who was drunk — fall down on his daughter and nearly
get run over by a hansom cab. The magistrate added that he was
determined to do all he could to prevent children being taken out at night
for begging. He thus sent the girl to the workhouse for a week, with the
proviso that she should subsequently be sent to an industrial school.
Thompson was remanded for a week, and then became the subject of
rigorous justice, being sentenced to six months' hard labour.[34]

---

[32] *Daily Telegraph*, 22 February 1856, p. 2.

[33] *Daily Telegraph*, 25 March 1870, p. 6.

[34] *Daily Telegraph*, 10 March 1875, p. 3; 18 March 1875, p. 3.

Evidence suggests that beggars and vagrants in the Victorian era might objectively be considered poor and socially excluded but at a time when welfare provision centred on the workhouse and the notion of pauperism, the division in the public mind between the deserving and the undeserving poor ensured that there was little sympathy for such elements in their midst. Thomas Alfred Peale of Spitalfields appeared before the magistrates charged with begging. He had been apprehended stopping passers-by and asking them for money. In his defence, he said that his friends had deserted him and that he had a wife and three children who were starving. Witnesses had nonetheless seen him go into a tavern where he had partaken of beer, bread and cheese. He was sentenced to 21 days' imprisonment.[35]

Such people were anathema to the emerging artisan class because of their drunkenness, their evident lack of the work ethic and their crass behaviour. Working-class consent to the police in the Victorian era was invariably tenuous and liable to breakdown at times of socio-economic crisis but there is evidence that the respectable working classes were only too willing to seek protection from the rough and criminal elements in their midst. The moralising mission of the police on the streets coincided neatly with the increasing enthusiasm of the artisan classes for self-betterment that has been described on various occasions from different influential sociological perspectives as embourgeisement and 'the civilising process'.[36]

Despite the best efforts of police and magistrates, supported by the respectable classes, begging and vagrancy did not disappear. It continued to be an intermittent problem in the first half of the twentieth century, but not at the levels that had caused such moralistic concern amongst the Victorians. Partly, this was because it was generally easier to attribute such episodes to particular, short-term, essentially political causes, enabling a greater sympathy for the indigent, rather than indignation at their supposed work-shy tendencies. For example, the Boer War (1899-1902) destabilised the economy and the job market to such an extent that there was a huge increase in begging and sleeping rough in London. Demobilisation following the First World War in 1918 produced both mass unemployment and disabled war veterans.[37] As a result, the inter-war years were

---

[35] *Daily Telegraph*, 21 May 1875, p.3.

[36] See: J. H. Goldthorpe, *The Affluent Worker in The Class Structure* (Cambridge University Press, Cambridge, 1968-9), 3 vols; N. Elias, *The Civilising Process*, vol. 1, *The History of Manners* (Blackwell, Oxford, 1978); N. Elias, *The Civilising Process*, vol. 2, *State-Formation and Civilisation* (Blackwell, Oxford, 1982).

[37] F. Williams, *Social Policy: A Critical Introduction* (Polity Press, Oxford, 1989).

characterised by the appeals of the war-disabled, their condition exacerbated by economic slump on an unprecedented scale, mass unemployment, the continuation of the Poor Law Act, the Board of Guardians and the dreaded 'means test'. In a word, poverty.

Following the Second World War, economic boom and full employment meant that few people needed to beg through necessity, and the sympathy for this class again eroded. The relatively few who were incapable of work were now beneficiaries of the new universal social security system. The substantially reduced ranks of beggars predominantly consisted of men with alcohol-related problems living in derelict buildings and sleeping rough.[38] A return to begging on a large scale occurred following the collapse of the long post-war economic boom and the retreat from the welfare state that epitomised the subsequent government response, but some realisation of the involuntary causation of this has not been a feature of public, let alone governmental, attitudes to this later development.[39]

Policing Begging and Vagrancy in Contemporary Society

From 1973 onwards, the growing world recession reintroduced mass unemployment to the UK. Moreover, increasingly tougher rules limiting welfare benefit to certain groups can be seen as a major reason for the explosion in the numbers of beggars to be found on the streets of London and other major cities.[40] The traditional vagrant with alcohol-related problems remains strongly represented.[41] Many are mentally ill, and their presence on the streets is at least partially explained by care in the community policies that closed down the institutions in which they were previously housed and cared for.[42] However, the great majority are the unambiguous victims of a post-economic boom restructured economy. Unable to find a job or having been made redundant, many were overwhelmed by a sense of disillusionment:

> Many have parents who have been unemployed for ages and they
> have seen no chance of getting a job themselves so they come onto

---

[38] See J. Conroy, 'Some Men of Our Time: A Study of Vagrancy', unpublished MA Dissertation, Department of Sociology, University of Leicester, 1975; P. Archard, *Vagrancy, Alcoholism and Social Control* (Macmillan, London, 1979).

[39] See B. Jessop, *Regulation Theory and the Transition to Post-Fordism* (Polity, Oxford, 1990).

[40] L. Rose, *Rogues and Vagabonds* (Routledge, London, 1988).

[41] J. Healey, *The Grass Arena* (Faber and Faber, London, 1988).

[42] A. Murdoch, *We Are Human Too: A Study of People Who Beg* (Crisis, London, 1994).

the streets.... Once on the streets they face stark options... begging is one.[43]

The significant defining characteristic of the vast majority of the new beggars on the streets since the 1980s has been their youth. Many are teenagers who have had to run away from home due to abuse, violence or the inability of parental income to support a child.

These people make their way to the cities and become involved in a 'street culture' that involves sleeping in doorways, hanging out, looking rough and begging.[44] The policies of the then Conservative government have been cited as explanation for the existence of this street subculture. Changes to social security entitlement in 1988 introduced as part of the neo-liberal assault on welfare dependency meant that 16 and 17 year-olds lost their automatic right to benefits and 18 to 24 year-olds saw a dramatic reduction in the money they received. Caroline Adams, from the charity 'Action for Children', estimated this legislative initiative to be a contributory reason why 75,000 16 to 17 year-olds had no source of income whatsoever.[45] Nick Hardwick, Director of Centre Point, responding to a speech by the then Prime Minister, John Major, who previously had been highly critical of beggars, commented:

> The reason young people beg is simple, they don't have any money. What does the Prime Minister expect them to do? Before 1988 surveys by Centrepoint found that none of them begged. Since benefits were changed for youngsters the numbers have risen steadily.[46]

Later in the year he added:

> Before 1988, you simply did not see young people begging and sleeping rough.... We used to get about 700 young people a year into the private rented sector. The day after the changes were introduced it became impossible to get anyone a private rented place and the begging and sleeping rough began.[47]

---

[43] *The Guardian*, 2 December 1992, p. 16.

[44] R. Hopkins Burke, 'Begging, Vagrancy and Disorder', in R. Hopkins Burke (ed.), *Zero Tolerance*; R. Hopkins Burke, 'The Regulation of Begging and Vagrancy: A Critical Discussion', *Crime Prevention and Community Safety: An International Journal* 2000, 2(2), pp. 43-52.

[45] *The Guardian*, 11 June 1994, p. 34.

[46] *The Guardian*, 28 May 1994, p. 1.

[47] *The Guardian*, 14 December 1994, p. 29.

The experiences of history have been repeated. Major economic and social upheaval has forced large numbers of people into poverty and home-lessness and many of these have taken to begging on our streets.

Furthermore, with the continuing experience of economic downturn, the official response increasingly moved away from any vestiges of humanitarianism. First, there were the changes to the welfare benefit system that provided the preconditions for people going onto the streets in order to beg. Second, there was the redefinition of these people as a social problem and increasing demands that something be done about them. It was a message that crucially gained support from politicians at both ends of the political spectrum seeking populist electoral support and it was in this context that 'zero tolerance' policing strategies targeting beggars and vagrants were first introduced in Britain.

There is undoubtedly a widespread assumption among the public that the welfare state looks after the poor and inadequate. Consequently, those found begging on our streets are widely considered by many members of respectable society to be shirkers and workshy, in this latter-day conceptualisation of pauperism, a contemporary undeserving poor. These assumptions are undoubtedly exacerbated by media stories that suggest beggars are in some way 'bogus'. For example, the Reverend Ken Hewit was reported as calling for the streets of South Kensington to be cleared of beggars, claiming that most are bogus: 'I have heard of beggars who collect £100 an hour.... When you consider that it is tax free, it makes an income of around £50,000 a year'.[48]

This author has mused elsewhere that the concept of the bogus beggar is a semantically interesting one that provokes speculation as to exactly what constitutes a *bona fide* beggar.[49] There appears to be a consensus that they should be penniless and preferably homeless. It is certainly criminal deception to falsely claim to be these things. For example, a man received a fine and a twelve month suspended prison sentence after it was discovered that he travelled in his 'L' registration Astra motor car from his home in Hereford to Sheffield each day in order to beg.[50] Nevertheless, there appears to be no consensus definition of a legitimate beggar. For example, a London magistrate urged the public not to give money to beggars as she had just sentenced a Bosnian woman for begging with her 14 month-old daughter.[51] She appears to have failed some unwritten residency test.

[48] *The Guardian*, 17 July 1993, p. 4.
[49] Hopkins Burke, 'Socio-political Context'; Hopkins Burke, 'Regulation of Begging'.
[50] *The Times*, 17 February 1994, p. 5.
[51] *The Times*, 29 May 1993, p. 5.

There are undoubtedly those who make false claims to their status, for example, those who proclaim that they are homeless when in reality they have accommodation. However, there appears little evidence to suggest that begging is a particularly lucrative way of life, and indeed the literature suggests that virtually all beggars have one thing in common, their poverty (although this may well be a relative concept).[52] On the other hand, general public assumptions of the adequacy of the welfare state, compounded by media stories of dishonesty, provide an excellent context of public legitimation for the introduction of the assertive, 'zero tolerance' policing of beggars and vagrants that has occurred in various constituencies in the UK since the mid-1990s.

Conclusions

It has been widely accepted by policing historians from all perspectives that the newly formed state-sector police service had a substantial impact on street incivilities and were implicated in a broader process of pacification or integration into Victorian society.[53] Orthodox accounts advise us that the police brought universal benefits, but especially to the weaker sections of society: revisionists note the opposite, the poor may have benefited in their capacity as victims of routine offences of theft and assault but in other respects they were the target of many police offensives.[54]

However, the essential focus of police attention was the lowest strata of the working class, those dependent on the street economy or irregular employment, those involved in vagrancy and begging, often drunk and disorderly, a threat either real or imagined to women, children and indeed, respectable adult males. Evidence suggests that regularly employed workers with aspirations of upward social mobility – the emerging 'respectable working class' – increasingly came to accept the legitimacy of the police actions that protected them from the non-respectable elements in their midst.

Police activity has always focused most heavily on the socio-economically excluded, the unemployed, vagrants and young men, those groups that have come to be termed 'police property'.[55] Undoubtedly, the

---

[52] Hopkins Burke, 'Socio-political Context'; Hopkins Burke, 'Regulation of Begging'

[53] R. Reiner, *The Politics of the Police* (Oxford University Press, Oxford, 2000) 3rd edn.

[54] B. Weinberger, 'The Police and the Public in Mid-Nineteenth Century Warwickshire', in V. Bailey (ed.), *Policing and Punishment in Nineteenth Century Britain* (Croom Helm, London, 1981).

[55] S. Cohen, 'The Punitive City', *Contemporary Crises*, 3, 1979.; P. A. J. Waddington, *Policing Citizens* (UCL Press, London, 1999); E. Cray, *The Enemy in the Streets* (Anchor,

increasing incorporation of the working class into the relatively 'good life' provided by a successful and inclusive capitalism that epitomised American and British society, particularly during the economic boom years between 1945 and 1974, helped to modify working class resentment at the nature of policing.[56]

In recent years, there have been profound structural changes in the political economy of Western capitalism. There has been the re-emergence of long-term structural unemployment and the socio-economic exclusion of increasing sections of the young working class. It is this group -- heavily represented among those currently involved in begging, vagrancy and invariably drunkenness and gross behaviour – who are the target of the zero tolerance-style policing strategies identified earlier in this chapter.[57] It seems that much of the widespread public support for these strategies comes from those groups of the respectable working class who welcome the protection from these non-respectable 'rougher elements' in their midst in very much the same way as their predecessors in the Victorian era.

New York, 1972); J. A. Lee, 'Some Structural Aspects of Police Deviance in Relations with Minority Groups', in C. Shearing (ed.) *Organizational Police Deviance* (Butterworth, Toronto, 1981).

[56] J. Young, *The Exclusive Society: Social Exclusion, Crime and Difference in Late Modernity* (Sage, London, 1999).

[57] Hopkins Burke, 'Socio-political Context'; Hopkins Burke, 'Regulation of Begging'

Chapter 5

Law and Disorder: Victorian Restraint and Modern Panic

Kiron Reid

Introduction

Keeping the peace and public order has always been a concern of governments. Doing this through establishing police forces in the modern understanding of the term had gained widespread acceptance by the middle of the nineteenth century. Initially a voluntary initiative, the County and Borough Police Act 1856 required all local authorities to set up police forces. However, in terms of legislation passed, Victorians did not resort to 'knee-jerk' legislation to increase state power as readily as governments of the latter part of the twentieth century. This chapter will consider the law and order policies of the late twentieth century along with examples from Victorian times, looking at the legal framework for clues to a greater comprehension of attitudes towards the desirable levels of state control past and present. The focus is the modern policy in England and Wales, using Victorian parallels to illustrate potential concerns about the policies and legislation for today.

The argument is that the crucial development in criminal justice policy in the 1990s has been an increase in state intervention, something which has been accepted by all key parties in the policy-making process, regardless of political faction. The chapter highlights the areas relating to public order law, disorder and police powers as significant areas where governments in the last decade have increased state involvement by extending the boundaries of the criminal law. This extension covers criminalising areas of behaviour not previously the subject of the criminal law, or increasing either police powers or state control of the police. Elements taken from the Criminal Justice and Public Order Act 1994, Protection from Harassment Act 1977, Public Order (Amendment) Act 1996, Crime and Disorder Act 1998 and others will show that rather than being a watershed in policy development, the 1997 General Election simply marked a continuity of policy that has developed throughout the 1990s. Whereas the 1980s were marked by significant debate about the boundaries of police powers and the boundaries of the criminal law, the 1990s demonstrate a general acceptance by lawmakers of increasingly authoritarian developments in the criminal justice process. The extent to which this has mirrored Victorian attitudes, with parliament arguably enacting similarly wide-ranging criminal law measures in statute provisions in the second half of the previous century, will be explored.

A trend has been evidenced throughout the 1990s where the criminal law has been extended to courses of conduct and formerly civil matters, or police powers have been extended, with cursory scrutiny by parliament – a move to criminalisation of or via the civil law.[1] An assertion that the boundaries of the criminal law have been extended over the last ten years may be regarded as something of a truism. While it may be agreed that this is what has happened, it is still useful to have that explained and documented. On the other hand, taking a more 'black letter' approach to legislative developments, it might be argued that it is not actually necessary to know about the political developments, as long as it is clear what the law is. However it is important for scholars in law and history, policy-makers and others to understand how government policy can affect the boundaries of the criminal law.[2] Much has been written about the Conservative party's criminal justice policies when in government, and subsequently, about New Labour's policies.[3] How different, in practice, have they been?

While the 1990s have not been as repressive as, say, the eighteenth century, the last Conservative government had reverted to the old common law view.[4] In Feldman's words, it saw 'public gatherings and public

[1] See for example A. Ashworth, 'Criminalising Disrespect', *Criminal Law Review*, 1995, p. 98; C. Wells, 'Stalking: The Criminal Law Response', *Criminal Law, Review*, 1997, p. 463; K. Reid, 'The Public Order (Amendment) Act 1996', *Criminal Law Review*, 1998, p. 864.

[2] J. Feinberg, *The Moral Limits of the Criminal Law*, vol. 4, *Harmless Wrongdoing* (Oxford University Press, New York, 1988). See also I. Loveland (ed.), *Frontiers of Criminality* (Sweet and Maxwell, London, 1995).

[3] On this continuity, see A. James and J. Raine, *The New Politics of Criminal Justice* (Longman, Harlow, 1998); I. Brownlee, 'New Labour – New Penology?', *Journal of Law and Society*, 1998, 25, p. 313; H. Fenwick, *Civil Rights: New Labour, Freedom and the Human Rights Act* (Longman, Harlow, 2000). This point was highlighted in K. Reid, 'Law, Order and the Increase in State Intervention in the 1990s', unpublished conference paper, SPTL Conference, Leeds, 1999.

[4] See D. Hay, 'Property, Authority and the Criminal Law', in D. Hay (ed.) *Albion's Fatal Tree: Crime and Society in Eighteenth-century England* (Lane, London, 1975); L. Radzinowicz, *A History of English Criminal Law* (Stevens, London, 1948), vol. 1, pp. 209-13; vol. 4, pp. 316-26. For an overview see A. Norrie, *Crime, Reason and History* (Butterworths, London, 2001), 2nd edn., ch. 2.

protest ... as a threat to good government rather than as a part of the democratic activity which today legitimises government'.[5] Allen and Cooper, for instance, have highlighted consequent establishment labelling of 'non-conformity as disorder'.[6] This is particularly true in relation to the Criminal Justice and Public Order Act 1994. Most of the restrictions on civil liberties in the 1990s have been justified by reference to widely-accepted allegations of uncontrolled growth in crime and disorder of the types discussed by Roger Hopkins Burke and Richard Stone. It is widely accepted that each generation perceives that society is under threat from some new menace which was not present before.[7] However, the actuality of the problems facing parliament in each period are, in fact, very similar.[8] Politicians now take similar attitudes towards generic social problems as did their forebears over a century ago, suggesting that the Victorians likewise dealt with them by also resorting to the law as a means of dealing with them. Such a continuity of policy in relation to the law raises important issues.

A key theme of this chapter is to illustrate an historical continuity of policy that largely supersedes differences in the governing political party, reflecting a general political consensus at least when it comes to dealing with what is perceived as 'bad', or anti-social behaviour. While 1997 marked a landslide victory for the opposition Labour Party, in one of the momentous election swings of the twentieth century, the switch in government illustrates the reality that dates which are recorded as great watersheds in history often turn out to be marked by a continuity of policy. Equally, continuity can clearly be seen in the periods 1832-42 and 1896-1906, despite governmental variations in party terms. The legislation passed speaks for itself. Far from marking a great change, 1997 will come to be seen as marking continuity in criminal justice policy. However, while accepting this continuity, there is an interesting discontinuity between the

---

[5] D. Feldman, *Civil Liberties and Human Rights in England and Wales* (Butterworths, London, 1993), 1st edn., pp. 802-3.

[6] M. Allen and S. Cooper, 'Howard's Way – A Farewell to Freedom?' *Modern Law Review*, 1995, 58, pp. 364-78.

[7] G. Pearson, *Hooligan. A History of Respectable Fears* (Macmillan, London, 1983); S. Cohen, *Folk Devils and Moral Panics* (Blackwell, Oxford, 1987), 3rd edn. See also, S. Chibnall, *Law and Order News: an analysis of crime reporting in the British press* (Tavistock, London, 1977); D. Boyle, *The Tyranny of Numbers* (Harper Collins, London, 2001), pp. 51-53. A recent study is P. Schlesinger and H. Tumber, *Reporting Crime: The Media Politics of Criminal Justice* (Oxford University Press, Oxford, 1994).

[8] Compare for example the end of the twentieth century, with the end of the sixteenth. See J. B. Black, *The Reign of Elizabeth 1558-1603* (Oxford University Press, Oxford, 1959), 2nd edn., pp. 264-7.

Behaving Badly

periods, in terms of the readiness of governments to resort to fresh legislation as a way of dealing with popular moral outrage caused by high profile bad behaviour of varying kinds.

Legislative Approaches

The table opposite details public order and police legislation enacted during the two periods, including measures that created new offences or that established new police powers. The table also includes measures about police accountability, and some general legislation that is important in illustrating Government criminal justice or criminal law policy (for example the Criminal Justice Act 1993). This list is not intended as an exhaustive inventory.[9]

Victoria reigned for 64 years. The table compares that *entire* period with the 22 years of the Conservative and Labour governments from 1979 to 2001 (one Act of the post-June 2001 parliament is included). It seems astounding that recent parliaments have passed more of these kinds of criminal justice legislation than did the Victorians. True, nineteenth century parliaments were also dealing with significant amounts of legislation to do with Ireland and the empire, as well as more legislation about Scotland than the case today, or even before devolution.[10] However, that extra geographical workload could not of itself explain the much readier resort to 'new' versions of legislation to deal with social problems today.

Omitting the Irish and Scottish Acts, the Victorians passed approximately 45 pieces of legislation on these areas. Given that the Victorian era saw the completion of the establishment of police forces it is not surprising that there was a lot of legislation in that area, including 17 on the Metropolitan Police. Some of the Acts were quite technical, such as the Metropolitan Police Act 1861 (about certain police pensions), rather than being about core criminal law and criminal justice issues. Apart from these

---

[9] Background on current sentencing law and policy can be found in M. Wasik, *Emmins on Sentencing* (Blackstone, London, 2001) 4th edn.; D. Wilson and J Ashton, *What Everyone in Britain Should Know About Crime and Punishment* (Blackstone, London, 1999); C. Clarkson and H. Keating, *Criminal Law: Text and Materials* (Sweet and Maxwell, London, 1998), 4th edn., Part I. A good historical survey from the legal perspective is in L. Radzinowicz and J. Turner, 'Punishment Outline of Developments Since the Eighteenth Century', in L. Radzinowicz and J. Turner (eds), *The Modern Approach to Criminal Law* (Macmillan, London, 1945). L. Radzinowicz and R. Hood, *A History of English Criminal Law* (Stevens, London, 1986), vol. 5, 'The Emergence of Penal Policy'.

[10] For example, the Constabulary (Ireland) Act 1851; the Police (Scotland) Act 1857; the South Africa Offences Act 1863. A modern example is the Criminal Procedure (Scotland) Act 1995. Re. detention and questioning the police, Part II 'Police Functions'.

Public Order and Police Legislation

Victorian (1837 to 1901)	1979 to 2001
Vagrancy Act 1838	Police and Criminal Evidence Act 1984
Special Constables Act 1838	Interception of Communications Act 1985
Metropolitan Police Act 1839	Public Order Act 1986
County Police Act 1839	Crossbows Act 1987
Canals (Offences) Act 1840	Criminal Justice Act 1988
County Police Act 1840	Criminal Justice Act 1991
Parish Constables Act 1842	Football Offences Act 1991
Transportation Act 1843	Criminal Justice Act 1993
Night Poaching Act 1844	Criminal Justice and Public Order Act 1994
Parish Constables Act 1844	Police and Magistrates' Courts Act 1994
Seditious Meeting Act 1846	Offensive Weapons Act 1996
Poor Removal Act 1846	Police Act 1996
Town Police Clauses Act 1847	Public Order (Amendment) Act 1996
Transportation Act 1847	Confiscation of Alcohol (Young Persons) Act 1997
Treason Felony Act 1848	Crime (Sentences) Act 1997
Parish Constables Act 1850	Knives Act 1997
Prevention of Offences Act 1851	Police Act 1997
Criminal Procedure Act 1853	Protection From Harassment Act 1997
Criminal Justice Act 1855	Crime and Disorder Act 1998
Metropolitan Police Act 1856	Greater London Authority Act 1999
County and Borough Police Act 1856	Criminal Justice and Courts Services Act 2000
Criminal Justice Act 1856	Football (Disorder) Act 2000
County Police Act 1857	Regulation of Investigatory Powers Act 2000
Metropolitan Police Act 1857	Anti-Terrorism, Crime and Security Act 2001
County and Borough Police Act 1859	Criminal Justice and Police Act 2001
Metropolitan Police Act 1860	
Metropolitan Police Act 1861	
Accessories and Abettors Act 1861	
Larceny Act 1861	
Malicious Damage Act 1861	
Forgery Act 1861	
Coinage Offences Act 1861	
Offences Against the Person Act 1861	
Garrotters Act 1863	
Metropolitan Police Act 1864	
Larceny Act 1868	
Prevention of Crime Act 1871	
Vagrant Act Amendment Act 1873	
Fugitive Offenders Act 1881	
Explosive Substances Act 1883	
Prevention of Crimes Act 1885	
Riot (Damages) Act 1886	
Inebriates Act 1898	
Vagrancy Act 1898	
Metropolitan Police Act 1899	

Metropolitan Police and Police Acts there were 19 major pieces of legislation. The total of 45 in 64 years is proportionately far fewer than the 25 passed in the last 22 years. The last two decades of criminal justice policy provide good insights into the sweep of influences on legislation.

The 1980s

Continuity marked government policy in 1979. The Royal Commission on Criminal Procedure had been established prior to the General Election and the subsequent report contributed to the debate around the enactment of the Police and Criminal Evidence Act 1984 (PACE).[11] Lord Scarman's report into the riots of 1980-81 greatly influenced the safeguards introduced.[12] However, with PACE there was much debate over the style of policing, safeguards and extent of police powers, a perspective also reflected on by David Bentley in his chapter. Civil liberties groups thought that the Act gave the police too much power; the police thought that it imposed too many burdens on them. In retrospect, therefore, and with the Act having stood the test of time, it can be concluded that the legislation was a sensible and workable compromise.[13] The same can be said about the Public Order Act 1986. There was again great debate over the Act but it has been generally accepted that the legislation was a clear improvement on what went before.[14] It put vague public order powers on a statutory footing, with a clear order of severity and reasonably clear *actus reus* and *mens rea* requirements. The redrafted offences are seen as more suited to modern conditions than the old broad and vague offences such as unlawful assembly and rout.[15]

---

[11] Cmnd. 8092, 198.

[12] *The Brixton Disorders 10-12 April 1981: Report of an Inquiry by the Rt. Hon. the Lord Scarman OBE*, Cmnd. 8427 (HMSO, London, 1981).

[13] See text and sources cited by S. Bailey, D. Harris and D. Ormerod, *Civil Liberties: Cases and Materials* (Butterworths, London, 2001), 5th edn. pp. 153-6. See also David Bentley's chapter in this volume for a different perspective.

[14] T. Gibbons, 'Annotations to the Public Order Act 1986', *Current Law Statutes Annotated 1986* (Sweet and Maxwell, London, 1986); R. Card, *Public Order – The New Law* (Butterworths, London, 1987); P. Thornton, *Public Order Law* (Financial Training Publications Ltd, London, 1987); A. T. H. Smith, *Offences Against Public Order* (Sweet and Maxwell, London, 1987).

[15] On the old law see J. Smith and B. Hogan, *Criminal Law* (Butterworths, London, 1965), 1st edn, pp. 552-61. On the new law see R. Card, *Public Order Law* (Jordan, Bristol, 2000); J. Marston and P. Tain, *Public Order Offences* (Callow, London, 2001). For a summary, see J. Smith and B. Hogan, *Criminal Law* (Butterworths, London, 1999), 9th edn, ch. 21.

'Knee-jerk' and poorly thought-out legislation was enacted in the 1980s, legislation passed in haste with all the problems that can bring.[16] This included criminal justice legislation rushed through following particular incidents such as the Criminal Justice Act 1988 or the Crossbows Act 1987. However, the product of parliament (if not the debate) shows that the 1980s was largely a period of rational legislation. At the end of this period, the Criminal Justice Act 1991 was a welcome example of reason from the Home Office. The new era was revealed when part of this Act was rapidly discarded in a new Act, the Criminal Justice Act 1993.

The 1990s

Unlike the 1980s where there was significant ideological argument, in response to the perceived problem relating to law and disorder post-1991, authoritarian development in the criminal justice process came to be accepted by most players in the policy-making process. It is easy to assume that this will find ready parallels in the Victorian period, but the reality is more complex. During the 1990s, government methodology for getting its agenda passed has been threefold. There has been greater centralisation (for example of the control over the police); there has been legislation passed in haste. This, in turn, stemmed from the apparent need to be seen to react to perceived problems (an example was increasing the sentences relating to knives), or to 'be tough' (such as policy moves on prisons; bail; and cautions of juveniles).[17]

This was done usually without any logical or rational basis – often entirely in contradiction, or without reference, to evidence from research, experts or the reality of the statistics used to justify the move (see Tom Williamson's chapter for further reflections). 'New Labour' used the same tactics as were utilised by John Major's Conservative governments, though it is argued that there are some positive signs in recent years of more reasoned criteria for law-making. The Criminal Justice and Public Order Act 1994 introduced wide offences to cover aggravated trespass, raves, and trespassory assemblies. It almost entirely ignored problems highlighted by the Report of the Royal Commission on Criminal Justice, as well

---

[16] On legislation passed in haste see K. Reid and C. Walker, 'Military Aid to the Civil Powers: Lessons From New Zealand', *Anglo-American Law Review*, 1998, 27, p. 133, notes 139-50.

[17] For example the Criminal Justice and Public Order Act 1994 ended the right to bail for repeat murderers and rapists (s. 25). This is despite the fact that these groups are unlikely to be given bail anyway; and murderers at least are less likely to re-offend (many murders being particular 'crimes of passion').

as ignoring evidence presented to the Royal Commission.[18] The Police and Magistrates' Courts Act 1994 led to some increased local accountability but overall less local democratic control over the police. One Act seemed a special case at the time in that it mixed criminal and civil law policies in the public order field – the Protection from Harassment Act 1997. It was, in fact, a forerunner of the style of legislation of the Crime and Disorder Act 1998, where the ambit of the criminal law is extended into previously civil matters, to deal with what is believed to be a pressing social problem. The Crime (Sentences) Act 1997 has set the scene for sentencing policy despite the change of political colour of government; and the Police Act 1997 has similarly marked a key change in policy, with the development of national policing structures and foreshadowing the increasing importance of Europol and European policing structures.

A key feature of the change since the 1980s was in relation to the Criminal Justice and Public Order Act 1994 and the Protection from Harassment Act 1997. The former was largely unopposed on its passage through parliament, because the Labour party in particular did not want to be seen as 'soft on crime'. The latter provided an interesting scenario: all the main parties vied to support this more restrictive legislation in order to be seen to be responding to soaring levels of social panic, highlighted particularly in newspapers (an issue discussed by Rowbotham and Stevenson in their chapter). Yet 'stalking' was no new phenomenon, and had even troubled the Victorians, though they had believed existing legislation to be (with suitable will to act behind it) sufficient. Later 'knee-jerk' legislation has included the Football (Disorder) Act 2000.

Coherent Law-Making?

Some academics previously have consciously stopped talking about 'the criminal justice system' and instead referred to the 'criminal justice process' given that the country has a piecemeal structure that has grown up particularly since Victorian times with no clear aims and objectives.[19] Certainly, the new Labour government in 1997 set about implementing the Conservative government's sentencing legislation and prisons' policy and its criminal records legislation. The Crime and Disorder Act 1998 as the first flagship piece of Labour criminal justice legislation, introducing anti-

---

[18] Cmnd. 2263, Viscount Runciman (HMSO, London, 1993).

[19] See for example, N. Padfield, *Text and Materials on the Criminal Justice Process* (Butterworths, London, 1995), 1st edn, p. 3. The Victorian era saw the growth of institutions such as the prison system. See M. Ignatieff, *A Just Measure Of Pain: The Penitentiary In The Industrial Revolution, 1750-1850* (Macmillan, London, 1978).

social behaviour orders (ASBOs), sex offender orders (which cover men engaged in consensual homosexual sex, as well as young persons who have consensual underage sexual intercourse), child curfews, and the abolition of the informal system of police cautioning for young people. This Act did, however, see some return to a more coherent form of law-making, in that it introduced a clear aim for the youth justice system in section 37.[20] The Act also put the importance of inter-agency co-operation on a clear statutory basis, including crime and disorder partnerships (section 5) and plans (section 6), and introducing a duty on local authorities to have due regard to the likely effect of the exercise of their functions on crime and disorder in its area. Part IV of the Act established the Sentencing Advisory Panel. Another measure of great importance was the Human Rights Act 1998, moving away from the previous British negative system of protecting rights.[21]

The role of the police is also significant here. The Victorians established the 'modern' police system, operating at local level on a county and borough basis as the current names still indicate.[22] However, centralisation of the police has gone on apace in the 1990s and into the twenty-first century, with the advent of national policing bodies for the first time (notably the National Crime Squad and National Criminal Intelligence Service), as well as the increased influence of the Home Secretary.[23] While Labour governments continued a trend initiated under Conservative governments, it has also remedied one accountability defect that was a hangover from the nineteenth century. The Metropolitan Police Authority was introduced for London by the Greater London Authority Act 1999, giving London for the first time a (part) democratic police authority, in a reflection of the changed reality of metropolitan government by this time.

The most striking comparison between the 1990s and the Victorian era is the continued enactment of piecemeal broad legislation. The Criminal Justice and Public Order Act 1994, for instance, can be directly compared with that unfortunately most enduring piece of nineteenth century criminal legislation, the Offences Against the Person Act 1861 (OAPA), passed

---

[20] Section 37(1). It shall be the principal aim of the youth justice system to prevent offending by children and young persons.

[21] See R. Stone, *Textbook on Civil Liberties and Human Rights* (Blackstone, London, 2000), 3rd edn.

[22] Clive Emsley, *Crime and Society in England 1750-1900* (Longman, London, 1996), 2nd edn, ch. 9; David Taylor, *Crime, Policing and Punishment in England 1750-1914* (Macmillan, Basingstoke, 1998).

[23] K. Reid, 'Current developments in police accountability', *Journal of Criminal Law*, 2002, 66, p. 172.

originally to 'consolidate and amend the Statute Law'.[24] Despite much debate, the Victorians never brought themselves to pass a criminal codification measure, and it is disappointing that there has still been no serious attempt to codify criminal law, ensuring that the enactment of piecemeal broad statutes continues apace, with the most recent example being the Criminal Justice and Police Act 2001.[25]

The Criminal Justice and Public Order Bill debated in 1994 was a real 'rag bag' of provisions. The Act itself (CJPOA) was 214 pages long, and contained 172 sections.[26] These included:

Stop and search in anticipation of violence. Section 60 allowed the police to stop and search for a limited period without reasonable suspicion if certain conditions were met. Reasonable suspicion was a key safeguard under PACE, designed to provide better protection for individuals than the common law.[27]

Attaching conditions to police bail. Section 27 extended the Bail Act 1976. This was superficially attractive as the police would be able to add conditions to bail without the individual having to be held in custody to go before the magistrates. It was anti-roads campaigners who highlighted that it could be used tactically by the police to neutralise individual protesters, by barring them from sites, with appeal only to magistrates who would generally agree with the police.[28] Some evidence to support this analysis came from the miners' strike of 1984-85 (police applying to magistrates for restrictive bail conditions on striking miners).[29] Thus section 27, rather than enabling bail to be given to people who in the past would have been

---

[24] For one critique see A. Reed and P. Seago, *Criminal Law* (Sweet and Maxwell, London, 1999) p. 353. On the reform proposals J. C. Smith 'Offences Against the Person: The Home Office Consultation Paper', *Criminal Law Review*, 1998, p. 321 detailing some of the offences under the OAPA that would be specifically replaced.

[25] J. Rowbotham and Kim Stevenson, 'Societal Distopias and Legal Utopias: Reflections on Visions Past and the Enduring Ideal of Criminal Codification', *Nottingham Law Journal*, 2000 9/1.

[26] On the passage of the Act through Parliament see F Klug, K. Starmer and S. Weir, 'Civil Liberties and the Parliamentary Watchdog: the Passage of the Criminal Justice and Public Order Act 1994', *Parliamentary Affairs*, 1996, 49. p. 536.

[27] The Act was subsequently widened by the Knives Act 1997 s.8, enacted by the Conservative government, brought into force by Labour, 1 March 1999: SI 1999 5; and by the Crime and Disorder Act 1998 s.25.

[28] Emma Must, anti-M11 extension campaigner, speech, National Critical Legal Group Conference, Bristol, February 1994. On magistrates see P. Darbyshire, 'For the New Lord Chancellor – Some Causes for Concern About Magistrates', *Criminal Law Review*, 1997, p. 861.

[29] N. Blake, 'Picketing, Justice and the Law' in B. Fine and R. Millar (eds), *Policing the Miners' Strike* (Lawrence Wishart, London, 1985), p. 114.

held in custody, has enabled conditions to be attached to bail for individuals who would not previously have been subject to restrictions on their freedom.[30]

Criminalising 'Bad' Behaviour?

It was not just 1990s legislation that introduced broad criminal offences. The Public Order Act 1986 criminalised conduct perceived to be disorderly or threatening – i.e. 'bad' behaviour in its widest sense. Section 5 of the Public Order Act 1986 introduced the very wide offence of 'harassment, alarm or distress' (discussed further below). Ashworth talked about section 5 'criminalising disrespect';[31] the CJPOA 1994 was all about criminalising diversity and dissent. The provisions that did this were those relating to travellers; aggravated trespass; trespassory assemblies; and raves. The key feature here is that conduct that was previously only the subject of the civil law has now been brought within the ambit of the criminal law. The powers granted were almost always wider than first suggested by the government, as A. T. H. Smith noticed when discussing (fairly ambivalently as regards the liberty of 'ravers' and 'new age' travellers) the new bans on trespassory assemblies: 'To level such a power at ravers and new age travellers is one thing; but the power is generalised in a way that has enormous implications for civil liberties'.[32]

A wide range of peaceful protest has been criminalised by section 68 (aggravated trespass), with police given very flexible powers of arrest by section 69. It was originally anticipated that government would single out hunt saboteurs to be criminalised, as Richard Stone discusses in his chapter.[33] In fact the offence enacted was very much wider than that.[34] Irrespective of whether one likes rave music or not introducing separate criminal laws to ban raves, such as section 65, may seem unduly authoritarian, but this section provided a police power to enforce a five-mile exclusion zone around potential sites. Designed to stop raves at night, roadblocks and exclusion zones could be put in to operation at any time.[35]

---

[30] *Criminal Statistics*, HMSO, London, 2001. These indicate that every year since 1994, numbers held in police custody have increased.

[31] Ashworth, 'Criminalising Disrespect', p. 98. See Bailey *et al*, *Civil Liberties*, pp. 490-3.

[32] [1995] Crim LR 19, p. 24.

[33] 'Briefing on the Criminal Justice and Public Order Bill' (League Against Cruel Sports, London, 1994).

[34] On road protests see B. Doherty 'Opposition to Road-Building', *Parliamentary Affairs*, 1998, 51, p. 370.

[35] s.63(1).

These measures are a manifestation of preventive justice, a concept with a long legal history, being in fact very similar to those used by means of breach of the peace powers during the miners' strike.[36] Other recent developments relating to the possession of knives, provide good examples of legislation passed in haste and their unforeseen effects, as well as an echo of the Garotters Act 1863, another flawed piece of legislation which neither eradicated its intended target offence, nor ensured good behaviour on the part of the police. The Offensive Weapons Act 1996 was introduced in response to public outrage following the fatal stabbing of London headmaster, Philip Lawrence, and the savage attack on Birmingham nursery nurse, Lisa Potts, and her class. Starting as a Private Member's Bill, government support ensured it came onto the statute book, increasing the penalty for carrying offensive weapons or knives and giving the police a power of arrest for both. Government amendments added during passage through parliament included making it an offence to carry a knife on school property; and establishing a police power to stop and search for knives on school property. Only eight months later the Knives Act 1997 was enacted, amending Section 60 CJPOA to allow the police to stop and search people in a particular area for a specified time if they believed they might be carrying knives (section 8). Had not the 1996 Act been rushed through, this measure could have been included in the same legislation.

The Public Order (Amendment) Act 1996 was introduced as a ten-minute rule bill in the House of Commons by Estelle Morris. Its first reading took only seven minutes on 18 June 1996; its second reading, the committee stage and third reading were all taken formally on 12 July.[37] Its second reading in the House of Lords was even quicker, and the Bill's third reading on 16 October was followed by Royal Assent the following day, widening the power of arrest for section 5 Public Order Act 1986.[38] There has been widespread criticism of section 5 – both for criminalising conduct that should not be regarded as criminal, and for its actual use by the police, not reflecting the use that parliament allegedly intended.[39] Most

---

[36] See *Moss v McLachlan* [1985] IRLR 76; the Dartford Tunnel case, *The Guardian*, 21 March 1984. Compare with the police operation around Stonehenge, 20-21 June 1985: NCCL, *Stonehenge*, quoted by N. Lacey and C. Wells, *Reconstructing Criminal Law* (Butterworths, London, 1998), 2nd edn, p. 138.

[37] *Hansard*, 1996, 279, col. 684-5; 1996, 281, col. 756.

[38] *Hansard*, 1996, 574, cols 1497-8.

[39] See Peter Thornton, *Decade of Decline: Civil Liberties in the Thatcher Years* (NCCL, London, 1989), p. 37. Ashworth 'Criminalising Disrespect', pp. 98-100; see also D. Brown and T. Ellis, *Policing low-level disorder: police use of section 5 of the Public Order Act 1986* (Home Office Research Study No 135, HMSO, London, 1994), the focus of Ashworth's article.

conduct covered by section 5 would already have been an offence under the Town Police Clauses Act 1847, section 28, but that was less useful to a police officer, as the power of arrest under the older statute was abolished by PACE. Section 5 was very controversial at the time of the passage of the 1986 Act but by 1996, an amendment to the power of arrest was obviously viewed as a simple and uncontroversial statutory amendment and paid cursory attention. The argument put by Estelle Morris in support of a broad public order offence was a sign of the change in Labour thinking on law and order issues, and a forerunner of the kinds of issues that the government would seek to tackle: 'many of my constituents express particular concern about an increase in abusive, threatening, disorderly and intimidating behaviour in the streets'.[40] It can be argued that none of this involves direct harm, but all give offence to other people, and the argument over whether conduct that causes 'offence' should be criminalised has long been at the heart of the debate on the limits of criminal law.[41] The Victorians had specifically penalised various forms of offensive behaviour in the 1847 Act.

Stalking is not a new phenomenon. Glanville Williams, in discussing binding over, cited the 1840 case of *R v Dunn* concerning a campaign of harassment by a man who would undoubtedly today be labelled 'a stalker'.[42] It was held, in the absence of any threat pleaded, that continual pestering of a woman by a man was not enough to establish breach of the peace. Lord Chief Justice Denman mused that 'Perhaps the law of England may be justly reproached with its inadequacy to repress the mischief, and obviate the danger, which the prisoner's proceedings render too probable'.[43] Harassment itself had only been recognised as a tort by the 1993 case of *Khorasandjian v Bush*.[44] At that time it could be argued that the civil law might be more effective at ending harassment than criminal law, which did not stop the appalling conduct by the defendant in *Khorasandjian*, since proving intention to the civil standard, on the balance of probabilities, was an easier option. However, in 1997, government acted to end the mischief that Lord Denman had highlighted

---

[40] *Hansard*, 1996, 279, col. 684.

[41] John Stuart Mill formulated his famous test in 1859: 'the only purpose for which power can be rightfully exercised over any member of a civilised community, against his will, is to prevent harm to others' J. S. Mill, *On Liberty* (J. M. Dent, London, 1972), p. 78.

[42] (1840) 12 Ad & E 599; 113 ER 939. Cited in 'Preventive Justice and the Rule of Law' (1953) 16 MLR 417 at p. 418.

[43] 113 ER 939 at pp. 948-9.

[44] [1993] QB 727. See J. Bridgeman and M. Jones, 'Harassing conduct and outrageous acts: a cause of action for intentionally inflicted mental distress', *Legal Studies*, 1994, 14, p. 180.

157 years earlier. Celia Wells emphasised the broad nature of the
Protection from Harassment Act 1997: 'The Act follows a pattern
witnessed in other areas (hunt saboteurs, joy-riding, and dangerous dogs
come to mind) of addressing a narrowly-conceived social harm with a
widely-drawn provision, often supplementing and overlapping with
existing offences'.[45] Section 2 created an offence of harassment (detailed
in section 1). Section 3 allowed a civil action for an actual or apprehended
breach of section 1, including grant of an injunction; breach of the
injunction without reasonable excuse leads to the defendant being guilty of
a criminal offence. In combining the criminal and civil law this was the
forerunner of the ASBO introduced a year later. Section 4 created the
offence of putting people in fear of violence, intended to be more effective
than the offence of assault on which the Victorians relied, as there is a
lesser *mens rea* and no requirement for immediacy as needed for a charge
of assault.[46] But again, the Act had wider effects than initially realised. In
DPP v Moseley, Selvanayagam and Woodling peaceful animal rights
protesters outside a mink farm were prosecuted for harassment,
demonstrating that the legislation had hit a much wider target than just
stalkers. Yet Home Office research has shown that the Act has led to action
against a large number of 'stalkers' when victims might previously have
had no effective legal remedy.[47]

New Labour – New Limits of the Criminal Law

In June 1997, new Home Office Minister, Mike O'Brien, argued that 'Yobs
hanging about on street corners and gangs of teenagers roaming shopping
centres put off customers and increase fear of crime'.[48] This speech further
marked the intention of establishing new boundaries to criminal law. In
Victorian times, fear of crime related equally to the perspective that
'gangs' of disaffected youths hanging around the streets encouraged crime.
Despite calls for action, no special legislation was introduced to deal with
the Victorian 'menace', however. Recent reaction has been different, as is
underlined by ASBOs.

---

[45] Wells, 'Stalking', p. 464.

[46] s.4(1), A person whose course of conduct causes another to fear, on at least two occasions,
that violence will be used against him is guilty of an offence if he knows or ought to know
that his course of conduct will cause the other so to fear on each of those occasions –
'ought to know' is subject to a reasonable person test, s.4(2).

[47] [1999] Times LR 9 June; J. Harris, *An Evaluation of the Use and Effectiveness of the
Protection from Harassment Act 1997* (Home Office, London, 2000).

[48] Home Office Press Release 147/97, 18 June 1997.

The Orders introduced under the Crime and Disorder Act 1998 add weight to the key theme that current government responses to publicly expressed disquiet about what is perceived as anti-social behaviour has been the imposition of criminal liability for such conduct, previously merely socially offensive. Worries about the long-term implications, as well as the immediate effects, of out-of-control children are not merely a modern phenomenon, the difference is that an Act now gives the criminal law the ability to target children. In the Victorian period, where parental supervision was held to have failed, the reaction of most magistrates was not to criminalise the vulnerable child, but rather to send them to a training institution of some sort, such as an Industrial Training School.[49] Now, breach of a civil law anti-social behaviour order is a criminal offence.[50] Initially few orders were taken out by the police or local authorities, so government guidance was issued to increase the use of ASBOs.[51] As with the 1997 Act: provisions on stalking, use of ASBO is advantageous to complainants as it is easier to prove anti-social behaviour via civil procedure. Of course, breach of an ASBO may be by conduct which would have been a crime anyway. But to the extent that the initial conduct and breach would not have been a crime, the boundary of the criminal law has been extended. Did government realise the implications of this *de facto* extension of criminal law? The cursory scrutiny by parliament of measures of criminalisation of or via the civil law would indicate it did not, even though members of both Houses of Parliament did highlight issues about the boundaries of the criminal law.[52]

Human rights issues may arise concerning ASBOs. Challenges are most likely under Article 8 of the European Convention on Human Rights on the grounds that terms of orders may breach the right to respect for private life. To judge whether such complaints about ASBOs might succeed, a comparison can be made between the role of ASBOs and the very old powers of binding-over Historically, binding-over has provided a controversial form of preventive justice.[53] For individual incidents of anti-social behaviour the police could use their powers to seek a binding-over order to restrain future anti-social behaviour, meaning that it has

---

[49] As when Sir Robert Carden sent a 'wretched' child who appeared before him to an Industrial Training School to remove him from parental corruption, *News of the World*, 6 January 1861, p. 7. See also Roger Hopkins Burke's chapter, this volume.

[50] *R (McCann and Others) v Manchester Crown Court* [2001] 1 WLR 1085.

[51] N. Warner, *Anti-Social Behaviour Orders: Guidance on drawing up Local ASBO Protocols* (Home Office, London, 2000).

[52] *Hansard*, Lords, 1998, 585, cols 512-4.

[53] Feldman, *Civil Liberties*, pp. 1083-4.

always been about the control of conduct and the regulation of future behaviour, preventive justice in other words. Blackstone talked about the requirement of obtaining sureties in the context of preventive justice:

> This preventive justice consists in obliging those persons, whom there is a probable ground to suspect of future misbehaviour, to stipulate with and to give full assurance to the public, that such offence as is apprehended shall not happen; by finding pledges or securities for keeping the peace, or for their good behaviour.[54]

Glanville Williams concluded that 'It is now distinctively a weapon to be used against those who have not broken the criminal law'.[55] In *Hashman v UK* binding over 'to be of good behaviour' was found to be in breach of the Convention as not giving sufficient guidance to the person subject to the order.[56] As they have a clear basis in statute, ASBOs are unlikely to be subject to the same challenge. Their application is founded on specific behaviour and the orders contain specific conditions – indeed, for each of these reasons ASBOs can be considered an improvement on binding-over.

There is one area where a Victorian call for action is still outstanding. Lord Warner gave guidance which emphasised that 'An ASBO is unlikely to be suitable for settling a private dispute between two or more neighbouring families (for example over boundary lines), unless the dispute escalates into anti-social behaviour'.[57] As the content of tabloid newspapers underline, disputes between neighbours remain a common cause of disharmony. The late Victorian Lord Chancellor, Herschell, made an appeal to the legislature for action in 1895, arguing that 'It might be very reasonable that there should be some law regulating the rights of neighbours in respect of trees, which, if planted near the boundary, necessarily tend to overhang the soil of a neighbour'.[58] The Crime and Disorder Act provisions were not intended to provide such remedy. However, government legislation along the lines suggested by Lord Herschell now seems likely following a 1999 consultation on high hedges.[59]

---

[54] *Commentaries on the Laws of England* 12th edn, (London, 1795), vol. IV, pp. 251-2.

[55] Glanville Williams, *Criminal Law. the General Part* (Stevens, London, 1961) 2nd edn, p. 427. See also Lane, LCJ, *Veater v Glennon* [1981] 1 WLR 567 at 574.

[56] [2000] Crim LR 185, ECtHR.

[57] Warner, *Anti-Social Behaviour Orders*, para 2.4.

[58] *Lemmon v Webb* [1895] AC 1, at p. 4.

[59] 'High Hedges: Possible Solutions' (DETR, London, 2000). Several private members bills on this failed to pass in the 1997-2001 Parliament. Department for Transport, Local Government and the Regions 'Trees and Problem Hedges', 7 December 2001 (website).

Will the new century be a more rational era? Though more legislation has been passed, and some of it has been shown to have had unexpected and negative consequences, not all of the evidence points to poor quality legislation. There are arguments that the government is rationally thinking about the boundaries of the criminal law rather than just putting forward populist policies. Inter-agency co-operation is one area of continuity of policy between the last two decades where governments have looked for solutions outside of 'knee-jerk' reactions. Inter-agency co-operation was promulgated by governments throughout the 1980s and 1990s and given statutory force in the Crime and Disorder Act. That Act also included support for rehabilitation and restorative justice. The establishment of the Sentencing Advisory Panel was a deliberate response to law reform calls for consistency in sentencing.[60] These examples demonstrate government taking advice, looking at evidence and applying clear principles to the development of legislation. The Human Rights Act must count as the most important example of the principled approach. What is needed in the new decade is a much more informed and considered approach to criminal justice legislation than has been the case in the 1990s. The Regulation of Investigatory Powers Act 2000 gives some police powers a statutory footing for the first time, potentially increasing accountability. On the other hand the Football (Disorder) Act 2000 and Anti-Terrorism, Crime and Security Act 2001 mirror the 1990s approach. It remains to be seen which approach will become more prevalent.

Were the Victorians more liberal than those in authority today? It may be that the Victorians did not proportionately pass as much criminal legislation as has been passed in the last 24 years. However, arguably, the powers the nineteenth century state needed already existed for the large part, enabling them to deal (as they saw it) relatively effectively with 'bad' behaviour merely bordering on serious criminality. The Vagrancy Act 1824 gave the police wide powers to deal with 'vagabonds, trespassers and loiterers'.[61] This included the section 4 offence of 'being a suspected person loitering with intent to commit an arrestable offence'. Not repealed until 1981, use of this provision in the Act had long had negative overtones. For instance, there is clear evidence that the powers of the 'Sus' laws were used until abolition in a racist way by some police officers.[62]

---

[60] Crime and Disorder Act 1998, s.81.

[61] See Home Office *Working Party on Vagrancy and Street Offences Working Paper* (HMSO, London, 1974) Appendix A 'Historical Background'.

[62] Vagrancy Act 1824, ss.4, 6. See Williams, *Criminal Law*, pp. 656-62; Scarman, *Report;* for a recent explanation of the 'sus' laws see Jack Straw's comments in debates on the Prevention of Terrorism (Additional Powers) Act 1996, *Hansard*, 1996, 275, col. 186.

The approach of the courts in reasserting oft-cited but often not observed traditional British values of individual liberty and tolerance has been an important issue in the last few years, as chapters by Roger Hopkins Burke and Richard Stone underline. Both periods considered in this volume dealt with major public order issues, from the reaction to the Chartists in the 1840s to the recent riots in northern towns dealt with by Tom Williamson. The Riot (Damages) Act 1886 introduced following Trafalgar Square riots of 1886 remains in force today.[63] *Beatty v Gillbanks* is often considered to be a leading authority in support of civil liberty in late Victorian Britain.[64] Some European Court of Human Rights decisions have supported individuals against vague common law powers.[65] Recently the higher courts have supported civil rights and traditional British constitutional protections without recourse to ECHR jurisprudence, with the decision of the High Court in *Redmond-Bate v DPP* providing a modern reassertion of *Beatty v Gillbanks*.[66] In *R v Chief Constable of Sussex, Ex parte International Traders' Ferry Ltd* the House of Lords reasserted the importance of the doctrine of police independence – potentially establishing a limit on political influence over the police.[67] Relating to trespassory assembly the House of Lords in *DPP v Jones* held that a peaceful non-obstructive protest on the highway is a reasonable user of the highway, is lawful and therefore not trespass for the offence of trespassory assembly, though previously it could have automatically been held to have been an obstruction of the highway.[68] Barendt argued that the House of Lords formulated 'a broad common law right of public assembly'.[69] A century from now 1999 may be

---

[63] The Act provides for compensation out of police funds for loss or damage to property in any house, shop or building, by any persons 'riotously and tumultuously assembled together' See G. Best, *Mid-Victorian Britain 1851-75* (Fontana, London, 1979), pp. 293-300.

[64] (1882) 9 QBD 308, see also Richard Stone, 'Unlawful Assembly', in this volume. Compare *O'Kelly v Harvey* (1883) 15 Cox CC 435; also the 1930s cases of *Duncan v Jones* [1936] 1 KB 218; *Thomas v Sawkins* [1935] 2 KB 249, for less pro-civil liberties decisions.

[65] Compare *Hashman*, above, with *Steel and Others v the United Kingdom*, [1988] Crim LR 893, ECHR.

[66] [1999] Crim LR 998, and D. Birch, 'Commentary'

[67] [1999] AC 418, HL reaffirming CA. On the relationship between the Shoreham decision and the law on public protest (including comparison with *Beatty v Gillbanks*) see Lord Cooke, 'Shoreham-by-Sea', in J. Beatson and Y. Cripps (eds), *Freedom of Expression and Freedom of Information* (Oxford University Press, Oxford, 2000).

[68] [1999] Crim LR 672. On the High Court decision see B. Fitzpatrick and N. Taylor, 'A Case of Highway Robbery?', *New Law Journal*, 1997, 147, p. 338.

[69] E. Barendt, 'Freedom of Assembly', in Beatson and Cripps (eds), *Freedom of Expression*, p. 162.

seen as a high point in liberal judgments by the higher courts. This tolerant attitude of the courts sits to some extent uneasily with an authoritarian attitude predominant in parliament.

Conclusion

Governments in the 1990s have passed more criminal justice legislation but on balance that is not because they are more authoritarian than the Victorians but because the Victorians had fewer wider statutes and wide common law powers to rely on. It is clear, however, that after a period of rational and clearly thought-out law-making in the 1980s, 1990s politicians have resorted to piecemeal, vague and wide legislation which echoes the Victorian unwillingness to pass the coherent measures argued for by, for instance, James Fitzjames Stephen. This trend is ameliorated by a few positive measures, notably the landmark and by a liberal era in the higher courts with the Court of Appeal even joining the judges of the High Court and the Law Lords in seeking to defend traditional British civil liberties. In that respect the courts today are putting more into practice what Victorian judges also preached.

Chapter 6

Moral Cancers: Fraud and Respectable Crime

Sarah Wilson

The ability to respond effectively to major fraud is of the highest priority to the Government. We recognise that, in recent years, the public has at times felt that those responsible for major crimes in the commercial sphere have managed to avoid justice. Even where fraud is detected, the present procedures are often cumbersome, and difficult to prosecute effectively.[1]

Introduction

This is a study of financial crime in society, and has at its heart the objective of demonstrating that fraud is a problem old and new. The work is constructed around the assertion that fraud is an activity problem which troubles society greatly today, but no more so than it did our Victorian ancestors. This assertion is itself couched within the proposition that while British society's encounters with fraud can be seen to have predated the nineteenth century, the Victorian experience of fraud is crucial to this discussion.[2] This represented fraud as a long-term and continuing threat to social and economic stability, as one leading financial commentator put it during the 1850s: 'From time immemorial clerks have been discovered embezzling the property of their employers'.[3] This chapter takes as its starting point the insistence that notwithstanding fraud's antecedence, the 'inauguration, development and rapid progress' of 'high art' crime which occurred from the middle years of the nineteenth century marked the birth of financial crime in its true modern sense.[4]

---

[1] The Lord Chancellor, Lord Irvine, 'The feasibility of a unified approach to proceedings arising out of major City fraud', KPMG Lecture, June 1998.

[2] Notably the South Sea Bubble.

[3] D. M. Evans, *Facts, Failures, and Frauds: Revelations, Financial, Mercantile, Criminal* (Groombridge and Sons, London, 1859).

[4] *Ibid*, p.1; see also Wilson, 'Invisible Criminals?' 'High art' crime is an early term for what

The classification of certain crimes as 'financial crimes' flows from the much broader conception of white collar crime. White collar crimes are believed by modern scholars to raise a number of fascinating issues in relation to law enforcement and the administration of criminal justice, with their often complex interactions with society and key institutions. The chapter aspires to reach beyond a consideration of fraud's numerous crimino-legal difficulties to link white collar crime literature and research for the nineteenth century with another burgeoning corpus of literature; that which is growing up around the onset and progression of twentieth century economic globalisation. The objective is ultimately to position fraud's complex relationship with society in the context of a rapidly changing world, past and present. Predictably, this has involved a consideration of current events for both periods, as the promises inherent in ever-greater technologicisation of society and economy are inherent to both periods, with their allusions to an age of insecurity.[5] Both time points are characterised by great excitement and promise, as well as anxiety, as the implications of a world without economic boundaries are explored, and an inability to predict the future becomes apparent. In seeking to link these broad themes together, this chapter is really a snapshot of Britain's encounters with fraud in two periods with powerful similarities.

The Intellectual Position of the Problem of Fraud Defined: Some Basic Considerations

Intellectual considerations of fraud featured strongly in Victorian literature with a focus upon intelligence, sophistication and social status and power as central characteristics. *The Times* financial journalist, D. M. Evans, spoke of the 'architects' of high art crime as characteristically highly respectable individuals who had tampered 'with weighty trusts reposed in them'.[6] He could see in their activities the 'qualities' of 'full mental culture... position... and character' aligned with 'ingenuity, perseverance, and artistic skill'. It was in the criminal activities of many of such people which Evans alleged showed how well their talents could be employed 'had they been properly directed'.[7] Over one hundred years later, at the dawn of the third millennium, what is now a large corpus of writings on

---

is now known as financial or City crime.

[5] L. Elliott and D. Atkinson, *The Age of Insecurity* (Verso, London, 1998).

[6] See Evans, *Facts*, where the remark was made specifically in reference to W. J. Robson, perpetrator of the Crystal Palace Frauds in 1856.

[7] *Ibid.*

City crime (and particularly white collar crime literature more broadly) suggests that in essence the nature of fraud, and consequently the nature of the fraudster *himself* as someone powerful, educated and possessive of a public persona, has changed very little. This is suggested during the Guinness trial in 1990, in the insistence of Justice Henry, that 'these were offences which by their nature could only be committed by the very rich with very great power over their corporate empires'.[8]

Over the past 30 years, scholars have focused on the 'big questions' of white collar crime's relationship with 'ordinary' or traditional types of crime and criminality, and also with society.[9] This focus pivots the much-alluded-to alleged 'special nature' of white collar crime, and the number of intellectual and practical questions which arise within this conception. In the context of financial crime, translations of these into issues raised include ones in relation to the nature of financial crime's activity; ones arising in the process of trial and punishment of its perpetrators; and questions of whether or not fraud and related crimes of dishonesty are 'real' crimes. The fundamental question underlying these is, whether white collar crime is somehow 'different' from ordinary crime, justifying its 'special' classification or whether it is nothing more than crime in the true sense, requiring its absorption into general criminological theories?[10] There is in short a remarkable lack of consensus beyond agreement that fraud is a huge problem for society.[11]

The 21st Century and an Increasingly Globalised World: The (Second?) 'Age of Insecurity'

Emerging from the pressures and opportunities created by globalisation can be seen the empowerment of the individual, and the corresponding role of government in facilitating the maximisation of individual potential. The underpinnings of this movement and the outgrowths from it can be most clearly illustrated with reference to the political economy of the current

---

[8] *R v Saunders; R v Parnes; R v Ronson; R v Lyons* [1990] Central Criminal Court, London.

[9] The debt of scholars to Edwin Sutherland's work is crucial, see E. Sutherland, *White Collar Crime* (Dryden Press, New York, 1949).

[10] D. Nelken, 'White Collar Crime' in M. Maguire *et al.* (eds), *The Oxford Handbook of Criminology* (Oxford University Press, Oxford, 1994) is a work which admirably draws together central literature and the essential issues and questions relating to white collar crime and its complex relationship with society.

[11] For example, while documenting the views of Wilson that fraud is not part of the real crime debate, Michael Levi insists that its characteristic absence from official recordings of crime meant that it was a 'dark figure'. See M. Levi, *Regulating Fraud: White Collar Crime and the Criminal Process* (Tavistock Press, London, 1986).

New Labour government. As a reflection of the need to maximise individual potential whilst distancing government from its traditional role as one of 'provider',[12] the Blair government is seeking a 'third way' between statist (or 'top down') brand of social democracy, which is characteristic of 'old' Labour, and the dismantling of government in favour of the operation of the free market which is favoured by political persuasions of the right.[13]

It is the idea of the global age as the second age of insecurity which is central, with its apparent precipitation of the disempowerment of the nation-state, and the accompanying 'hollowing out' of its autonomy of action.[14] In this manner, the modern historical equivalent can be found in the parallel development in Britain which peaked in the Victorian age, as the balance of power gravitated away from the localities and towards a centralised organisation of government functions.[15] This pattern was, of course, inextricably linked with the industrial revolution and the modernisation of the economy through capitalist development. Here, this age can be seen as harbouring many of the same insecurities and difficulties as the present one, but of course 'travelling' in the opposite direction. The grapple for state control period was also inextricably linked to Britain's occupation of central stage in providing the lead for world industrialisation. The modern parallel for this can of course be found across New Labour's reform agenda, with a particularly salient example taken from a speech of the Chancellor of the Exchequer, the Rt. Hon. Gordon Brown MP:

> The changes we face in the twenty-first century economy involve permanent economic revolution: continuous and rapid innovation that compels unprecedented flexibility and adaptability in skills and knowledge. Increasingly every good and every service will be exposed to relentless global competition. And to equip ourselves best to meet and master these challenges, we need a pro-enterprise and pro-opportunity Britain.[16]

Remaining initially with the events at the turn of the nineteenth century, the onset and progression of the capitalist economy did of course come

---

[12] A. Giddens, *The Third Way*.

[13] *Ibid.*

[14] G. Wilson and S. Wilson, '"Responsible risk takers": Notions of Directorial Responsibility – Past, Present and Future', *Journal of Corporate Law Studies*, 2001, 1, p. 211.

[15] D. S. Eastwood, *Governing Rural England: Tradition and Transformation in Local Government 1780-1840* (Clarendon Press, Oxford, 1994).

[16] Rt. Hon. Gordon Brown, MP, Newspaper Conference, *The Times*, 22 July 1999.

with corresponding enhancements in opportunity for individual wealth. For D. M. Evans, and others like him,[17] it was this which provided the social and economic context for the inauguration of 'high art' crime. The shift away from the nation's agrarian economy and its adoption of the capitalist doctrine represented a huge source of excitement, and held the promise to revolutionise all quarters of social and economic life, but the progress implicit also became the source of insecurity. The appearance of financial crime in its modern form during the 1840s highlighted both sides of the 'progression' coin, and also the ironies which this harboured. It was clear to the commercially literate, and even the moderately intelligent, that the capitalist economy promised unprecedented personal wealth. Yet the middle years of the nineteenth century established beyond doubt that it was also the lifeblood of activity which could undermine, and even destroy it. The implications of fraud for society on the eve of its status as the world's leading industrial nation were frightening, and, just as is the case today, the problem of fraud can be seen to have cut across a number of social and economic institutions.

Fraud as a Modern Problem: The Central Issues and the Globalising Influences

The influence which the problem of fraud can be seen to have in the calibration of modern policy can be illustrated on a number of levels, and at a *macro* level is well illustrated with reference to the present climate characterised by New Labour government's reforming zeal. As has already been suggested, the rhetoric and the proposed agenda for reform originate in the promotion of Britain as a key player in the newly-emerging world market place – the extent of the vision is vast. Cutting across the entire social and economic spectrum, the 'enterprise culture' proposals for reform can be seen both as an endorsement of the opportunities presented by the knowledge economy, and the promotion of the UK as a most suitable location for the development of business in a fast-changing world.[18]

---

[17] See for example *Hansard* entries for the period and also opinion expressed in the leading 'companies' publication of the day, the *Law Times' Joint Stock Companies Journal*.

[18] The principal initiatives targeted are those of training and education, the development of high technology; the promotion of regional and community growth; the promotion of awareness of e-business; the promotion of small business and the strengthening of European and Global connections through the fostering and development of entrepreneurship in the UK and forging partnerships with world business. See for example *Opportunity for All in a World of Change: A White Paper on Enterprise, Skills and Innovation*, Cm 5052, 2001.

As part of this broad calculation, the need for harsh responses to fraud's presence can be seen to have crept into the proposed reforms to bankruptcy law currently at White Paper stage.[19] This movement seeks to depart from the present legal position whereby no distinction is made between honest and unlucky individuals who become bankrupt and those who have acted irresponsibly or actually fraudulently.[20] In turn, reforms which are proposed thus resolve to introduce a new regime within which the consequences of bankruptcy are determined by whether the bankrupt has behaved honestly in his dealings, but has been unlucky, or has acted irresponsibly, negligently or even dishonestly. Under the proposed regime, those in the former category are to be given every incentive for quick rehabilitation whereas those who have acted without responsibility shall be dealt with more harshly than at present, and with early discussions indicating that those who have acted dishonestly, being subject to restrictions of up to 15 years.[21] This rethinking of the bankruptcy position is indicative of recognition of the ability of fraud to damage Britain's social and economic prospects.

At a more fundamental level, modern perceptions on the problem of fraud into the twenty-first century clearly focus on the transformation of the transactional culture of business which has been created by a revolution in technology. Such concerns have also turned towards the ways in which this huge transformation in communications is permeating beyond the commercial sectors and intruding into everyday life. Warning of these dramatic changes was given in earnest during the 1980s, both in the literary explorations of academics, and also in policy initiatives which resulted in the inception of the Serious Fraud Office in 1988.[22] The Serious Fraud Office came into being as a result of perceived lack of public confidence in the ability of the criminal process to respond with efficacy to the occurrence in society of financial crimes. This assessment of public opinion was aired firstly during the early 1980s in the wake of the appointment of the Fraud Trials Committee chaired by Lord

---

[19] The underlying *raison d'être* for enterprise culture is very much motivated by the challenges associated with globalisation, and the reforms are in turn located within the framework provided by third way politics.

[20] Such a rationale also underlies New Labour's promotion of the 'responsible risk taker' concept for company directors. See G. Wilson, 'Business, State and Community'.

[21] The proposals relating to reforms in bankruptcy law can be found in *Opportunity For All*, ch. 5.

[22] M. Levi, *The Prevention of Fraud*, Crime Prevention Unit, Paper 17 (HMSO, London, 1987); pursuant of the Criminal Justice Act 1987, and resultant of the Report of Lord Roskill's Fraud Trials Committee.

Roskill to conduct an investigation into the present regime for the management of fraud, and to make recommended changes. The Committee identified a number of difficulties which appeared to interfere with the effective management and prevention of fraud in the UK. As a result of this enquiry the Serious Fraud Office, a 'unified organisation' for the investigation and prosecution of serious fraud, was 'born'.[23] The Committee introduced its work through its contention that:

> The public no longer believes that the legal system in England and Wales is capable of bringing perpetrators of serious frauds expeditiously and effectively to book. The overwhelming weight of evidence laid before us suggests that the public is right. In relation to such crimes and to the skilful and determined criminals who commit them, the present legal system is archaic, cumbersome and unreliable.[24]

It is clear from the Roskill Committee Report itself, as well as from commentary generated by it and which was contemporaneous with it, that key questions in the formulation of modern fraud policy relate to a 'twin' set of issues. These issues relate firstly to the conceptual difficulties surrounding fraud as a 'type' of *crime*, and one which is in many ways different from other types of criminality, and secondly, ones pertaining to the 'type' of *person* engaged in such criminal activities. What is striking in this dual exploration of the Victorian period alongside the events of the closing years of the twentieth century is the same clustering of key questions around the type of crime and the type of criminal.

The Victorian Discovery of Fraud

The events which are alleged to comprise the Victorian 'birth' of modern financial crime were enormously influential at the time, and moreover can be seen to have precipitated a number of developments in what might now be regarded as the institutional machinery against fraud. The most important of these was the use of criminal proceedings in allegations of criminal conduct in the context of business dealings, with the criminal *cause célèbres* believed to be the historical ancestor of the modern serious fraud trial.[25] It was this which perhaps represented the most important step

---

[23] Lord Roskill had originally recommended that this unified body should also be responsible for 'all [these] functions' which included detection of serious fraud, but the detection function was ultimately dropped from its remit.

[24] *Report of the Fraud Trials Committee* chaired by Wentworth, E. Bart., Lord Roskill (1986), HMSO, London.

[25] S. Wilson, 'In Defence of Respectability: Financial Crime, the "High Art" Criminal and

ever in the emergence of modern responses to fraud, and was the clearest demonstration of Victorian will to question very publicly the manner of its progress as a capitalist nation. In addition, our Victorian forefathers can be seen to have made the first tentative steps in the formulation of coherent sentencing policies in respect of people who did not really fit prevailing social and cultural perceptions of criminals.

It has been contended elsewhere that it was the boom in railway companies during the 1840s which provided the immediate context for the Victorian legal and social recognition of financial crime.[26] It was following the exposure of widespread dubious business activity during the boom that the criminal law came under growing pressure to 'intervene'. The response was quite spectacular, and according to D. M. Evans, '[the offences of] fraud and forgery and misappropriation are called into existence, with all their frightful and heavy legal responsibilities'.[27] Victorian society responded by acknowledging the presence of 'high art' crime, and bestowing on the earliest criminal trials the task of defining its remit, by working through important deliberations, during which criminal offences can be seen to have come into existence, and others given a modern meaning and application.[28] The body of evidence from the trials makes it plain that this discovery of large-scale dishonesty in business dealings was deeply shocking, in terms of the conceptual difficulties entailed in the acceptance of a crime which had arisen from the operationalisation of capitalist doctrine, and one which represented a sophisticated manipulation of it, counting amongst its perpetrators the cream of respectable society.

Today and Yesteryear: Conceptual Difficulties with the Problem of Fraud

How much has changed? Lord Roskill's 1986 Report painted a picture of absence of public faith in the machinery in place to counter the occurrence of fraud in the British economy. Strong allusions to the persistence of such a state of affairs were made in the Law Commission's 1999 Report on the law relating to fraud and deception entitled *Legislating the Criminal Code*.[29] The 1999 Report reveals that concerns raised during the 1980s in

---

the Language of Criminal Charges 1850-1880' in I. Inkster *et al* (eds), *The Golden Age: Essays in British Social and Economic History, 1850-1870* (Ashgate, Aldershot, 2000).

[26] S. Wilson, 'Invisible Criminals?'.

[27] Evans, *Facts*.

[28] S. Wilson, 'In Defence of Respectability'

[29] Law Commission Consultation Paper *Legislating the Criminal Code: Fraud and Deception* (No. 155), 1999.

relation to fraud's mutability and enforcement of the laws against it continue to echo today, almost word for word, just as they do for the rhetoric for the Victorian period. This includes worries about the ability of fraud to threaten commercial interests, and damage Britain's reputation as a safe place to do business, witness the claims of the Institute of Chartered Accountants:

> business fraud is a growing problem that affects everyone both in the private and public sectors.... The cost to the country is huge in terms of those who pay for it and the loss of reputation as a safe place to do business.[30]

A prosecutor's perception of the problems associated with fraud, with emphasis placed on the influence of technology can be gleaned from the statement of Rosalind Wright, Director of the Serious Fraud Office, that 'Commercial fraud is fast-growing and an ever more threatening phenomenon. It is a negative force to be reckoned with in the world'.[31]

The discourse surrounding the nineteenth century fraud trials is highly revealing of the wider concerns shared by the Victorians. It is striking that the importance of business profitability to a capitalist economy such as that of Victorian Britain was not, apparently, regarded by key Victorian public figures as providing a justification for avoiding state intervention in the daily regulation of business. Business management could not remain a matter of private concern. This is underlined by the complete absence of any proposition to the contrary in addresses made by the judiciary during the trials. Even the most pro-capitalist addresses made in parliament were met by ones of equal strength which warned of its dangers, and especially highlighted the problem of fraud and its wider implications for the nation.[32] Indeed, key players in the earliest trials used the business dimensions to emphasise its wider signficances, and to elevate business fraud into a highly public matter, as is emphasised by the precise nature of the charges which were brought against individuals and the direction of the discourses generated in the courtroom. Indictments often explicitly charged that the intention of a fraudster had been to misrepresent information to the public as a whole, as well as to shareholders. This perspective was reinforced in the proceedings themselves by direct and

[30] Institute of Chartered Accountants, Press Release, February 1998.
[31] R. Wright, 'What does the future hold for the SFO?' *Serious Fraud Office Information*, 1998.
[32] Perhaps the most heated exchanges of opinion on the danger of 'modern' conditions for business activity providing breeding grounds for fraud occurred in debates on the case for limited liability, and the passage of legislation on this in the mid-1850s.

specific reference to activities such as falsifying accounts, information being matters of 'public concern' and 'public mischief'.[33] Thus, a public dimension to business activity was clearly established in the Victorian period. This included intimations on occasions of particularly high profile incidents that such behaviour constituted a fraud on society, as Baron Alderson made plain in passing sentence in 1855 upon the London bankers Strahan, Bates and Paul: 'A greater or more serious offence could hardly be imagined in a great commercial community like this'.[34] This concern to protect the integrity of the economy in the wider interests of the nation is directly analogous with today's concerns on representing Britain as a safe place to conduct business.

Victorian cases such as that of Strahan, Bates and Paul, guilty of embezzling client money, caused little difficulty for the presiding judge in directing juries. Many cases were not so clear-cut. In several trials where money had been 'lost' in transactions which were not necessarily *prima facie* criminal, and where the source of the alleged illegality was the information which misrepresented a business reality to the public, a number of complex considerations clearly operated.[35] An underlying tension was that it was investment activity which supported and advanced Britain's capitalist economy. The desirability of a blanket castigation of 'undesirable' business activity had to be carefully weighed against the need to encourage entrepreneurialism within commercial circles. Such tensions remain for today. The key difference is not that these difficulties have conceptually become easier over time, but that during the Victorian period, the actors lacked the benefit of the legal and cultural parameters which are in place today, as a result of experience dating back to the nineteenth century as well as to the present.[36]

---

[33] See the trial of the directors of the Royal British Bank, February 1858, at the Central Criminal Court in London on charges relating to conspiracy and intention to misrepresent and deceive.

[34] Evans, *Facts*.

[35] Two which have been used in this study are the Royal British Bank trial and the City of Glasgow Bank trial.

[36] Fiduciary responsibilities in the Law of Trusts were of course well established in a line of case law descending from *Keech v Sandford* (1726) Eq. Cas. Abr. 741. However, while much thrust within many of the trial proceedings was expressly or impliedly oriented towards fiduciary obligations, professional opinion was not convinced that liability in equity would necessarily arise in relation to these trials. See 'Commentary upon the Tipperary Bank Case', *Law Times' Joint Stock Companies Journal*, 19 September 1857. Today, company directors are subject to a common law duty of skill and care objective in nature in a way that would scarcely be imaginable in the nineteenth century, the facility for the disqualification of company directors is provided in the Company Directors Disqualification Act 1986.

Fraud and a Different Type of Criminal: Understandings Past and Present

A very popular scholarly pursuit in recent times has been to undermine the connection between respectability and white collar crime.[37] At the same time however, there is also a cluster of literature which suggests that the link between high(er) social status and crimes of fraud is as strong as ever, and seeks to warn of the dangers which this presents. In policy discourses, Rosalind Wright has warned recently against the dangers of 'justice by social status' in her assertion that:

> It cannot be allowed... that there is one way of dealing with blue-collar crime — the burglars, the car thieves and the armed robbers and another, much softer option, for the more sophisticated 'suits' who, with a press of a computer key, and no blood being shed, get away with millions.[38]

Such concerns might be dismissed as being typical of institutions which are 'pushing' a particular agenda. The Serious Fraud Office is an investigative and prosecutory body, and one which is still recovering in the aftermath of its 'darkest hour' during the mid-1990s, following a number of highly publicised acquittals of equally high profile cases.

However, such concerns are mirrored almost exactly in the work of the Law Commission, a very different organ pushing a very different agenda, and also in a number of highly respected academic studies, such as the one in 1991 conducted in the USA. According to this study, perceptions of white collar crime, and particularly the white collar criminal as the polar opposite of the common criminal, mean:

> as much as we have come to see street crime primarily as the work of disadvantaged young men from broken families and decaying neighbourhoods, white collar crime has been linked to advantaged older men from stable homes living in well-kept communities.[39]

---

[37] See for example H. Croall, 'Who is the White Collar Criminal?' *British Journal of Criminology* 1989, 30, pp. 157-74; S. Shapiro, 'Collaring the Crime, Not the Criminal: Reconsidering the Concept of a White Collar Crime', *American Sociological Review*, 1980, 55, pp. 346-65; see also Nelken's amusing rendition in 'White Collar Crime' of red, white, and khaki coloured collars to illustrate the futility of an obsessive focus upon misleading attributes of a highly complex type of criminal behaviour.

[38] Rosalind Wright, Director of the Serious Fraud Office, 'Fighting Fraud in the UK — the interaction of the criminal and the regulatory process', Speech, Financial Regulation Industry Group Reception, London, May 2000.

[39] D. Weisburd, S. Wheeler, S. Waring, and N. Bode, *Crimes of the Middle Classes: White Collar Offenders in Federal Courts* (Yale University Press, New Haven, 1991).

The most recent humanisations of concerns about social polarisations in justice can be found in the trial of Ernest Saunders *et al* resulting from the so-called 'Guinness affair' directors in 1990 and that of the Maxwell brothers in 1995-96. In the earlier trial, the four Guinness defendants were found guilty *inter alia* of theft and false accounting. Although a subsequent analysis of their sentences ranging from four years imprisonment (reduced on appeal to a maximum of two and a half years), fines of between £3-5 million, and the loss of a knighthood (in the case of Sir Jack Lyons) argued persuasively that the punishments were adequate, the trial generated much interest in the punishment of respectable criminals.[40] A *Daily Express* headline, 'Disgraced!' was obviously intended to strike a chord with its right-of-centre, comfortably-off readers, but in the subsequent commentary it also sought to demonstrate the opinion that there was 'one law for the rich'.

In the broadsheet, 'quality' press, a headline in *The Times* reported 'Lyons *Escapes* Jail with £3m Fine' (emphasis added).[41] In similar vein, although the trial of the Maxwell brothers over complicity in the 'dealings' of their late father, Robert, ended in the acquittal of the defendants, considerable interest was generated in the status of the accused, including the sharp contrasts between 'criminals' like the Maxwells and others who were treated visibly very differently by the criminal process.[42] The aftermath of the Maxwell trial moved Michael Levi to remark that, despite some longer sentences which had been meted out, there was 'much delusion about the lack of seriousness with which fraud is being taken by the courts'.[43]

The issues raised in both these trials in relation to the (comparative) social superiority of those standing accused of financial crimes have their nineteenth century equivalents in the fraud trials of middle and late years of the century, which became public accusations of criminality levied against the cream of Victorian society. On trial during these immensely important proceedings were key figures in the commercial community, including many respected bankers and businessmen; including for example, Strahan, Bates and Paul, and the directors of the Royal British Bank. Those exposed also included John Sadlier, MP, who lost his position

---

[40] M. Levi, 'Sentencing White Collar Crime in the Dark?: Reflections on the Guinness Four', *Howard Journal of Criminal Justice*, 1991, 30, 4, p. 257.

[41] See Levi, 'Sentencing', for an account of the press reporting and its directions and points of reference.

[42] R. Bosworth-Davies, 'Thinking the Unthinkable', *New Law Journal*, 1995, June, p. 811.

[43] M. Levi, 'Regulating Fraud Revisited' in P. Davies *et al.* (eds), *Invisible Crimes: their victims and their regulation* (Macmillan, Basingstoke, 1999).

in Lord Aberdeen's Treasury as a result of his dubious mercantile dealings.[44] In these trials of Victorian commercial and polite society's great and good, attention was drawn to activity which was not confined to the so-called criminal classes.[45] It was a type of crime characteristically perpetrated by respectable people, it was dishonesty which required education, and was alleged to be deliberate and calculated in design and execution (though most defendants pleaded necessity in their defence).[46]

When opening the case against London bankers Strahan, Paul and Bates in Bow Street magistrates court, prosecuting barrister Mr. Bodkin remarked that those who now stood at the bar were 'not prisoners such as are usually seen in that position, but gentlemen'. In the Central Criminal Court, the prosecuting Attorney-General reminded those assembled that the prisoners had 'hitherto maintained a high position in society'.[47] While it might seem obvious to suggest that because so much attention was given to the defendants' social position their criminal conduct was being correspondingly downplayed, this is probably far too simplistic.[48] Esteem and probity were always very closely aligned with confidence and trust. This emphasis had a central role in contemporary questioning of prevailing social and cultural assumptions on crime and criminality, but also, there is the suggestion that this rhetoric added to the gravity of the charges.

Fraud and the Criminal Process: Victorian and Modern Sentencing Patterns

It is clear today, both from official and less formal discourses, that alleged demonstrations of judicial lenience accorded to convicted fraudsters is a source of societal unease. This unease occurs across a spectrum of views, at one end of which are the generalised accusations of 'rich man's law', moving to better-considered commentary relating to proportionality, and questioning whether the punishment actually reflects the gravity of the offence.[49] There is much evidence that Victorian judges struggled with

---

[44] Evans. *Facts.*

[45] For 'typical' depredators, see *Report of the Rural Constabulary Commissioners* 1839 Parliamentary Papers XIX, p. 169.

[46] See the City of Glasgow Bank trial, University of Glasgow Business Archive Centre, UGD Class/108 11.

[47] The trial of Strahan, Bates and Paul as transcribed in D. M. Evans, *Facts, Failures and Frauds.*

[48] Wilson 'In Defence of Respectability'

[49] See, for example, Bosworth-Davies, 'Thinking the Unthinkable'; also the works of Michael Levi, notably Levi, 'Sentencing'; Levi, 'Regulating Fraud'; M. Levi, 'Fraudulent

similar tensions. Several cases suggest that judges could demonstrate lenience in the administration of custodial penalties, making explicit their intention to stop short of what the law and policy would allow. Their harsh verbal attacks upon the guilty, including acknowledgement of the damaging nature of fraud, did not translate into actual sentencing. Lord Campbell, for instance, in the trial of the Royal British Bank directors, attributed his decision to 'pass milder sentence than I otherwise should' on the fact that the case before him was the first prosecution of such a nature.[50]

Examination of the big 'City' fraud trials of the nineteenth century which were the first modern trials of serious and complex fraud reveal that expression of current societal concerns about white collar crime were voiced then.[51] They illuminate many deep insecurities about the nature of the crime and the nature of the criminal which predominate current discourses, and about the accommodation of respectable crime and the respectable criminal within British culture. In respect of sentencing policy and practice, almost 150 years on from these earliest large fraud trials, and writing in relation to the outcome of the trial of the former Guinness directors in 1991, Michael Levi commented on the wider difficulties in the sentencing of white collar criminals:

> The charge of social bias in favour of the rich and the powerful is one that exercises sentencers emotionally and socio-politically. The spotlight on white collar offenders means that... judges are sensitive to prospective media and social criticism.[52]

He added that such crimes committed by 'people with no prior convictions' raises 'in an acute form the conflicts between principles of social equity and *general* deterrability... and *individual* deterrence and rehabilitation'.[53]

This assertion is perhaps the clearest and most accurate reading of the totality of the 'problem' of fraud (as a category of white collar crime) in society, with powerful resonances reaching beyond questions of sentencing, drawing together concerns underlying formal policy and less official discussions of policy and principle. According to some modern

---

Justice?: Sentencing the Business Criminal', in P. Carlen and D. Cook (eds), *Paying for Crime* (Open University Press, Milton Keynes, 1989).

[50] Evans, *Facts*.
[51] For instance, the Serious Fraud Office's original remit was defined in relation to such conduct.
[52] Levi, 'Sentencing'
[53] *Ibid.*

scholars, there are intuitive inclinations towards demonstrating lenience towards people who, prior to their contact with the law, have been characteristically 'model' citizens in every respect. But this is coupled with the demand for severity arising from the nature of their criminal activity, which does have the capacity to 'hurt' its victims, and undermine society at large and the economy. This gives rise to a tension between the diametrically opposed factors of lenience and severity, and the resultant discomfort and uncertainty in sentencing in the sentencing process is coined as the 'paradox of lenience and severity'.[54]

Fraud as a Moral Cancer: Conceptions Old and New

This consideration of the presence of fraud in society has not attempted a comprehensive consideration of the intellectual and practical problems associated with fraud's operation in modern society. It has instead sought to provide insights into fraud's impact upon society and economy, past and present, through reference to a number of particularly telling examples. Some modern conceptions of fraud elevate it to something which is beyond mere 'criminal activity', as a 'social phenomenon'[55] Most recently, this has occurred through the deployment of the language and imagery of 'disease' and 'debilitation' to illuminate fraud's negative impacts on the fabric of society.[56] Subsequently the growth and disease metaphors have been developed by City commentator Brian Widlake who postulated that fraud was a growing cancer within (and thus, by implication spreading through) our society.[57] Whilst this language of disease and debilitation was not developed by the Victorians in relation to financial crime, it would be a mistake to presume that this signals acceptance of the proliferation of fraud. In their determination to respond to activity which interfaced with the capitalist doctrine and the operation of *laissez faire* so strikingly, and contradicted them far more subtly, our nineteenth century ancestors leave a legacy which puts beyond doubt their fears and concerns as they came to terms with the implications of a 'new' type of crime.

---

[54] S. Wheeler, D. Weisburd, and N. Bode, 'Sentencing the White Collar Offender: Rhetoric and Reality', *American Sociological Review*, 1982, 47, pp. 641-59.
[55] Nelken, 'White Collar Crime'
[56] A. Bequai, *White Collar Crime: A Twentieth Century Crisis* (Lexington Press, Massachussets, 1978).
[57] B. Widlake, *Serious Fraud Office* (Little Brown and Co, London, 1995).

Chapter 7

The Blast of Blasphemy: Government, Law and Culture Confront a Chill Wind

David Nash

The crime of blasphemy and blasphemous libel has a history which has reflected the changing concerns of the state in all countries where it has had a significant presence. England is no exception to this, but the uniqueness of its situation is that English legal jurisprudence in this area combines a strange mixture of authoritarian defence of morals and protection of individual opinion. Where most other countries have, in the contemporary world, made the state neutral in this matter or have more actively devolved power to individuals, English law finds itself pushed into maintaining this ambiguous dichotomy.[1]

In reflecting the changing concerns of society at large, blasphemy in England has mutated from a criminal mechanism designed to ensure religious conformity, through brief status as an issue of national security to become, from the late nineteenth century onwards a matter for the scrutiny of public opinion. The last of these phases has made the offence, and society's attitudes to it, more responsive than ever to social and cultural climates of change. This chapter will discuss this last phase with particular reference to two cases; each of these occurring at either end of this period. The first of these, the celebrated *Freethinker* case, *R v Ramsay and Foote* (1883), was fundamentally important in altering the case law of blasphemy and blasphemous libel.[2] Arguably it was from this moment that the intrinsically tight relationship between Church and State found its bounds loosened sufficiently to allow liberal secular opinion to

---

[1] The history of blasphemy is best approached through the following works, L. Blom-Cooper, *Blasphemy: An ancient wrong or a modern right?* (Essex Hall Bookshop, 1981); H. Bradlaugh-Bonner, *Penalties Upon Opinion* (Watts and Co, 1934); C. Kenny, 'The Evolution of the Law of Blasphemy', *Cambridge Law Journal* 1, 1922, pp. 127-42; L. W. Levy, *Treason against God: A History of the Offense of Blasphemy* (Shocken, New York, 1981); L. W. Levy, Blasphemy, *Verbal Offense Against the Sacred from Moses to Salman Rushdie* (Knopf, New York, 1993); G. D. Nokes, *A History of the Crime of Blasphemy* (London, 1928); D. Nash, *Blasphemy in Britain 1789–Present* (Ashgate, Aldershot, 1999).

[2] (1883) 15 Cox CC 231.

expand. However, reasons for studying the second of these cases in a comparative context is precisely the reverse of the reasons for studying the first. This case, the equally-celebrated *Gay News* case of 1977 and 1978, similarly altered the law, but in this instance restored the law to the condition it was in before the *Foote* case.[3] This latter judgment and its assumptions about the finite and indissoluble nature of religion and religious belief closed the door to endlessly liberal progressive legal interpretations of culture and cultural development which had otherwise characterised the twentieth century. But it also demonstrated how responsive a law like blasphemy is to issues that centre around public opinion relating to bad behaviour and precisely how such opinion might be harnessed and manipulated.

Bear in mind here that the history of the crime and phenomemon of blasphemy and blasphemous libel in England has been expressly guided and shaped by certain forms of nationalist self-image and isolationist agendas. These images have over the last two centuries sought to portray wayward tendencies within society as firstly un-English/British and secondly as explicitly foreign forms of dangerous cultural invasion. Issues of national identity have bequeathed an important legacy to the modern period as British culture made great efforts to make blasphemy and blasphemers alien entities. From an earlier reliance upon the direct use of authority the 'crime' has come to embrace issues of public opinion which have themselves influenced defendants, legal practitioners and judges in their interpretation of the law. This interest in, and appeal to, public opinion has itself had two sides. While the law seeks to reflect the religious beliefs and moral concerns of the population at large, defendants have equally been swift to invoke liberalising public opinion and the modernising 'spirit of the age' as a justification for their actions.

The power of public opinion was enhanced and given increased legal credence through the adoption and promotion of ideas of the 'casual encounter' evident in these cases. It was an enduring fear that dangerous tendencies could lie in wait to ambush the unwary. On the specific occasions when the legal conception of blasphemy was invoked, it has also been possible to see assumptions behind its operation that utilise explicitly English nationalist discourses. Finally, the 'resolution' of the blasphemy problem beyond the end of the twentieth century still involves a declaration and assertion that British culture is somehow unique, superior and in need of vigilant defence: a situation that, once again, has given enhanced power to the phenomenon of public opinion. This is in spite of the integration of the European Convention on Human Rights into British law and the

---

[3] *R v Lemon* [1979] AC 617.

supposed adoption of pan-European cultural values associated with wider issues of tolerance.

Freethinking and Religious Authority

The legal system considered here is English law, but the history of blasphemy in the British Isles is a story about the elision of cultural standards. The English and Scottish legal systems remain different and retain different conceptions of blasphemy (and the situation is different still in Northern Ireland), yet this is an area of life in which an English standard of morality has been swiftly invoked with almost unanimous appeal and approval.[4] One particular mindset which aided and abetted this elision has been a readiness to appeal to the phenomenon of empire as both comforting bulwark and as solemn duty riddled with foreboding. Even the dissolution of this empire has coincided with imperatives for integration with Europe. This in itself has been an episode about which opinion has been, to say the least, divided. However, it is especially clear that globalised cultures have introduced new fears while re-awaking much older isolationist moral discourses. Where once Europe threatened generations-old imperial markets, its new threat to Europeanise morals and standards of tolerance threatens a sweeping away of the inherited moral order that the idea of the British empire still nurtures and sustains.

The laws against blasphemy originated in the laws against heresy. The development of blasphemy as an offence was ostensibly a function of the developing close relationship between Church and State in England in the final quarter of the seventeenth century. As a species of political and moral order the law increasingly came to defend religion as the religion of the land established by law. The Blasphemy Statute (9 and 10 William III) was passed at a time of wider concerns about the maintenance of internal order and perceived threats of foreign invasion to the integrity of the state.[5] This legacy has had important consequences for the long-term history of blasphemy. With these concerns in mind, Sir Matthew Hale gave his famous judgment, explicitly describing religion as 'part and parcel of the laws of the land'. This suggested that the sanctity of the state was provided by a religious settlement which, by definition, it was 'bad behaviour' not to accept without question.[6]

---

[4] For an introductory discussion of the separate character of blasphemy in Scottish Law see G. Maher, *Blasphemy in Scots Law* (Scots Law Times, 1977), p. 260. See also Viscount Dunedin, J. L. Wark, *et al*, *Encyclopaedia of the Laws of Scotland* (W. Green and Son, Edinburgh, 1928), pp. 68-70.

[5] Levy, *Blasphemy*, p. 221; Nokes, *Blasphemy*, p. 48.

[6] See Levy, *Blasphemy*, pp. 220-1, Nash, *Blasphemy*, pp. 32-7.

Thus the treatment of blasphemy as a crime and its perpetrators as criminals emanates from fear and insecurity, not from confidence. It may have begun as a species of articulated and legislated authoritarian fear, but by the twentieth century attitudes to this area of concern had come to rely upon the capricious nature of public opinion. A surrender to the power of public opinion also provided, towards the end of the nineteenth century, evidence of a genuine desire to create an active and consensual 'populist' state which itself was often contrasted with the lack of such developments in other European countries. One explanation for this particular reaction was that Britain has, in a genuine sense, been isolated from a culture of criticism that surfaced as especially virulent anti-clericalism in mainland Europe. The British state emphasised its providential distance from the religiosity of continental Europe through the law of blasphemy's protection for only the Established Church of England.[7]

The blasphemy cases of the early 1880s contained a significant flavour of imported European anti-clericalism. The first genuinely tabloid and ribald atheist paper, G. W. Foote's *Freethinker*, borrowed its cartoons from the French anti-clerical activist Leo Taxil's *La Bible Amusante*. These were adapted and sometimes redrawn parodies of biblical events or lampoons of clerical targets designed to suit a British audience, focusing upon the supposed ridiculousness or the immorality and barbarism of particular biblical passages.[8] Foote understood the shock tactics involved in attempting to use this material, associated with continental anti-clericalism; he was also quite aware of the fear generated by its provenance. Indeed Foote used this opportunity to lament that England had not developed a sufficiently virulent anti-clerical culture.

> We in England have Comic Histories, Comic Geographies, and Comic Grammars, but a Comic Bible would horrify us. At sight of such blasphemy Bumble would stand aghast, and Mrs Grundy would scream with terror. But Bumble and Mrs Grundy are less important personages in France, and so the country of Rabelais and Voltaire produces what we are unable to tolerate in thought.[9]

It was particularly important that this issue of Foote's *Freethinker* arrived upon the desk of the Home Secretary, Sir William Harcourt, at the same

[7] Demonstrated in the 1830s by the 'Gathercole Case', *R v Gathercole* (1838) 2 Lew CC 237, where a supposed libel against a Catholic nunnery was dismissed because the law was deemed to protect only the Christian religion as established by law. See Hypatia Bradlaugh Bonner, *Penalties Upon Opinion* (London 1934), p. 64.

[8] In one cartoon, 'Jehovah's Day of Rest' Foote's anglicised version gave the Almighty a copy of the *Freethinker* to read. See D. S. Nash 'Laughing at the Almighty' in Wagner Lawlor (ed.), *The Victorian Comic Spirit* (Ashgate, Aldershot, 2000).

[9] G. W. Foote, *Prisoner for Blasphemy* (Progressive Publishing Co., London, 1886) p. 20.

time as a host of challenges to domestic British morality, discussed in chapters by Gavin Sutter and Tom Lewis. There were threats from Irish dynamitards and a more lingering and protracted fear of continental sources of depravity.[10] Harcourt was confronted with a contemporary report from the Metropolitan Police which suggested that the supply of pornography, particularly from France, had now run out of control and the panic induced by suggestions of a white slave trade in young girls focused on Belgium.

Behind all this was a highly popular and easily-motivated conception that Britain's attachment to Christianity was supremely valued, unique and actively despised by foreigners who were jealous of the special dispensation it had given Britain.[11] Some of this same language survived to be spoken with renewed vigour by Mary Whitehouse in the infamous Thorsen incident of 1977. Here the Home Secretary was persuaded to deny Danish film director Jens Jurgen Thorsen entry on the grounds that his proposal to film 'The Sex Life of Christ' in Britain would outrage public morals.[12] However it is also obvious that a clear element of national self-image lay in the adoption and promotion of the 'casual encounter' concept within the legal definition of blasphemy. This phenomenon was ostensibly the heightened concern that challenges to moral and religious authority were waiting to cause fear and trepidation when they pounced upon the unsuspecting. The Foote/*Freethinker* blasphemy case of 1883-4 contained a number of crucial allusions to this idea. Foote deliberately used his cartoons to shock, liking to portray the reactions of religious authority interacting with his works. A number of concerned letters to the Home Office describe the fear of women, minors and workmen encountering the material in the street. One correspondent was quick to suggest that an attack upon religion constituted an attack upon wider conceptions of English culture.

> Permit me with much respect to call your attention to the enclosed Blasphemous periodical which prompted by curiosity I purchased in Holborn on Friday last... That such an infamous periodical so calculated to bring religion into ridicule and disrepute, can be disseminated in our public thoroughfares without restraint – while in other respects the supervision of our national morality is ostensibly the subject of such rigorous supervision, appears somewhat strange.[13]

---

[10] See PRO/HO 45 9536/49902.

[11] For the longevity of such views and Anglicanism's role in sustaining a celebrated constitutional gradualism see David Hempton, *Religion and Political Culture in Britain and Ireland From the Glorious Revolution to the Decline of Empire* (Cambridge, 1996), ch. 1.

[12] Mary Whitehouse, *Quite Contrary* (Sidgwick and Jackson, London, 1988), p. 47.

[13] PRO/HO 45 9536/49902, Letter, Walter Grover to Harcourt, 13 August 1882, enclosing

This aspect of the *Freethinker's* shock tactics even made its way into popular novels, with the hero of Mrs. Humphrey Ward's *Robert Elsmere* sent reeling by his 'casual encounter' with the paper.[14]

Foote was eventually indicted for publishing a Christmas copy of the *Freethinker* containing a comic-strip life of Christ and articles blatantly attacking the message and ultimate value of Scripture.[15] Foote's case appeared to have been one which caught the imagination of liberal progressive England. While Foote and his co-defendants Ramsay and Kemp were incarcerated, Sir William Harcourt received a number of petitions and letters requesting clemency and remission of sentence. Most notable was one containing a significant list of names from the worlds of religion, law, medicine, academe and politics. While the appearance of radical MPs such as P. A. Taylor is hardly surprising there were also representatives of local government. Prominent clergy and nonconformists such as the President of the Congregational Union and the Baptist Union, A. M. Fairbairn and R. Glover, were also signatories.[16] Although this petition was content to suggest that the sentence and government reaction to the offence had been excessive, others went further. Foote himself had encouraged a discourse whereby the offence of blasphemy was portrayed as contrary to the 'spirit' of the age. A significant number of petitions using these precise words flowed into the Home Office from Manchester, London and parts of the north east.[17]

The Foote case was fundamentally important because its alteration of case-law (which regulated the law until the late 1970s) made the very idea of the 'casual encounter' still more important to the operation of the law. The last of the particular offences for which Foote stood trial was heard before Justice Coleridge, who chose to interpret the law differently to the judge in Foote's other cases (Justice Ford North). Coleridge was prepared to

---

copy of the *Freethinker* 13 August 1882, portraying Jesus casting out devils as 'The Devil Doctor'. See also PRO/HO 144 114/A25454 for complaints that the material in Footes *Freethinker* was finding its way into the hands of children.

[14] See Joss Lutz Marsh, '"Bibliolatry" and "Bible Smashing": G. W. Foote, George Meredith, and the heretic trope of the book', *Victorian Studies*, 34, 3, pp. 315-36.

[15] There is not room to consider the courtroom arguments intrinsic to this case: this chapter aims to investigate the effects of the individual judgments in such cases. More detailed accounts of the numerous cases against Foote can be found in Nash, *Blasphemy*. Foote's own account is available in Foote, *Prisoner*; also G. W. Foote, *Defence of Free Speech, being a three hours' address to the jury in the court of Queen's Bench before Lord Coleridge, on April 24, 1883* (London, 1889); G. W. Foote (ed.), *Comic Bible sketches reprinted from The Freethinker*, Part 1 (London, 1885).

[16] See PRO/HO 144 114/A25454, letters protesting against the treatment of Foote and the verdict against him and Ramsay. Item 258 Petition, Mr. James Sully to Harcourt, 9 May 1883.

[17] See PRO/HO 144 114/A25454 items 69, 75, 86, 106, 113, 125, 126 and 206.

abandon the implicit Church-State relationship created by Hale for the first time, and persuaded the law to accept that criticism of Anglican Christianity was permissible in some circumstances. Coleridge argued that 'if the decencies of controversy are observed, even the fundamentals of religion may be attacked without the writer being guilty of blasphemy'.[18] The verdict created the so-called 'Coleridge dictum' which departed significantly from the previous history of the offence by suggesting 'matter' that was published or spoken was not a determining factor in producing a successful prosecution but rather the 'manner' and the intention of the speaker or publisher was crucial. This was a curious change on one level since the offence of blasphemous libel sat in English criminal law alongside other species of libel, all of which required proof of the substance of an accusation rather than an investigation of the manner in which it was made. This emphasis on 'manner' made the 'casual encounter' increasingly central to the offence. The precise issues discussed were no longer important, but their published or spoken context and the reaction of any audience became crucial, since it was the immediacy of the first reaction to words or images that was now the crucial test of blasphemy.

Looking at the issue of blasphemy as constituting a simple dichotomy between a fearful establishment and a dangerous 'law' other would be to dramatically oversimplify matters. It would also be a mistake to assume the law and the establishment had an unimpeachable monopoly on Englishness and that blasphemers accepted their irredeemably stigmatised foreign identity. Blasphemers often saw themselves as protecting English liberties against dangerous innovation. G. W. Foote regularly argued that his own apparent vulgarity and want of taste was matched by the new style of evangelism of Booth and the Salvation Army, and that his own strident reaction was more than matched by that of the public at large.[19]

The issue of the 'casual encounter' survived into the twentieth century. Summing up in the *Gott* case of 1921, Justice Avery demonstrated the climate of fear that the law simultaneously preserved and encouraged.

> You must put it to yourself, supposing you received by post some abominable libel upon yourself...what is your first instinct? Is not the instinct of every man who is worthy the name of a man... to thrash the man or the woman who has written a libel on him? and that is

---

[18] (1883) 15 Cox CC 231. The jury were, however, discharged after some hours deliberation as they were unable to agree. See also Sir James Fitzjames Stephen, *A History of the Criminal Law of England* 3 vols (London, 1883), II, pp. 474-6.

[19] The Salvation Army had been a widespread cause for public concern in the period leading up to the Foote cases. See PRO/HO 45/9613/A9275. See also Richard Stone's chapter in this volume.

why the law says that it is calculated to provoke a breach of the peace.... You must ask yourself if a person of strong religious feelings had stopped to read this pamphlet, whether his instinct might not have been to go up to the man who was selling it and give him a thrashing, or... use such language... that a breach of the peace might be... occasioned, because that would be quite sufficient to satisfy this definition.[20]

It is also true that the rejuvenating and reinvented blasphemy law and its intended operation after 1884 also indulged some assumptions which were particularly 'English'. The Coleridge judgment inherited some of the classical arguments about British culture, reinforcing a clear distinction between an intellectual 'high' culture and a dangerous, ribald coarse street culture. Its intention was to clearly protect the former and to vanquish the latter. The failure to repeal the law also stemmed paradoxically from an underlying belief in the progressive evolution of the British constitution and religion's vital role in this evolution. Home Office opinion in the twentieth century considered that the development of modern society would leave blasphemy law as an anachronistic dead letter. Moreover the religion protected by law was Anglican Christianity which was also considered to be in a condition of progressive evolution and inevitable secularisation.

The Cultural Conception of Blasphemy

This phenomenon was alive well into the late twentieth century, and was given a new lease of life when Mary Whitehouse had a 'casual encounter' with a copy of the homosexual newspaper, *Gay News* which landed on her doorstep, sent by a concerned sympathiser. While by this stage the statute law of blasphemy had been repealed in 1967, Mrs. Whitehouse found that what remained was still a useful tool in some hands. The remaining Common Law conception of blasphemous libel constituted an awkward half-way house between a privatisation of the law seeking to protect the outraged Christian feelings of individuals while seeking state sanctions and archaic conceptions of a universal state church and religion to do so. The offending copy of *Gay News* contained the poem 'The Love that Dares to Speak its Name' by the respected poet James Kirkup. It portrayed Christ as a promiscuous homosexual and dwelt upon the homosexual fantasies of the centurion at his crucifixion. Kirkup claimed that this unconventional retelling was intended to extend the possibility of Christian salvation to the gay community. Mary Whitehouse and a number of other commentators saw it as an affront to their Christian beliefs to see Christ identified with

---

[20] *R v Gott* (1922) 16 Cr App R 87.

sexual activity, particularly with homosexual activity. Acting under a statute of 1866 which required the consent of a judge, she instituted a private prosecution against Denis Lemon, the editor of *Gay News*, and also against the publisher Gay News Ltd.[21]

The trial took place astride the weekend of 9 July 1977, the first airing of the whole issue for over two generations. In approaching the case Justice Alan King-Hamilton refused to allow consideration of expert evidence which might argue that the moral climate of the country had significantly altered since the last consideration of the crime in the 1920s. However his summing up contained a re-invention of the 'casual encounter' argument which once more specified the importance of the immediate context of offence in an astonishingly theatrical manner, reminiscent of the melodrama which surely underpinned its initiation in the previous century;

> When, therefore, ladies and gentlemen, you are considering this poem, you must try to recapture in your minds the impact it made upon you when you first read it... what would your reactions have been had you first read it or had it read aloud to you in your home, or a friend's home, or in a public house?... after over a week you are used to it. It is the first reaction you must try to recall. A medical student present at his first operation quite frequently... faints at the sight of blood, the shock; but after a time he gets used to it and it does not mean anything to him. So you must not judge it by what you think about it now; it is your first, immediate reaction, because that is the time when, if at all, your anger or anybody else's anger might well be aroused or their resentment provoked.[22]

The reaction of public opinion in relation to the *Gay News* case became polarised around the cultural cleave created by Coleridge — only the difference was that the earlier definitions of polite and impolite had been reversed. Polite culture was identified with an intellectualism which attempted to suggest discourses of tolerance, ecumenism and the need to embrace and include. The recent liberalisation of Christianity through works like *Honest to God* and the *Myth of God Incarnate* was seen as evidence that heterodox spirituality was to be encouraged and accepted.[23] Alongside this

---

[21] Levy's is a succinct account of the proceedings of the trial in accessible form although Nicholas Walter's should also be consulted. See N. Walter, *Blasphemy in Britain: The Practice and Punishment of Blasphemy, and the Trial of 'Gay News'* (London, 1977); N. Walter, *Blasphemy Ancient and Modern* (Rationalist Press Association, London). See also Geoffrey Robertson's memories of the case: G. Robertson, *The Justice Game* (Vintage, London, 1999).

[22] Original unpublished typescript of Justice Alan King-Hamilton's summing up in *R v Lemon*, in author's possession.

[23] *The Times*, 29 June 1977.

was a progressive argument that society itself was becoming more secular and could withstand questioning of values that were not as central as they once had been. This was opposed by an emotional suspicion of liberal Christianity which argued in favour of a more literalist reading of scripture and interpretation of religious culture and its function. This interpretation became more obviously capable of colonising public space through its prayers outside of court and appeal to the raw emotion of religious feeling. The triumph of this latter interpretation was sealed by King-Hamilton's hostile attitude to expert evidence and the expert testimony of witnesses. His argument that the jury could decide for themselves without intellectual argument simultaneously enshrined the twin ideas of the two cultures and the casual encounter.

The issue of blasphemy has not been resolved in contemporary Britain. The existence and operation of the law and, perhaps just as importantly, the cultural conception of blasphemy still involves a declaration and assertion that British culture is somehow different and superior. This still endures despite the integration of the European Convention on Human Rights into British law. The resolution of the *Gay News* case involved a crucial alteration of the law that undermined the Coleridge distinction between 'matter' and 'manner'. Henceforth the task of the prosecution in any blasphemy case has centred on proof of publication rather than any assessment of a publication's supposed effects or the intention of its producers. Perhaps the most important long-term effect has been to make purveyors of culture more responsible for their actions. But a clash is almost inevitable since the relocation of religion in England into the private sphere is itself more likely to make unorthodox explorations of spirituality and its alternatives (this making of worlds) more likely. It is worth considering how far this change in the law shelved further serious consideration of its intention and contemporary applicability. A Christian outlook which, as we have already seen, was moving away from literal belief as a method of modernising religion might well have had a significantly different part to play in the history of religious toleration if the *Gay News* case had been resolved differently. The Coleridge judgment and its issues about 'manner' would have focussed consideration upon public order issues and those relevant to breach of the peace in a post-*Gay News* world. In such an atmosphere, and with such concerns prevalent, it is easy to see how dialogues about religious feelings and personal belief might well have created arguments for the extension of the blasphemy law to cover other faiths. As it was, the return to a situation where the law looked more like it did in the days of Matthew Hale changed its focus. Thus the law has been expressly concerned with the *fact* of publication as proof of the offence.

In this climate the fact that such an offence has to be committed against Christianity has escaped legislative action and indeed the production of relevant case law. Thus attempts to move against Salman Rushdie's *Satanic Verses* quickly foundered.[24] In 1989 the Home Office declared that the state would no longer involve itself in state prosecutions for blasphemy.[25] This has not stopped agencies of the state taking action in areas around the issue of blasphemy and blasphemous libel. Despite the peculiarities of the Rushdie case, writers in Britain since 1945 have been generally tolerated but hysterical concerns about the impact of the moving image means that film-makers are often treated with suspicion. Such purveyors of (admittedly diverse) religiously inspired cinema such as Jens Thorsen, Monty Python and Martin Scorsese have all discovered this. Many of these concerns have been highlighted by the resolution of the 'Wingrove case' in 1996 – an instance in which Europe for the first time took issue with the living British legal concept of blasphemy. Nigel Wingrove's film 'Visions of Ecstasy' (based on the ecstatic visions of St Theresa of Avila) was refused a classification by the British Board of Film Classification (BBFC) and was, as a result, banned from sale or public display in Britain under the Video Recordings Act 1984. Wingrove appealed to the European Court of Human Rights arguing that the BBFC had effectively denied him freedom of expression, guaranteed in Article 10 of the European Convention as well as unlawfully exercising prior restraint. Wingrove's submission was initially accepted, but overturned in November 1996 following a government appeal.[26]

The Board had significantly departed from the law as it had previously been understood. 'Visions' was refused a certificate because it 'might' be blasphemous, a contention which undermined all previous thinking about the power, sanctity and sense of public opinion. Up to this point the Home Office and many clerical and lay commentators had been comfortable with the law's existence as a common law offence since placing the initiative with the public at large provided an instant form of regulation and public censorship. By allowing material into circulation the attitude of the public could be relied upon as an effective measure of what was permissible and what was not. While this had been the accepted official opinion for most of this century it is easy to forget that it was founded upon a model of

---

[24] See *R v Chief Metropolitan Magistrate ex parte Choudhury* [1991] 1 All ER 306.

[25] Alan Travis, *Bound and Gagged: A Secret History of Obscenity in Britain* (Profile Books, 2000).

[26] *Wingrove v UK* (1996) 24 EHRR 1; (19/1995/525/611), Judgment Strasbourg 25 November 1996. See also Helen Fenwick, *Civil Liberties and Human Rights* (Cavendish, London, 2002), ch. 6.

secularising Christianity. This enshrined the notion of how far toleration was seen to be progressing rather than how far religious doctrines deserved to be upheld. This was generally reflected in the law's contention (at least until the *Gay News* case) that the 'manner' of blasphemy was the most important element. Successive governments had historically thus relied upon the discretion and sobriety of public opinion to regulate sensibly the moral outlook and, in extreme cases, pretensions of religious sections of society.

The final decision reached by the European Court was that Britain could retain and continue to exercise such jurisdiction under the conditions of the 'Margin of Appreciation'. This proviso effectively limited the jurisdiction of the European Court of Human Rights in areas perceived to be culturally unique and valuable to an individual member state. In some respects the implication of such a decision argued obliquely that religion should again be considered to be 'part and parcel of the law of the land' a phrase used in the Hale Judgment. It also suggested that the control and regulation of religious opinion was an important part of Britain's cultural heritage which was in profound need of protection – a view which the Archbishop of York in a letter to *The Times* in 1996 went some way towards endorsing.[27] However all of this has put Britain out of step with Europe.

The Wingrove case prompted the human rights group 'Article 19' to investigate blasphemy laws in Britain and elsewhere in Europe. 'Article 19' could find no other examples of a healthy and thriving culture of blasphemy prosecution. Denmark had allowed public showings of Thorsen's 'Sex Life of Christ'; Norway was in the process of abolishing the relevant section of its penal code. German law contained a clear sense of breach of the peace alongside a strong conception of intention to insult belief. It was also clear that adults had a legal right to view or encounter material they were briefed about in advance. In Belgium, Spain, France and Italy the powers lay dormant and arguably were only waiting for overdue repeal. Moreover the powers adopted by the BBFC appeared to be without parallel in the countries surveyed. The report thus concluded that Britain's current practices were 'incompatible with the guarantee of freedom of expression provided by Article 10 of the European Convention of Human Rights'.[28]

This appeared to give legislative sanction to the law, through the Court's acceptance of the 'margin of appreciation', that Britain is somehow culturally distinct from the rest of Europe. Its impact has fed the enduring

---

[27] *The Times*, 29 March 1996.

[28] Article 19 and *Interights, Blasphemy and Film Censorship: Submission to the European Court of Human Rights in Respect of Nigel Wingrove v The United Kingdom*, London 1995.

belief in a cloistered historical self-definition of one country's own culture as emphatically different and beyond question. Moreover the effects of Europeanisation and globalisation upon the nation-state have prompted the redefinition of its national characteristics to draw precisely upon those laws like blasphemy that are capable of rejuvenating traditional state nationhood. Britain thus appears to have lived with a legacy of fear and arguably this persists in a form of Euroscepticism that turns particularly around the issue of religion and morality. Over the last century or so this has shared psychological space with a belief in the sanctity of the religio-imperial mission. This heady cocktail has, at various points in the history of the nation, come together when under threat to influence the nature and character of English and British nationalism.

The long-term history of blasphemy in Britain is an historical defence of an enduring and arguably institutionalised cultural cleave in society. The law still distinguishes between polite and unruly forms of doubt and expression in a manner that is surely anachronistic. British law's obsession with elements of recoil, shock and 'casual encounter' means that opposition to blasphemous works often appears highly theatrical. The Muscular British Christianity of the Victorian era is, in these incidents, always rejuvenated and made to do battle with effete, bizarre and dangerous foreign spirituality or subversive *émigré* doubt. In contemporary Britain, through the 'margin of appreciation', the existing law diverges from Europe since it places responsibility upon the providers of culture. Many, if not all, European countries place greater premium upon the responsibility and critical faculties of individuals in making their way through modern cultural encounters. Popular suspicion of Europe should be underrated at the peril of governments and politicians brave enough to meddle in this area since the uniqueness of Britain is viewed as an enduring, and intensely popular, cultural truism.

In the late 1990s the Newcastle-based Christian Institute voiced suspicion about the dangerous moral invasion that European law represented. This, in a supposedly secularised age, is enduring testimony to the power of religion to enter and mingle with dialogues about nationalism, identity and morality. The Institute argued that 'Unlike the system of common law employed in many member states (including the UK) which is based on the Judeo-Christian ethic, the law of the EU and of the Convention is based on the values of liberal secular humanism'. Expanding upon these concerns it feared 'our obligations under the Convention and the EU' about 'the morality of all member states is being brought down to a lower level'. Instead of 'all states being brought up to the best standard... the worst standard to be found in any state is starting to be imposed as the norm. Immorality tolerated in a minority of states is being sought as a "right" in

Behaving Badly

all states'. Thus it suggested the European courts were 'left with only notions of "rights" and "equality"' to judge issues, meaning '"total equality regardless of ethics" must be the logical outcome'. This was dangerous since 'Civilisation itself requires conformity to principles of good social order to survive. For this, absolutes of right and wrong are essential'.[29]

Conclusion

The English Channel has in the popular mind stopped Hitler and Napoleon but it also provides a comfortable cultural buffer from dangerous European conceptions of tolerance in equal measure. With the reverberations of the Salman Rushdie case an uncomfortable recent memory, the claim of ethnic minorities to a British citizenship that retains within it an historically-sanctioned religious inequity is problematic. The presence and demands of new ethnic and religious communities for equal rights that go with a supposedly sacred British citizenship have added new dimensions to the nature of the debate about English/British identity and the concepts of 'good' and 'bad' behaviour which underpin it. Far too much has been said of the process of nation-building and not enough about those who feared, or even actively wanted, the nation's rapid demolition before their own eyes. Blasphemy provides probably the most fundamental sense of conflict between the issues of freedom versus responsibility. What, for example is the real role of the artist in a culture that still demands levels of intellectual policing? How should artists' rights be balanced with the needs of the wider community? In a world ambivalent about globalisation how do we all cope with those who are unable to accept or effectively use their empowerment? Do they need (deserve?) protection? We might also ask how far wider and deeper standards of tolerance should protect those individuals and nation-states that are prepared to appropriate and misuse the status of victim? Britain has avoided answering these questions by ignoring them and sweeping them into an increasingly anachronistic and desolate isolationism. However the writ from Europe now runs over the cliffs of Dover and the clock is ticking.

---

[29] This was displayed at the organisation's website (http://www.christian.org.uk/menu.htm) in late 1998 and early 1999. The Christian Institute can be contacted at The Christian Institute, 26 Jesmond Road, Newcastle upon Tyne, NE2 4PQ (e-mail: info@christian.org.uk).

Chapter 8

A Dangerous Obsession?
Gambling and Social Stability

Mike Ahearne

Introduction

As Cornish succinctly observes, 'Gambling has always tended to occupy an equivocal position in national life, attracting both massive public participation and continuous criticism on moral, social and economic grounds'.[1] In comparing attitudes to gambling between the Victorian age and the current era, this chapter focuses on the following broad themes: firstly, discussion of the basis of the various objections to gambling, noting the shift in perception of gambling's problematic nature, from a rampant social malaise afflicting large tracts of society, to its present medicalised confinement within a relatively small sector of the community. Secondly, the legal status of gambling will be considered alongside attempts by government to initially regulate and latterly deregulate its various forms. Thirdly, the development of gambling as a burgeoning industry generating considerable employment and state revenue is traced. Finally the persistent connection between gambling and scandal is explored. Though these broad themes are highlighted, they also impinge upon and intertwine with one another, with fundamental underlying issues such as social class.

Before delving into these areas it is necessary to establish the territory to be covered here by the term 'gambling', and to offer some explanation for the evident paradox that sees gambling persist and flourish in the face of widespread condemnation, particularly since the activity almost invariably involves the loss of money, property, or indeed both, and has also implications for the respectable standing of the persistent or excessive gambler. This latter aspect is most germane to the Victorian era, when hostility to gambling was at its peak, but is not without resonance today.[2]

---

[1] D. B. Cornish, *Gambling: A Review of the Literature* (Home Office Research Study No 42, HMSO London, 1978), p. ix.

[2] For a fuller discussion on the persistence of gambling see D. M. Downes, B. P. Davies,

Many would argue, with some justification, that the dividing line is hardly discernible between speculation in the financial markets and business on the one side (discussed in Sarah Wilson's chapter) and more conventionally-understood forms of gambling on the other. Certain comparisons between the two are thus inevitable, but here the term gambling is confined to its more conventional application, referring to activities such as betting on sports and games, or playing the lottery or bingo etc. Within this definition it may also be useful to distinguish between 'hard' and 'soft' forms of gambling. The latter typically refers to such activities as buying lottery tickets or doing the football pools where an outlay is made but subsequent losses cannot be chased after the results are known. The former refers to activities such as betting on horses, casino games, playing fruit machines or buying scratch cards, which permit repeated opportunities to gamble and where, theoretically, losses are only limited to the amount of cash, property or credit to which the player has access.

In explaining the endurance of gambling in the face of both widespread criticism and financial loss, one can readily see that at an individual level, gambling, as well as being an interesting and occasionally rewarding pastime, can also provide opportunities to exercise such elements as skill, judgment, and levels of risk-taking and excitement which are not regularly attainable in 'ordinary' life. Additionally, gambling offers a constant source of hope, albeit often misplaced. A universal characteristic of the gambler is a willingness to believe in luck and the possibility that one can sometimes get something for nothing. This theme is central to Devereux's observation that gambling activity becomes more ubiquitous and more intense the further it is distanced, *in any direction,* from what he terms the 'Protestant work ethic'.[3] This point sits particularly well with a Victorian England where gambling was seen as largely the preserve of the upper and lower classes, leaving an articulate and often ascetic middle class as its fiercest critic. By contrast, with regard to the later twentieth century, the more gambling assumes the mantle of a legitimate leisure industry of significant proportions, the more it can be opened up to middle class participation. These themes will gain contextual clarity as the chapter unfolds.

M. E. David and P. Stone, *Gambling, Work and Leisure* (Routledge and Kegan Paul, London, 1976) pp. 11-28.

[3] Edward C. Devereux, Jr., 'Gambling and the social structure: a sociological study of lotteries and horse racing in contemporary America', unpublished PhD thesis, Harvard University, 1949.

The Basis of Objections to Gambling

To the extent that one can safely generalise, the over-arching backdrop to events in mid-nineteenth century Britain was that of a nation outwardly confident in its position, epitomised by the Rhodesean assertion that to be born British was to win first prize in the lottery of life (the terminology is interesting given the chapter's subject matter). However, beneath the confident exterior inevitably lurked doubts and insecurities which related to the source of any potential threat to the stability of this order. While a watchful eye could be kept on foreign affairs for any impingement on British interests, the most potent threat came from within, in the form of the less palatable consequences of industrialisation and rapid urbanisation. The plight and vulnerability of the urban poor, crammed together in the expanding centres of industry and commerce, were graphically chronicled by such eminent contemporaries as Mayhew.[4] Their comments emphasised that for the authorities of the day, the control of the lower classes was of paramount importance. Policy emerged from the often uneasy blend of the classic Victorian credos of *laissez-faire*, paternalism and suppression.

Garland has argued that one of the aims of Victorian social policy was to drive a wedge between what were regarded as the respectable working class or the deserving poor and those perceived as members of the dangerous classes.[5] Much of this can be seen as a direct response to anxieties about working class crime – a familiar theme within our own society. But a broader concern was to regulate the habits of the urban working classes, specifically their newly-acquired leisure pastimes. With regard to gambling, the two concerns meld since gambling, irrespective of its own legal status, was identified as a potent precursor to crime. It was believed it could precipitate members of the respectable working class into the chasm occupied by the dangerous and criminal classes; the various social misfits comprising the amalgam of all that was antithetical and offensive to the Victorian social, moral and economic order.

Before addressing the issue of gambling directly, it is worth adding that the growing power assumed by the respectable middle class could afford a greater toleration of upper class gambling. The aristocracy and gentry still retained considerable wealth and political power, and so also retained their functionality for the interests of the capitalist order.[6] There was an

---

[4] Henry Mayhew, *London Labour and the London Poor* (Penguin, Harmondsworth, 1985).

[5] D. Garland, *Punishment and Welfare* (Gower, Aldershot, 1985) pp. 38-9.

[6] W. D. Rubenstein, *Men of Property. The Very Wealthy in Britain since the Industrial Revolution* (Croom Helm, London, 1981).

accompanying belief very apparent in the fiction of the day that the feckless element within the upper classes could be safely left to squander their fortunes if they so chose, particularly if they did so with due aristocratic grace and discretion.[7] They might set an inconvenient bad example to the lower orders, but the parallels were not so dangerous as the lessons afforded by the crash to ruin of ancestral oaks as a result of gambling excess.

Pre-Victorian opposition to gambling was already extensive. Lotteries, which had had a long and often chequered history, were officially banned on grounds that they were riddled with corruption and no longer an efficient method of raising government revenue. However, there is no denying the evangelically strong moralistic undertones to the move. The language of the 1808 Select Committee Report which paved the way for the 1823 and 1826 Acts making lotteries illegal spoke of lotteries inducing idleness, poverty, dissipation, madness and crime.[8] Such high moral sentiments were vociferously endorsed by the Anglican Church and Nonconformity. Munting notes that 'the moves against lotteries were consistent with the emerging hostility to gambling of any kind which was becoming more and more evident in the early nineteenth century'.[9] However, while the evangelical dimension was clearly present, it was quite as much a practical reaction to the excesses of eighteenth century gambling. Entering the Victorian era, arguably the real *emergent* hostility came from the middle classes and was based more on economic and social grounds than moral evangelicalism.

It would also be more accurate to say that these hostilities were not so much ranged against gambling *per se* but rather the consequences of excessive gambling. Certainly one focus of significant interest to the Victorian establishment was the pressure placed on the legal system by gambling disputes not just in terms of their volume but also the, at times, absurd nature of these disputes. Downes *et al* allude to the wonderful example given in evidence to the Select Committee on Gaming 1844 whereby the full pomp and majesty of the English court was invoked merely to rule as to whether or not a particular individual had successfully managed to jump backwards over a table.[10] In seeking to suppress the most negative *forms* of gambling, those that were ancillary to race

---

[7] See for example, Evelyn Everett Green, *In Pursuit of a Phantom* (Religious Tract Society, London, 1900).

[8] Garland, *Punishment*, p. 31.

[9] R. Munting, *An Economic and Social History of Gambling in Britain and the USA* (Manchester University Press, Manchester, 1996).

[10] *Ibid*, p. 32.

meetings and on-course betting aroused particular opposition for their injurious effect on the sport itself. Pedestrian access to racetracks were thronged with betting booths offering a variety of gambling games to entice the gullible, for example.

However, the primary interest was directed at the lives of the urban poor not simply because of their perceived potential to undermine the smooth running of the social and economic order, but also from a measure of paternalistic concern for the very real misery and hardship that were frequently the result of working class gambling. Devereux's astute analysis of the relationship between the frequency and intensity of gambling activity and its location relative to the core values of the Protestant work ethic fits snugly into Victorian England, with gambling largely the preserve of the idle rich and the desperate poor. Both groups were far removed from 'Victorian' values and were testament to the vagaries of chance and the fact that merit was not always the arbiter of fortune. The masses of poor working people crammed together in big cities were always prone to succumbing to the escape routes offered by alcohol and gambling. Crucially for them, unlike their rural counterparts for whom leisure time remained contingent on the seasons, industrialised wage labour had created a reshaped leisure environment.

The reality of a rapidly expanding urban population heightened the perceived threat posed by gambling, since there can be no doubt that gambling was an extremely popular device, by which the urban poor could wring some hope from apparent pervasive hopelessness and enjoy their leisure time. Within this framework, the moral debate tended to cast the urban poor as the victims of gambling and moralistic bile was directed at those who promoted it, such as bookmakers, tipsters and gambling operators and at the profligacy of the idle rich and the example it set. It should be noted too that when, towards the final quarter of the nineteenth century, Britain began to feel the pinch of challenges to her trading eminence from Germany and the USA, objections to gambling by the poor began to be also couched in terms of its impact on efficiency and its consequent capacity to erode national economic fitness and competitive edge.

It was in the spirit of the age that in Victorian England, gambling was seen as a pressing social problem requiring some form of state intervention and regulation. But it was targeted intervention. While as a social problem it could afflict all areas of society – neither the middle class nor women and children were immune to the allure and pitfalls of gambling – it was at either end of the social structure where the effects were most acutely experienced. However, the view prevailed that the fortunes of the upper classes had been protected as far as was reasonably possible by eighteenth century legislation. In any case, the rich were, generally, sufficiently buffered from the worst consequences of gambling, minimising the need for too much intrusion on their gambling habits. This left those of the working class exposed to the full brunt of state efforts at suppression.

This in many respects is virtually the converse of the situation which pertains regarding current attitudes to gambling, and both the extent and nature of objections to it have a very different emphasis. In a climate ushered in by the permissive legislation of the 1960s, the ever-burgeoning gambling industry has enjoyed an increasingly symbiotic relationship with governments of all hues. In this climate of toleration and expansion, a new way of defining and dealing with the problematic aspects of gambling has become necessary. The dynamics of this shift can be illustrated by a revised application of Devereux's functionalist approach. If gambling is to be repackaged as an acceptable leisure pastime, and in the new lottery's case actively encouraged, then the omnipresent problems associated with it must be isolated anew in areas where they can be safely acknowledged, leaving the overall enterprise to flourish. In this scenario it is not gambling itself in the form of a social malaise that is the problem so much as a particular type of gambler; one who can be seen as different, separate. The gambler as 'exceptional' is one who can be diagnosed as suffering from some sort of disorder related to his/her psychological make-up.

In reviewing the literature on pathological gambling (so-called), Griffiths comments 'that 'normal' or 'social' gambling is of no moral danger to most individuals in society'.[11] He points out that pathological gambling was first recognised by the American Psychiatric Association as a mental disorder in 1980 and adds that 'adopting a medical model of pathological gambling in this way displaced the old image that the gambler was a sinner or a criminal'.[12] The notion of the diseased gambler gripped by some psychic dysfunction has, of course, a much longer history. One of the earliest and best-known incarnations was Dostoyevsky, but as Jeffrey Bernard perceptively observed on behalf of the gambling fraternity: 'No-one ever seems to have tumbled that what was so bloody despicable about Dostoyevsky is that he was a really lousy punter. Not unusually bad, really awful. You wouldn't have passed the time of day with him in a betting shop'.[13] While the sciences (a questionable claim some might say) of psychology and psychiatry were still embryonic in the Victorian age, in the

---

[11] M. Griffiths, 'Pathological gambling: a review of the literature', *Journal of Psychiatric and Mental Health Nursing*, 3, 6, 1996, p. 347.

[12] *Ibid*, p. 348.

[13] J. Bernard, *Talking Horses* (Fourth Estate, London, 1987), p. 105.

post-war period, input into 'problem gambling' has been all but colonised by these disciplines, triggered largely by the work of Bergler.[14]

Much of this input emanates from America, the headquarters of the psycho-therapy industry, but its influence has been widely felt in this country. While it is beyond the scope of this chapter to comment in any detail on the more questionable aspects of much of this research – the frequently inadequate size of samples, the curious methodologies sometimes employed and the conflicting findings often generated – there can be little doubt that the cumulative effect has been to entrench the perception of problem gambling within a medical model. Griffiths has argued for a more eclectic approach which recognises the importance of social and environmental factors and thus predicts problem gambling increasing as gambling activity in general expands. However, the construction of the pathological gambler is convenient for the interests of both the betting industry and the government, since it enables the problems associated with gambling to be confined within a small minority that could not reasonably be allowed to dictate overall policy. How the attitudes to gambling outlined in this section were articulated, translated into policy and the reactions of various sections of society is the subject of the following section.

The Legal Status and Regulation of Gambling

The general picture that emerges of the gambling practices in early Victorian England which aroused such moral indignation was one of excessive gambling conducted by both rich and poor despite the fact that much of it was actually illegal. Margetson points to 'the game of hazard which, although illegal, was played by everyone, even bishops and Ministers of the crown'.[15] As well as the gambling booths and houses associated with race meetings, much of this went on in the numerous gambling houses that flourished in London despite their own illegal status. The rich could indulge themselves in the opulence of clubs such as Crockfords where, Margetson suggests, 'it was nothing for a gentleman to lose £30,000 or £40,000 in a single evening', while the poor would be fleeced in the 'copper hells' as the lower-class gaming houses were known.[16] It is tempting then to think that the gambling activities of the

---

[14] E. Bergler, *The Psychology of Gambling* (Hillard Wang, New York, 1957).

[15] S. Margetson, *Leisure and Pleasure in the Nineteenth Century* (Cassell and Co., London, 1969), p. 67.

[16] *Ibid*, p. 14.

upper and lower classes were conducted in entirely separate spheres, but all commentators would concur with Best's observation: 'Rich and poor, aristocracy and underworld, were never closer together than at the prizefight, the cockpit, the rat-catching, the race-track, and the demi-monde saloon and casino'.[17] Indeed it was often the case that the rich would sponsor such typically working class pursuits as prize fighting and dog fighting simply to extend their own repertoire of gambling opportunities.[18]

It was against this backdrop that the Select Committee on Gaming was convened in 1844. Its principal concerns were; the use of the courts' time in settling gambling disputes; the impediments to the police built into existing legislation in the enforcement of laws against gaming houses; and the example set to the poor by the profligate gambling habits of the upper class. Ultimately the latter preoccupation, though receiving much consideration, was not translated into subsequent legislation – presumably the evidence from the Chairman of the Middlesex Quarter Sessions held sway: 'I do not think that one apprentice more or less would go to the copper hells because the first gentleman in the land did or did not gamble'.[19] The Committee did not seek to suppress betting itself, declaring that such a move would be 'repugnant to the general feelings of the people... an arbitrary interference with the freedom of private life'.[20] Nor were its aims particularly class distinctive. Much evidence was presented by the police illustrating the difficulties they faced in enforcing the law against gaming houses, but in seeking to redress this situation the Committee expressed the hope that, when armed with extended powers, the police would raid both upper and lower class versions of these establishments. However, the testimony of Admiral Rous, as staunch a supporter of horse-racing as he was opponent of gaming, presaged what would become an important theme as the century progressed: 'betting (on horses) is not offensive: quite the reverse. England would not be fit for a *gentleman* to live in if it were prohibited'.[21] Downes *et al* also suggest that the work of the Committee effectively made a demarcation between financial transactions in the business community and straightforward gambling.[22]

[17] G. Best, *Mid-Victorian Britain 1851-1870* (Fontana Collins, Glasgow, 1979), p. 221.

[18] For an excellent account of Victorian gambling pursuits see K. Chesney, *The Victorian Underworld* (Readers Union, Newton Abbott, 1970), pp. 267-306.

[19] 'Minutes of Evidence', *Report*, 1844 Select Committee on Gaming, para. 616.

[20] *Ibid*, p. v.

[21] *Ibid*, para. 3098, parenthesis and italics added.

[22] *Ibid*, p. 33.

The upshot of the Committee's deliberations was the Gaming Act 1845 which greatly facilitated the ability of the police to act against the gaming houses and other forms of illicit gambling, and created the expectation that they should so do. That the legislation achieved a significant level of success at least in that regard is illustrated by Ludovici:

> The journalist, George Augustus Henry Sala (1828-1895) writing about his boyhood days, recalled how the West End of London swarmed with gambling-dens, how gambling booths were freely dotted about every racecourse and how the racecourses were infested by thimble-riggers. By the 1860s Sala could rejoice that these no longer existed.[23]

The Act also provided that gambling debts were to be no longer recoverable in law thus severing the association of gambling with the legal system (a situation that pertains to this day). However, this was to have an altogether less satisfactory consequence that may well have had a bearing on the demise of the copper hells.

With gaming houses subjected to more stringent policing and credit betting no longer protected by the legal process, cash betting became the most expedient form of wagering for punter and entrepreneur alike. The result was a veritable explosion of betting houses. With them, a far clearer distinction could be drawn between upper and lower class gambling. Betting and particularly horse-betting in upper class circles had for some time been conducted either on a private basis between individuals, or increasingly at the racetrack or Tattersalls, where some bookmakers such as the legendary 'Leviathan' Davis had established a reputation for straight dealing unlike many of the 'bad hats' who passed themselves off as genuine layers.[24] As Chesney notes, in such arenas 'a man's reputation for settling-up was precious... defaulters' names were punctually posted, and the news travelled fast'.[25]

However, at the other end of the class spectrum things were altogether different. The betting houses or listers as they were termed, which often operated ostensibly as cigar shops, displayed lists of the day's runners on the walls, and money along with betting instructions would be passed through pigeon holes. Whether or not they would still be there the next day to pay out any winnings was likely to be even more uncertain than the outcome of the actual races. As 'The Druid' (a turf writer called Henry

---

[23] L. J. Ludovici, *The Itch for Play: Gamblers and Gambling in High Life and Low Life* (Jarrolds, London, 1962), p. 155.

[24] The famous sales ring where, according to the Tattersalls Committee's rules, all betting debts should be settled each Monday. 'Layers' were bookmakers.

[25] Ludovici, *Play*, p. 283.

Hall Dixon) observed: 'From 1850 to the end of 1853, the listers were in their glory; and at any one period, about four hundred betting houses were open in London alone, of which, perhaps, ten were solvent'.[26] *Punch* dubbed the listers 'ripe-for-jails' and the final verse of their poem *'The Betting-Office Frequenter's Progress'* published in 1852 expressed the sentiment admirably:

> And once again I see this youth,
> No betting-book is there
> The prison scissors close have cropped
> His once luxurious hair
> They tell that 'cleaned' completely 'out'
> He closed his short career
> By bolting with his master's till,
> When 'settling' time drew near.
> I see him shipped – the Government
> His passage out will pay:
> And at some penal settlement,
> He'll spend his Settling Day.[27]

Inevitably the authorities felt obliged to intervene and the Betting Houses Act 1853 which banned the listers was passed without debate. In his speech to the House, the Attorney General echoed the view of *Punch*, albeit in rather more strident and formal terms: 'There was not a prison or a house of correction in London which did not every day furnish abundant and conclusive testimony of the vast number of youths who were led into crime by the temptation of these establishments'.[28] There were suggestions that licensing the houses would be the most expedient course of action. However the Attorney General felt that this would not only discredit the government but also would compound the problem rather than reduce it. The Act thus cemented a situation that would endure for over a century, whereby working class gambling was criminalised while the upper class could indulge their passion quite legally. And the wealthy, in addition to their penchant for horse racing, from 1845 onwards began to switch their speculative interests to the Stock Exchange with the advent of so-called railway mania, as discussed by Sarah Wilson.

There can be little doubt that although the Act was suppressive it was also paternalistic in its rationale, but the extent to which this was appreciated by its 'beneficiaries' must be in doubt. Arguably the views of common people were succinctly stated by George Moore's eponymous

---

[26] Cited, J. Ashton, *The History of Gambling in England* (Duckworth, London, 1898), p. 210.

[27] *From the Early Years of Punch: Racing* (Constable and Robinson, 2000), p. 56.

[28] *Hansard*, 1853, 871, col. 129.

protagonist in his novel *Esther Waters* in which the moral position on gambling is an important theme. Esther provides a moral challenge to the status quo when she asks:

> What's the difference between betting on the course and betting in the bar?... Then the betting that's done at Tattersalls and the Albert Club, what is the difference? The Stock Exchange, too, where thousands and thousands is betted everyday. It is the old story – one law for the rich and another for the poor.[29]

While the Act may have been effective in terminating the existence of betting houses it was virtually useless in curbing betting itself. As Ashton observed: 'Children can lay their pennies and errand boys their sixpences, and throughout the length and breadth of the country, the curse of betting permeates every rank, and, I am sorry to say, spares neither sex'.[30] As a consequence of the Act working class gambling took to the streets, with betting conducted via the street bookies and their runners and gambling games like pitch-and-toss becoming a regular part of street life. The Metropolitan Streets Act 1867 and the Street Betting Act 1906 aimed to curb such activities, but with no great success as the police were both unwilling and unable to enforce the laws to any significant degree. It is noticeable too that when prosecutions were reported in the press, the accounts tended to be factual, accepting gambling's illegality as a given, even in newspapers like the *Daily Telegraph*, then a left-leaning radical organ for the working classes.[31] An overtly moralistic stance in such papers was only taken when the gambling activity broke the Sabbath, reflected also in the heavier penalties for such cases.[32] It was not until the 1960s that both the unfairness and impracticality of Victorian legislation was officially acknowledged in law with the restoration of the legal status of off-course betting.

Since the 1960s the most significant piece of legislation relating to gambling has been the National Lotteries Act 1993 which resurrected the lottery and other related scratch-card games as an aspect of national life. While rumblings of moral indignation were stirred up amongst some Church leaders and a group of Labour MPs who voiced concerns in the press about the government profiting from gambling, the most vocal

---

[29] Cited S. Magee (ed.), *Runners and Riders. An Anthology of Writing on Racing* (Methuen, London, 1993), p. 291.

[30] *Ibid*, p. 215.

[31] *Daily Telegraph*, 1 March; 14 September; 30 September 1870; 13 April; 16 April; 15 July; 1 September; 19 October 1875; and *Illustrated Police News*, 1 May 1869.

[32] *News of the World*, 18 February 1872; *Illustrated Police News*, 24 April 1869, focusing on 'the Sunday gambling nuisance'

objections came from pools promoters, bookmakers and some charities who feared a possible reduction in their own revenues.[33] The introduction of the lottery represented a notable shift in attitude to gambling on the government's part, from penalising it via taxation to actively promoting it. For many, despite its undoubted general popularity, it was merely a cynical ploy to raise revenue without increasing direct taxation – an interesting development, given government's previous rejection of gambling as an effective source of revenue. To assuage the concerns of other interested parties, the government made some tax concessions to pools companies and permitted the extension of betting shop opening hours to cater for evening racing during the summer months. This, as Munting notes, meant that 'for the first time since the early nineteenth century not only was central government itself sponsoring and encouraging popular gambling, it was also allowing a general broadening of the market for mass gambling'.[34] Interestingly, since the advent of the National Lottery, calls to Gamblers Anonymous have increased by some 17 per cent and research conducted for the Society for the Study of Gambling found a significant increase in problem gambling after the launch of the lottery.[35] This study also indicated that those on an income of less than £12,000 and poorly educated were especially vulnerable to problems associated with the lottery and scratch cards.

The Rise and Rise of the Gambling Industry

'It is usually conceded that social policy considerations should where necessary take precedence over other ones but, so far as policy in relation to gambling is concerned this has not always been the case. Instead, policies have tended to reflect the influence of fiscal, economic and commercial pressures'.[36] This assertion is arguably something of an understatement given the regularity with which successive governments' have pandered to the interests of the betting industry since the 1960s. It is explained in part by Munting's observation: 'Although governments in various forms had attempted to limit popular gambling they had few scruples about exploiting it'.[37] While the gambling business has

---

[33] *The Guardian*, 25 January 1993.

[34] Magee, *Runners and Riders*, pp. 87-8.

[35] Robin-Marie Shepherd and Hamid Ghodse, 'Gambling Behaviour Before and After the Launch of the National Lottery and Scratch Cards in the UK: a pilot study', Society for the Study of Gambling, *Newsletter*, 33, 1995.

[36] Cornish, *Gambling*, p. 245.

[37] *Ibid*, p. 13.

progressively assumed corporate status since the 1960s, the roots of this process can be traced back a century or more. As Downes *et al* note, 'from the 1850s on, betting and horse-racing became increasingly interdependent and increasingly big business'.[38] Given the legislation of 1853 this apparent paradox was fuelled by a number of factors such as improvements in communications like the telephone and telegraph services, the increasing coverage given to racing by the press, the organisation of a racing calendar and the building of grandstands to cater for the growing numbers of people who could access courses as the railway network expanded.

From its relatively humble origins in the likes of 'Leviathan' Davis and the army of backstreet bookies, bookmaking has become a corporate affair with the current dominant players, Ladbrokes, Hills, and Corals owned respectively by the Hilton Group, Nomura Bank and Bass Charrington. Collectively the gambling industry exercises considerable clout – hardly surprising given its estimated annual turnover of some £25 billion, yielding the government over £1.5 billion in revenue, not to mention the many thousands of jobs it provides.[39] The industry looks set for considerable further expansion with the arrival of internet betting allied to the solid international reputation of Britain's bookmaking firms. There is every reason to suppose that the UK will become the centre of a massive global gambling market offering virtual casinos and a huge array of betting opportunities. Gordon Brown's decision to abolish the nine per cent betting tax imposed on punters in favour of an overall tax on bookmakers' profits was clearly made with these developments in mind.

The spectacular growth in the betting business has occurred in the wider context of the general shift in economic activity from manufacturing to service and leisure, as well as development of an increasingly secular society and a shift away from direct taxation of the individual. This has seen the erosion of the long-standing class divisions once inherent in gambling. Many aspects of the industry, from its promotion and participation to the ownership of racehorses, is now reliant on middle class involvement – a reflection of a shift in the perceptions of the general financial sector to viewing risk-taking as increasingly ethical. Little wonder that in such a climate moral objections to gambling now form a very small voice crying in a very large wilderness.

---

[38] *Ibid*, pp. 38-9.
[39] www.homeoffice.gov.uk/cepd/gambleg.htm (accessed 10 August 2001).

Gambling and Scandal

This chapter would not be complete without allusion to the enduring relationship between gambling and scandal – the fundamentals of 'bad' behaviour. It is something of an irony that even while the Select Committee on Gaming was sitting in 1844 the 'sport of kings' was rocked by the revelation that the Derby winner of that year, Running Rein, was a four-year-old masquerading as a three-year-old.[40] In his concluding remarks at the ensuing court case, the trial judge commented that 'a most atrocious fraud has been proved... and I have seen gentlemen associating themselves with persons much below them in station... if gentlemen will condescend to race with blackguards, they must expect to be cheated'.[41] The listers were also a constant source of scandal, never more so than in 1851 when one proprietor named Dwyer, who hitherto had established an unusually sound reputation within this most questionable fraternity, disappeared without trace along with some £25,000 he had taken in bets on the victorious favourite for the Chester Cup. Dwyer's modern-day counterpart appeared, albeit briefly, in the form of a bogus bookmaker at the 1997 Derby. This individual, having taken some £10,000 by laying over the odds on the two favourites – the rather appropriately named Entrepreneur and Benny The Dip – slipped away with the proceeds while the race was in progress, never to be seen again. One of the most notorious scandals of the nineteenth century was the Tranby Croft baccarat case of 1890 in which Lieutenant Colonel Sir William Gordon Cumming was accused of cheating at baccarat whilst staying as a guest at Tranby Croft, the home of the shipowner Arthur Wilson. Cumming was ruined after unsuccessfully suing his accusers for slander, but not before society was shaken by the discovery that the Prince of Wales was one of those present and duly called as a witness.

The involvement of women in any form of deviance is still likely to be viewed as problematic. While it was the case that poor working class women who succumbed to the temptations of gambling were seen through paternalistic eyes, it should not be overlooked that many a Victorian lady of good society could be undone at the bridge-table. Itzkowitz relates the salutory insight of J. M. Hogge of the National Anti-Gambling League on the matter, 'young girls have been induced to play... it is not without knowledge that even virtue itself has been sacrificed to satisfy the suggestion of male friends who have gallantly paid such debts on their behalf'.[42] In recent years

[40] The Derby is confined to three-year-olds racing at level weights. A four-year-old would be expected to concede some twelve pounds in weight to a younger horse.

[41] Cited, Chesney, *Victorian Underworld*, p. 280.

[42] David C. Itzkowitz, 'The (Other) Great Evil: Gambling, Scandal and the National Anti-

snooker and football have been tarnished by betting related scandals, while the racing industry, having been hit by the scandal of horse doping and the fiasco of the botched investigation and failed prosecution that followed, is about to become embroiled in a fresh furore.[43] This concerns allegations by a trainer that some of the country's most prolific and successful stables have been using erythropoietin (better known as EPO, the subject of much controversy in the athletics world) to improve the performance of their horses.[44]

However, in modern times such affairs have rather paled into insignificance when compared to the exposure of massive bribery and corruption in the world of international cricket (is nothing sacred!), all of which has been linked to the activities of major betting and bookmaking rings in India and the Far East. The whole sordid affair has cohered around the involvement of South Africa's former captain Hansie Cronje, but the scandal's tentacles have reached all corners of the cricketing world. While the British, in time-honoured fashion, have sought to distance themselves from any direct involvement in such unseemly goings-on by identifying it as a 'foreign problem', many associated with the game are less than convinced that English players have not had their noses in this particular trough. With scandals such as these – and many more might have been included – it is a certainty that not only will gambling continue to be a regular feature of national life, but also, however respectable its veneer may seem, it will never lose its capacity to shock and induce outrage. Even if now legal, it remains on the edges of the cultural definitions of 'bad' behaviour, requiring (as in the case of the Lottery) a justification (of the profits going to 'good' causes) to gloss over the unacceptable dimensions of the pastime. The apparent discontinuities of official attitudes towards gambling thus disguise important continuities.

Gambling League', in Kristine Ottesen Garrigan (ed.), *Victorian Scandals: Representations of Gender and Class* (Ohio University Press, Athens, 1992), p. 237. The National Anti-Gambling League was formed in 1890. According to Itzkowitz, for all its endeavours the League was an entirely marginal organisation attracting little support.

[43] See *The Guardian*, 11 December 2000, for a full account.

[44] *Racing Post*, 11 December 2001.

Chapter 9

Legislating Morality: Victorian and Modern Legal Responses to Pornography

Tom Lewis

Introduction

At first sight the Victorian legal response to the publication of obscene and indecent materials would appear to have been strong and unequivocal. The period saw the passage of the first 'Lord Campbell's Act' of 1857. The term 'obscene' was accorded a legal definition for the first time in *R v Hicklin*.[1] In the same case it was decided that the motive of the publisher of obscene material, no matter how laudable, was not a relevant consideration in determining a charge of obscene libel.

There were also a plethora of high profile prosecutions and a steady stream of less high profile ones. It was partly the perceived repressiveness of this legal regime which provoked D. H. Lawrence to launch, early in the twentieth century, his blistering attack on 'the grey ones, left over from the last century, the century of mealy mouthed liars... of purity and the dirty little secret'.[2] Our own more permissive age is often contrasted (favourably or unfavourably) with what is perceived in the popular imagination to be this repressed, repressive and yet hypocritical regimen.[3] Despite the hyperbole of the nineteenth century rhetoric it will be argued that the *legal* response to obscenity was in fact deeply equivocal and that

---

[1] (1868) 3 QB 360. The 'deprave and corrupt' test.

[2] D. H. Lawrence, *Pornography and Obscenity* in *Selected Literary Criticism*, A. Beal (ed.) (Heinemann, London, 1967) p. 47.

[3] For example, I. Tang, *Pornography, the Secret History of Civilisation* (Channel 4 Books, London, 1999), see S. Marcus, *The Other Victorians. A Study of Sexuality and Pornography in Mid-Nineteenth Century England* (Meridian, New York 1974) for the 'repressive hypothesis'. Contrast M. Foucault, *The History of Sexuality* (Vintage, New York, 1980), vol. 1, and his 'proliferation of discourses' about sexuality.

this ambivalence was largely due to anxieties and tensions which centred around the public/private dichotomy. It will be intimated, in passing, that many of the same tensions and anxieties which helped sculpt the Victorian legal response to pornography have affected, and still affect, our own.

Technology and 'Urban Mass Culture'

The second half of the nineteenth century saw rapid growth in 'urban mass culture', with the issue of obscenity representing one of the most problematic aspects.[4] Improvements in printing technology, the abolition of stamp tax in 1855 and the tax on paper in 1861, made for cheaper and more plentiful publications. Increasing literacy meant that there was a wider reading public, though the invention and development of photography meant that this was not a prerequisite to the consumption of much material. The penny post and the railways meant that traders could send circulars and set up mail-order operations which facilitated plentiful and speedy distribution across the whole country.[5]

The President for the Society for the Suppression of Vice (the 'Vice Society') observed in 1871:

> Our difficulties have been greatly increased by the application of photography, multiplying at an insignificant cost filthy representations from living models, and the improvement in the postal service has further introduced facilities for secret trading which were previously unknown.[6]

The police court reports of Orders made for the destruction of the stock in trade of Holywell street pornographers under Lord Campbell's Act recount in exact detail the industrial scale quantities seized.[7] In 1874 130,248 obscene photographs and 5,000 obscene slides were seized at the premises of Henry Hayler.[8] When William Dugdale's premises were raided in 1868, the constables *and* staff of Bow Street police station spent the *whole day* unfolding and burning the condemned matter and succeeded in destroying only half. *The Times* explained, presumably to ward off suggestions that the unfolding was motivated by prurience, that 'to burn a quantity of paper

---

[4] L. Nead, *Victorian Babylon. People, Streets and Images in Nineteenth Century London* (Yale, New Haven, 2000), part 3.

[5] For example, *R v Judge*, *The Times*, 27 March 1865.

[6] *The Times*, 2 November 1871.

[7] Holywell Street, off the Strand, was the centre of the trade.

[8] *The Times*, 20 April 1874.

folded into quires would be a most difficult and uncertain process and it was therefore necessary to separate them to ensure perfect combustion'.[9]

The development of new technologies in the twentieth century has seen the continuation and repetition of these patterns of anxiety. There is a sense that the law is too slow and too cumbersome to cope with the bewildering pace of change. For example the increase in the popularity of domestic video recorders in the early 1980s (184,542 units were imported in 1979 as compared to 2.4 million in 1983) contributed greatly to the 'video nasty' media panic which resulted in the passage of the Video Recordings Act 1984.[10] The debates clearly indicate how the law was perceived to be 'painfully inadequate in dealing with developments in porno-electronics'.[11] The growth of the internet in the late twentieth century provides an even more vivid example of uncontrollable rapid technological change with which, it is perceived, the law is unable to cope.[12]

Legal Rhetoric

The language used in the Victorian legal discourse on obscenity in all its manifestations was extreme. The recurring metaphors were those of poison, pollution and infestation. An extract from a typical criminal indictment for obscene libel states that the defendant intended to:

> vitiate and corrupt the morals of the people... to incite and encourage them to indecent practices... to debauch, poison and infect the minds of the youth and to bring them into a state of wickedness lewdness and debauchery.[13]

Lord Campbell likened the traffic to 'poison more deadly than prussic acid, strychnine or arsenic'.[14]

Surprisingly, given the hyperbole, apart from general references to moral degradation and occasional vague statements that the 'sure preliminary to the downfall of the nation was the general indulgence of lust and sensuality on the part of the people', it was never made clear, in the legal discourse at least, what the evil was that the law was attempting

---

[9] *The Times*, 7 August 1868.

[10] *Hansard*, Commons, 1983, 48, col 536; see also, for example, *ibid*, col. 544 for comments of John Powell MP

[11] *Ibid*.

[12] See the US case of *Reno v ACLU* 117 S.Ct. 2329, 138 L.Ed.2d 874.

[13] *R v Carlile* (1845) 1 Cox C.C. 229.

[14] *Hansard*, 1857, clxv, col. 103.

to combat.[15] Presumably among the range of concerns were the dangers of masturbation, the promotion of promiscuity and the loss of shame but this was rarely if ever made explicit.[16] The very aim or object of the criminal law was elusive in the extreme.

The language of the modern debate is perhaps less colourful than the Victorian, although references to 'moral sewage' are not uncommon.[17] The aims of the modern law however remain equally opaque. Much of the debate is now couched in terms of 'harm' rather than moral degradation. The plethora of legal instruments and the profound logical inconsistencies within and between them are well-documented and indicative of a lack of any certainty or uniformity in aim.[18] An example can be drawn from the world of video classification. In 1999 seven explicit videos with titles such as *Horny Catbabe, TV Sex* and *Office Tart*, were refused an 'R18' classification by the British Board of Film Classification (BBFC) pursuant to its powers and duties under sections 4 and 4A of the Video Recordings Act 1984.[19] The distributors appealed successfully to the BBFC's Video Appeals Committee (VAC). The BBFC applied for judicial review of the VAC's decision. Justice Hooper held that the VAC had applied the correct statutory criteria and was entitled to conclude, on the present evidence, that the risk of the videos being viewed by, and causing harm to, young persons was insignificant. Thus an 'R18' classification should be granted.[20] The decision caused uproar. The National Viewers and Listeners Association claimed that it would 'open the floodgates to hardcore pornography'.[21] The Home Secretary condemned the decision and a Consultation Paper was published.[22]

Central to the argument of the critics of the decision was the belief that exposure to pornography causes harm to children. The BBFC therefore commissioned research into this question from 38 psychiatrists,

---

[15] *R v Shove* (1872), *The Times*, 10 February 1872.

[16] It was widely believed that masturbation would lead to a terrifying array of ailments from acne to insanity and death. See William Acton, *Functions and disorders of the Reproductive Organs* (J. and A. Churchill, London 1857).

[17] For example, *Hansard*, Commons, 1983, 48, col. 535, speech, Gareth Wardell.

[18] See G. Robertson, *Obscenity* (Weidenfeld and Nicolson, London, 1979); Williams Committee Report on Obscenity and Film Censorship 1979, (HMSO 7772).

[19] The 'R18' category is special and legally restricted classification primarily for explicit videos of consenting sex between adults. Such videos may be supplied to adults only in licensed sex shops.

[20] *R v Video Appeals Committee of the British Board of Film Classification, ex p British Board of Film Classification* [2000] C.O.D 239.

[21] *The Times*, 17 May 2000.

[22] *Home Office, Consultation Paper on the Regulation of R18 Videos*, July 2000.

psychologists and social workers active in the field of diagnosing and helping disturbed children. While

> the majority did feel that watching pornography would be harmful to any child and that they should be protected from it... they were able to quote very little in the way of evidence to support this belief, either from their own caseloads or those of their colleagues... determining the harm pornography does is not easy because it is necessary to disentangle it from other features of a child's situation, especially as the majority of children being exposed to pornography are also being harmed in other ways.[23]

It would seem that while there is a strong *sense* that exposure to pornography is harmful, especially to the young, the exact nature of this harm is no more tangible now than in the nineteenth century.

They 'Protest too Much'

With regard to the substantive law perhaps the most striking fact, given the extreme nature of Victorian rhetoric, was that mere possession of obscene matter was not a crime. Indeed in *R v Dugdale* it was decided that even possession with *intent* to publish was not an offence.[24] For an offence to be committed some positive act, like procuring, was required. The freedom to consume obscenity in private was not restricted. *The Times* summed up the position in 1857: 'If a man, more energetically nasty than his fellows should have succeeded in getting together a library or gallery of dirty things, he will [and, the implication is, should] be left in full fruition of it'.[25]

The main substantive offence in relation to obscenity throughout the period was the common law offence of obscene libel. The Obscene Publications Act 1857 did not change the substantive law. Rather it gave magistrates power, if a complaint upon oath was made, to grant a warrant to the police to search for and seize materials reasonably believed to be obscene and held for the purposes of publication for gain and the publication of which would be a 'misdemeanour and proper to be prosecuted as such'. Magistrates were further empowered to make orders

---

[23] BBFC Press Release 2000.

[24] (1853) 1 EL & BL 435. In some respects the modern position is more restrictive. Under s.2(1) Obscene Publications Act 1959 as amended by the 1964 Act it is an offence if a person 'has an obscene article for publication for gain'; and under s.160(1) Criminal Justice Act 1988 it is an 'offence for a person to have any indecent photograph or pseudo-photograph of a child in his possession'.

[25] *The Times*, 23 July 1857.

for destruction of any such obscene materials seized although publishers were entitled to attend in order to oppose such applications and had a right of appeal.

It is significant that such an important weapon in the state's armoury to protect *public* morality was the product of a private member's bill. Lord Campbell first raised the issue of obscene publications during the debate on the Sale of Poisons Bill and requested that the government take steps to stop the sale of publications of so 'pestilential a character'. Lord Cranworth, the Lord Chancellor, dismissed the need for legislation, for the law as it stood was 'quite sufficient' to put down such publications. It was for the 'Attorney General to enforce the law as he thought fit'.[26] It is clear that this was not an area in which the government wished to become ensnared. Consequently Lord Campbell, supported by the Vice Society, introduced the Bill himself.

The lack of government initiative in this area remains a persistent feature. The Indecent Displays (Control) Act 1982 and the Video Recordings Act 1984 both resulted from private members' bills (although both ultimately received government support). In respect of the latter, numerous comments by MPs bemoaned government inaction and delay. For example Gareth Wardell (who had previously, unsuccessfully, attempted to introduce his own private member's bill on the subject) commented:

> The Government have lacked – I use these words carefully – intestinal fortitude in their approach to this rapidly growing social problem, and the House is deeply conscious of the heavy responsibility laid at the Government's door for the long delay.[27]

The former Home Secretary Jack Straw is on record as having said of the internet that the present law represents a 'flexible regulatory tool' which has managed to adapt to changing times and tastes.[28] The government perceives, or says that it perceives, the current law to be up to the task. As in 1857 it has no wish to become ensnared in the mire of reform.

The 1857 Bill was vigorously opposed. The former Lord Chancellor, Lord Lyndhurst, considered that this area should be left well alone by the legislature: '[the Bill] will wholly fail in its object... it is unwise and

[26] *Hansard*, 1857, clxv, col. 103.

[27] *Hansard*, Commons, 1983, 48, col. 537; 1984, 57. The Act itself was in part the result of lobbying by Mary Whitehouse and her National Viewers and Listeners Association, see J. Petley, 'A Nasty Story', *Screen*, 1984, 25, 2, 68. Note the 'savage attack' in the *Daily Mail*, 25 February 1983, on Home Secretary William Whitelaw's unwillingness to support Wardell's Bill, relying instead on voluntary self-restraint in the video industry.

[28] A. Travis, *Bound and Gagged* (Profile, London 2000), ch. 12.

imprudent to poke into these questions and agitate the public mind in respect of them'. The problematic question of the distinction between worthy and beneficial art and literature on the one hand and degrading and polluting obscenity on the other was a prominent concern. The danger was especially acute when reliance was being placed, in the initial stages, on the uneducated opinion of an informant or a policeman. The copies of old masters, the ancient classics, the Restoration dramatists and the French novelists would all be at risk.[29] Another ground for opposition centred on the powers of search and seizure that the Act would bestow on the agents of the state. In the Commons, Sheffield MP John Arthur Roebuck said:

> It was an attempt to make people virtuous by Act of Parliament; but it could never succeed. A man who had a taste for this class of... publications... would get them in spite of all the laws they could pass. They would, therefore, not prevent mischief being done, while there was great danger of making mischief by an undue interference with the affairs of private life, by encouraging an abuse of power.[30]

One honourable Member who certainly did have a 'taste' for such publications was Monckton Milnes who, later in life, housed his large collection of erotica at Fryston Hall near Pontefract. He stated the Bill to be a 'clumsy method of meeting the evil, one totally alien to the habits of this country, and certain, in the end to be disgustful to the English people', adding 'the Bill would never have reached its present shape if Honourable Members had had the manliness to state what were their real opinions on the subject'.[31]

By contrast, the moral and political climate in parliament in 1983 meant that there was very little opposition during the passage of the Video Recordings Bill. Denis Howell MP seemed to sum up the 'liberal' position:

> Many people have old-fashioned ideas about censorship that I once had myself. However, my ideas have rapidly changed. I used to believe that every man should be his own censor. With the advent of the video coming directly into the home, I find that it is no longer a defensible position.... Parliament must say – no one else can – what people should be allowed to buy or hire for exploitation and visual showing to children and young people.[32]

If the proposition that obscenity was a serious threat to the life of the nation, or at least a serious threat to public morality, were to be taken seriously then it would be natural to expect the state agencies, in the

---

[29] *Hansard*, 1857, clxv, cols. 331-2; 336.

[30] *Ibid*, 1857, clxvii, col. 1475.

[31] *Ibid*.

[32] *Ibid*, Commons, 1983, 48, col. 550.

absence of any specific identifiable *victims* of crime, to take a pro-active part in the investigation of offences and obtaining warrants for search and seizure and orders for destruction. As much seems to have been indicated by Lord Chancellor Cranworth in 1857 when dismissing Lord Campbell's call for government action.[33] Only on rare occasions, however, did the police take the initiative: for example immediately after the passage of the 1857 Act itself.[34]

When publications were openly sold on the public street causing annoyance to passers-by action could also be taken under the Metropolitan Police Act 1839.[35] Overwhelmingly the initiative was left to voluntary effort, notably in the form of the evangelical Vice Society.[36] In order to obtain evidence the Society used paid *agent provocateurs* and tactics of entrapment. They were perceived by their opponents as being at best interfering busybodies and at worst akin to the Spanish Inquisition, threatening the very essence of English liberty.[37] The role of private initiative remained prolific in the twentieth century. In particular the role of Mary Whitehouse and the National Viewers and Listeners Association is worthy of note.

Legal Certainty

As was predicted by the opponents of Lord Campbell's Bill in 1857, the problem of how to distinguish between works of high art and classic literature (which were beneficial and uplifting) and obscenity (which was depraving and corrupting) recurred throughout the latter half of the century. Time and again defendants pointed to paintings hanging in public galleries or marbles in the Crystal Palace and challenged their prosecutors to distinguish them from their own publications. Indeed in many cases these publications were copies of those very works of art themselves.[38] An

---

[33] *Ibid*, 1857, clxv, col. 103.

[34] *The Times*, 3 February 1868.

[35] *The Times*, 2 February; 15 August 1870.

[36] See B. Harrison, 'State Intervention and Moral Reform in the Nineteenth Century' in P. Hollis (ed.), *Pressure from Without* (Edward Arnold, London, 1974); E. Bristow, *Vice and Vigilance* (Rowman and Littlefield, New Jersey, 1977).

[37] See Joseph Knight, Letter, *The Athenaeum*, 29 May 1875, cited Bristow, *Vice and Vigilance*, p. 48. Isabel Burton, widow of Sir Richard Burton the explorer and translator of the *Arabian Nights* and *Karma Sutra* was terror-stricken at the prospect of being investigated by the Vice Society, see M. Lovell, *A Rage to Live* (Little Brown and Co, London, 1998), p. 688.

[38] *R v Shove* (1872) *The Times*, 10 February 1872.

adequate answer to this conundrum is difficult to discern. *The Times* claimed that there may be a 'difficulty about a definition in words [but] there is none as to the application in particular cases of that unwritten definition which is graven in the hearts of mankind, broad as common sense, and deep as the wellsprings of morality and cleanliness'.[39] But this was not really good enough for a legal regime that prided itself on certainty. As the jurist James Fitzjames Stephen put it, 'the criminal law is... the most powerful and... the roughest engine which society can use for any purpose.... Before an act can be treated as a crime it must be capable of distinct definition and of specific proof'[40]

These were criteria that the law of obscenity found it very difficult to meet. The *Law Times* in 1860 commenting on the prosecution of a Mr Plataner for selling stereoscopic slides of the nude statues at the Crystal Palace stated:

> the offence... by its very nature was incapable of definition – being to a great extent a matter of individual opinion... it was dangerous to the liberty of the subject to make a law which might at future times be used by puritanical persons for suppression, not merely of that which we all agree to be indecent, but of art itself which puritans hold to be equally indecent with the indecencies universally admitted to be such.... If views of the statues are indecent much more must be the statues themselves... the word indecent is so indefinite, so much a matter of mere opinion, that it depends upon the accident of a judge, or the chance composition of a jury.[41]

Fitzjames Stephen commented that:

> A man may disbelieve in God, heaven, and hell, he may care little for mankind or society, or for the nation to which he belongs – let him at least be plainly told what are the acts which will stamp him with infamy, hold him up to public execration, and bring him to the gallows, the gaol or the lash.[42]

But this was precisely the problem. In the law of obscenity the individual was not 'plainly told'.

This problem persists. Lack of certainty and clarity suffuses the whole area. The line drawn between art and obscenity is scarcely more easy to discern today than it was in the nineteenth century. This obscurity is well

---

[39] *The Times*, 23 July 1857.

[40] James Fitzjames Stephen, *Liberty Equality Fraternity*, R. J. White (ed.), (Cambridge University Press, Cambridge, 1967), p. 141.

[41] 'Law Notes', *The Times*, 26 November 1860.

[42] James Fitzjames Stephen, *A History of Criminal Law in England*, 3 vols (Macmillan, London, 1883), III, pp. 366-7.

illustrated by the case of *R v Gibson and Sylverie*.[43] Peter Gibson, an artist, made a sculpture entitled 'Human Earrings' out of freeze-dried human foetuses of three or four months gestation. These were exhibited at the Sylverie's gallery. The two were prosecuted under the common law offence of outraging public decency. This offence had not, up until this point, been used against artistic works. The Obscene Publications Act 1959 (OPA) had been passed in part in order to afford protection to works of artistic or literary merit.[44] Section 4 provides for a 'public good' defence for such items. However, no such defence exists under the common law offence of outraging public decency. Section 2(4) provides that publishers should not be proceeded against by way of the common law where the essence of the offence is that the matter (contained in the impugned article) is 'obscene'. Thus it is intended that all prosecutions for obscenity should be funnelled through the OPA with its concomitant public good defence. This, on the face of it, would seem to have prevented a common law prosecution of Gibson and Sylverie. However the term 'obscene' has more than a single meaning in English law. There is the statutory meaning, derived from Lord Cockburn's judgment in *Hicklin* and defined in Section 1 OPA – the 'deprave and corrupt' test.[45] There is also a broader, everyday meaning of obscene – 'namely something which constitutes a serious breach of recognised standards of propriety on account of its tendency to corrupt morals or on account of its indecent appearance or its tendency to engender revulsion or disgust or outrage'.[46] It was never claimed that the earrings in *Gibson* would be likely to 'deprave and corrupt' anyone, meaning they were not 'obscene' in the Section 1 OPA sense. Rather they fell within the broader 'disgust and outrage' meaning. This version of the term, the Court of Appeal held, was not the one being referred to in Section 2(4) which consequently did not apply so as to prevent the prosecution under the common law. Gibson and Sylverie were therefore not able to put any arguments based on the artistic merit of the work and their convictions under the common law offence were duly upheld. Whatever the merits of the outcome of the decision in *Gibson* the case well illustrates the continued uncertainty surrounding the distinction between art, obscenity and indecency in English law.[47]

---

[43] [1990] 2 QB 619.

[44] See the preamble to the Act.

[45] The meaning of this test itself is distinctly unclear and fraught with difficulty, see Robertson, *Obscenity*.

[46] *R v Gibson* [1990] 2 QB 619 per Lord Lane, p. 442.

[47] See reports of the cases of: the University of Central England and Robert Mapplethorpe's Book, *The Guardian*, 1 October 1998; the Saatchi Gallery and Tierney Gearnon's

The Real Concern

The main spur to action by the Victorian legal regime, it seems, was not the existence or consumption of obscene materials *per se*. Rather, it was the fact that salacious materials were becoming increasingly available to a much wider reading and viewing public. More they were becoming available in *public space*. In short obscenity had become democratised and publicised. What particularly horrified Lord Campbell at the trial of William Strange in 1857 and convinced him that something needed to be done was the fact that what were essentially salacious gossip magazines, *Paul Pry* and *The Women of London*, were being 'sold publicly in the streets of London for a penny' while 'hitherto there had been some check on such publications arising from the high price which was extracted for them'.[48] After 'without hesitation' delivering the jury's guilty verdict the foreman added that they 'considered these cheap publications had a far greater tendency to demoralise the public than... others which were sold at a higher price'. At the trial of Frederick Shove at the Middlesex Sessions in 1872 for publishing the *Days Doings*, Mr Besley for the prosecution commented that this publication:

> was far more dangerous and more calculated to deprave and corrupt the minds of the people than the most filthy photographs which were sold at high prices and... with the utmost secrecy. In the one case the youth of both sexes could see the exciting pictures in shop windows while in the other it must be the act of a person of depraved mind to seek out the vendor.[49]

Sir William Bodkin, the Assistant Judge, stated that the suggestion that 'statues or paintings could be copied with impunity was ill-founded... [but] the idea of boys in the public street selling these papers was a scandal to the age'.[50]

It was not simply that the wares were now cheap. Open display of visual images in shop windows on the public streets meant that consumption could take place without the need for even a purchase – by the mere movement through the space of the street.[51] It was all very well for the

---

photographs, *The Guardian*, 10 March 2001. See also Susan Edwards' chapter in this volume.

[48] *The Times*, 11 May 1857.

[49] *The Times*, 10 February 1872.

[50] *Ibid*; see also '*Aze* and *Duk's*', *The Times*, 6 June 1868; 'Obscene Valentines', *The Times*, 11 February; 15 February; 18 February, 1869; 'The Ferret case', *The Times*, 29 January; 2 February, 1870.

[51] Nead, *Victorian Babylon*, part 3.

educated middle class male to peruse it in the privacy of his study. He was believed to have 'character' and objectivity and the facility of self-denial. This supposed ability is well illustrated by H. S. Ashbee's 1877 catalogue of classic pornographic works, the *Index Liborum Prohibitorum*, whose introduction alone stretches to 74 pages and is heavy with footnotes. The whole work is based on this premise of middle class male control. Indeed Ashbee himself argued that acquaintance with the classical works of erotica can only be beneficial on the grounds that virtue never tested is no virtue at all. He added:

> Let me not be misunderstood. I do not mean to say that [indecent] books... should be put into the hands of young people, far from it, but I do assert that it is necessary and profitable for the student to know such books as it is for the naturalist to be acquainted with the less known and less lovely members of the animal kingdom... the wood-louse being (in my opinion) as worthy of study as the elephant.[52]

It was all very well, therefore, for the middle class man to indulge himself with expensive works of erotica in the privacy of his study. It was quite another for cheaper, milder forms to be visible openly in the public streets, or to fall into the hands of women and children within the sanctity of the home itself.

Many of the same concerns infuse the modern debates. As Gavin Sutter's chapter also underlines, it was partly the ease and cheapness with which videos could be acquired by children that caused the disquiet which gave rise to the Video Recordings Act. In the Bill's Second Reading, Graham Bright, MP, said:

> In recent years there has been considerable growth in the sale of video equipment and the availability of video recordings. Retail outlets have sprung up in large numbers; many of these rent, rather than sell, video cassettes often as cheaply as £1 or £2 an evening. Therefore it is easy for children to get hold of and play video material. I have received hundreds of letters explaining how youngsters have clubbed together with their pocket money and got hold of these recordings.[53]

Victorian concerns over the display of indecent matter in public space also have modern resonances.

In 1979 one of the main recommendations of the Williams Committee was that the display of offensive material in public space, such as the

---

[52] Pisanus Fraxi, *Index Liborum Prohibitorum* (Privately Printed, London, 1877. Facsimile by Charles Skilton Ltd, London, 1960).

[53] *Hansard*, Commons, 1983, 48, col. 523.

unrestricted display of pornographic magazines on the shelves of ordinary newsagents, should be restricted. Its Report stressed that the

> paternalistic protection of other adults is... not the motivation of the test. However, paternalistic protection in the literal sense, the protection of children and young people, is a proper and very important aim of the law in this area, one which has been put to us by many witnesses.... There may well be material which responsible parents would not want to be available to children and young people, and this is properly something to be restricted.[54]

In instances where even relatively mild sexual imagery intrudes into *public* space the public reaction is often very hostile. The poster advertising 'Opium' perfume, depicting the model Sophie Dahl lying on her back cupping one breast in her hand and wearing nothing but gold stiletto-heeled shoes, was ordered to be withdrawn by the Advertising Standards Authority after receiving hundreds of complaints.[55]

The Public and the Private

The key to understanding the Victorian's ambivalent legal response to obscenity lies in the tension inherent in the public/private dichotomy. There was great concern to respect the sanctity of the private domain. This was seen as a key element of English liberty. Famously John Stuart Mill expressed this in his classic work *On Liberty* as the freedom to conduct 'experiments in living' irrespective of alleged immorality, as long as conduct did not cause direct harm to others.[56] In *Liberty Equality Fraternity*, Fitzjames Stephen rejected Mill's distinction between self-regarding and other-regarding acts and scathingly attacked the 'harm condition'.[57] However Stephen, like Mill, was also anxious to protect the private domain. He discussed, for example, the prosecution of John Wilkes for obscene libel in 1768, for his *Essay on Woman*. The prosecution had been brought despite the fact that the work had only been published privately to his friends in his own house. Stephen had no 'objection whatever' to the *principle* of this type of prosecution. But, he added, 'the reason why such acts should go unpunished is, that no police or other

---

[54] *Ibid*. The Indecent Displays (Control) Act 1982 was passed partly in response to the Williams Committee, 1979, making it an offence to display publicly 'any indecent matter'.

[55] *The Guardian*, 19 December 2000.

[56] J. S. Mill, *On Liberty*, S. Collini (ed.), (Cambridge University Press, Cambridge, 1989).

[57] *Ibid*, p. 137.

authority can be trusted with the power to intrude into private society, and to pry into private papers'.[58]

Thus, while Mill and Stephen had fundamentally differing perspectives, they agreed that the private domain ought to be respected. It is this concern that perhaps helps explain the ambivalent legal response to obscene publications, and why the authorities, for the most part, only became exercised in cases of indecency and obscenity blatantly in the public domain.[59] In the Victorian age the middle class 'cult of domesticity' reached its apogee.[60] The home and family were seen as a haven for the middle class male from the impurity, amorality and hustle and bustle of the public world of business and industry. Industrialisation and urbanisation meant that the work place became separated from the home in a world in which much of men's power resided in the ability to pass at will between public and private space and in which the lives of middle class women were concentrated in the domestic realm.[61] In 1865 John Ruskin wrote that the home 'is the place of Peace; the shelter, not only from all injury but from all terror doubt and division... a vestal temple, a temple of the hearth watched over by the Household Gods'.[62] The notion of privacy is absolutely central to this ideal of the domestic sphere as haven from the polluted public world.

One of the main reasons that obscenity was so loudly reviled was because it was perceived to be a direct threat to this ideal of domestic bliss. As Justice Grove said in sentencing a Gloucester solicitor convicted of obscene libel for running a mail-order pornography business, such material was 'likely to produce immorality, to prevent domestic happiness, demoralise young people, and deter them from entering marriage and respectability and calculated to bring serious and long continued injury to those whose minds are allowed to feed upon such garbage as this'.[63] The President of the Vice Society put it similarly in 1871:

---

[58] *Ibid*, p. 160.

[59] A modern version of the Mill/Stephen debate can be seen in the celebrated 'Hart/Devlin debate' of the 1960s. See H. L. A. Hart, *Law, Liberty and Morality* (Oxford University Press, London, 1963); P. Devlin, *The Enforcement of Morals* (Oxford University Press, London, 1965).

[60] J. Tosh, *A Man's Place. Masculinity and the middle class home in Victorian England* (Yale, New Haven, 1999).

[61] J. Walkowitz, *City of Dreadful Delight: narratives of sexual danger in late-Victorian London* (Virago, London, 1992).

[62] Cited in E. Trudgill, *Madonnas and Magdalens: the origins and development of Victorian sexual attitudes* (Heinemann, London, 1976).

[63] *R v Draper*, Gloucester Chronicle, 12 August 1876.

> It penetrates the retired habitations of simplicity and innocence; it falls into the hands of all ages and ranks and conditions, but it is peculiarly fatal to the unguarded minds of the youthful of both sexes and to them its breath is poison and its touch death.[64]

Obscenity was a fatal poison aimed directly at the very core of middle class domesticity and respectability.

Herein lies the central paradox of the Victorian legal response to obscenity. For the concept of privacy to mean anything at all it must necessarily entail the freedom to be able to read and view whatever one wants, unmolested in the sanctity of one's own home. The law was caught between polar aims. On the one hand it was necessary to protect the home from the pollution of obscenity – the product of the public world of industry, commerce and technology. After all, if this material was encountered and 'consumed' in the public streets from a shop window by children, wives and servants, or still worse if it was actually acquired by them as a result of its cheapness and availability, it would lead to the excitement of uncontrollable lusts, masturbation, promiscuity and the ultimate downfall of the home. But on the other hand the law was desperately concerned lest it interfere with the privacy of the freeborn Englishman – the freedom to read and view whatever he wanted in his own private domain.

The paradox is given a further twist by the fact that the very mass availability of pornography was due to the very same technological, industrial and social advances that made the age so wondrous – and for that matter created the impetus for the separation of private and public worlds and elevation of the cult of domesticity in the first place.[65] Given the stresses upon the law, pulled in such opposing directions, it is not surprising that the legal response was decidedly ambivalent.

Conclusion

Echoes of this nineteenth century paradox can be discerned in the modern legal regime. Of course there are massive differences, not least the advent of feminism, and the development of human rights.[66] But the tension between attempting to protect the vulnerable (both in private and public space) on the one hand and the desire to preserve privacy and the benefits

---

[64] *The Times*, 2 November 1871.

[65] Tosh, *Man's Place*.

[66] In particular note the feminist critique of the public/private dichotomy. See N. Lacey, 'Theory into Practice? Pornography and the Public Private Dichotomy', *Journal of Law and Society* (1993), p. 93.

that technological advances can bring on the other hand is still apparent. The modern law in this area is notoriously confused and incoherent.[67] It is perhaps not too fanciful to suggest that this is due in part to the persistence of the same tensions which troubled our Victorian ancestors.

---

[67] Report, Williams Committee, ch. 2, para 23. This concluded that 'the law in short is a mess'. Little has been done in the intervening years to require a reappraisal of this conclusion.

Chapter 10

Penny Dreadfuls and Perverse Domains: Victorian and Modern Moral Panics

Gavin Sutter

Introduction

The decades between 1850 and, roughly, the 1890s, were a time of change for Victorian England. People believed themselves to be living in the most modern of ages, at the high point of human development. Similar beliefs abounded at the tail end of the twentieth century; indeed a number of parallels may be drawn between the two time periods. During the Victorian era, literacy and mass communications became more widespread than ever before. David Vincent, based on a study of English literacy and popular culture throughout the period 1750 to 1914, has demonstrated that, from roughly 50 per cent of the population being unable to sign their own names, by the early years of the twentieth century England had become a (more or less) universally literate country. A comprehensive postal system, alongside cultural phenomena such as the sending of Valentines, Christmas cards, and half-penny postcards, was developed, being both a reflection of and a stimulus to, growing literacy in the country.[1] Literacy levels, rising during the Victorian era, were no doubt greatly boosted by the arrival of compulsory education in the 1870s. Advances in the printing industry included low cost, machine pressing and printing of paper, leading to an availability of cheap literature to the newly-literate masses. Also, by the 1860s, a wide rail network had spread across the country, providing a means of rapid distribution over a much wider geographical area than previously possible. Mass circulation of cheap newspapers, periodicals and other publications became a reality for the first time.

Advances of a similar scale in the dissemination of information were made during the last two decades of the twentieth century. Computer

---

[1] See David Vincent, *Literacy and Popular Culture in England 1750-1914* (Cambridge University Press, Cambridge, 1989).

literacy developed at an extreme rate, coinciding largely with the birth of what we now know as the internet. The modern internet began in the 1960s as a US government/military project, designed to ensure that in the event of nuclear war a network of official communications could be maintained; the system was by design decentralised in order that destruction of any one point in the network could not disable the whole. This internet eventually came to be used as an academic tool, however, as a mass cultural phenomenon the internet only arrived in the early-mid-1990s with the development of the user-friendly world wide web. Population figures for the internet are difficult to quantify: such has been the rapidity of its growth 'that there is now no precise count of the number of users', indeed it may well now be impossible to ever reach an accurate estimate.[2] It has, however, been estimated that by the middle of the last year of the twentieth century, 2000, global internet population had reached 300 million.

Over this period, the internet developed as an important research tool for academics: many academic and professional journals began to publish online. University libraries made their catalogues available over the internet; public libraries too began to place their catalogues online (a process which continues today). In keeping with the trend towards more open government in the UK in the 1990s, the Houses of Parliament and government departments developed websites detailing latest news and government reports, bills before parliament, lists of MPs, the ever-increasing number of statutes in force, and so on.[3] With a little technical capability, easily to be attained, anyone with occasional access could not only view this information (and much else besides), but also easily acquire free webspace, publish a homepage, and develop a voice in a forum with a potential audience of millions. Bulletin boards and real-time chat-rooms allowed great potential for enriching communications across cultural boundaries between users in different countries or even continents. Again, mass communications were available to the population at large in a way unprecedented.

In both eras, there were many to champion the new access to information for the masses. The educative benefits of free expression and exchange of information online have been much trumpeted in recent years. The G-7 Ministerial Conference on the Information Society at Brussels in July 1994 considered that

---

[2] G. Basque, 'Introduction to the Internet', E. Mackay, D. Poulin and P Trudel (eds), *The Electronic Superhighway: the shape of technology and law to come* (Kluwer Law International, The Hague, 1995), pp. 7-19.

[3] See http://www.housesofparliament.gov.uk.

for those able to exploit it, the information society is already a liberating experience which widens individual choice, releases new creative and commercial energies, offers cultural enrichment and brings greater flexibility to the management of working and leisure time.[4]

In the nineteenth century too, the benefits of the press were much commented upon. It was widely believed that the press served as a moral guide to the masses; in 1839, one commentator claimed:

It is to the Newspapers – the Press – therefore, that we stand at this day and hour, so immeasurably indebted for our knowledge and sense of moral duty... the People respect its advice and information, its praise and dispraise, because they know by experience, which teaches better than the schoolmaster at home.[5]

Some years later, in 1863, another remarked:

Freedom of printing and publishing – provided always that private character be not slandered, public morality be not assailed, and political treason be not fomented – is the inalienable birthright of every civilised nation... certain members of the publishing fraternity... have devised liberal things for the purpose of encouraging authorship, and have then striven to issue to the public the best of books, at the lowest possible prices... Let all who have thoughts utter them; and let those who only think they have be tested by the voice of public opinion.... Absolute free trade in books, so far as the removal of commercial obstacles can secure it, is our motto. Have we not means of cheap publishing such as the ancients never dreamed of?[6]

However, not all were fervent believers in the power of newly affordable works for good; there were those who sounded the note of caution:

Whatever tends to render the conditions of social existence more favourable – physically, intellectually or morally – has an *educative tendency*. The character of the ordinary literature of the working classes – the possession of the means of comfortable support, habits of economy, the character of the streets and dwellings, the kind of amusements – all exercise a most potent influence in educing or stunting the faculties and moulding the character... The new publishing industry has much to answer for of both good and ill.[7]

[4] 'G-7 Ministerial Conference on the Information Society', *Conference Theme Paper* (1995).

[5] A Student At Law, *The Fourth Estate: or the Moral Influence of the Press* (Ridgeway, London, 1839), pp. 9-12.

[6] Counsels to Authors, *Plans of Publishing, and Specimens of Types* (William Freeman, London, 1863), Introduction, pp. 3-4.

[7] James Hole, *Light, More Light! On the Present State of Education amongst the working classes of Leeds, and how it can best be improved* (Longman, Green, Longman and Roberts, London, 1869), p. 107.

Another, writing in 1858, put it succinctly: 'Our new publishing industry has shown itself to be a blessing, but also a curse'.[8] These words have been echoed by many commentators referring to the range of content available on the internet in recent years; Janet Reno, while US Attorney General during the Clinton Administration, stated the views of many when she said 'information technology, like other human creations, is not an unqualified good'.[9]

A balanced, cautious approach to new technologies and the uses to which they may be put is, of course sensible. However, not all critics of new media throughout history have been rational or balanced in their judgment. Both the arrival of cheap weekly publications in the Victorian era and the internet at the end of the twentieth century were subject to much hysteria, emphasising their supposed negative social effects, even blaming them for a range of social ills.

Anatomy of a Moral Panic

The classic definition of a moral panic remains that given by Cohen, as cited in the Introduction by the editors.[10] Interpreting this, the following comments can be made about the major elements of a moral panic:

- ○ The identification of a (perceived) threat to the established order – usually the threat will be identified with specific reference to children,
- ○ There will follow 'a spiralling escalation of the perceived threat through the media and censorship lobbying',[11]
- ○ Public hysteria may result in some form of legal action or law making; at the very least there will be some greater or lesser influence upon how the legal process is perceived,
- ○ The moral panic will fade from view either as public interest wanes or a new panic appears over the horizon; often a combination of both.

---

[8] Samuel Day, *Juvenile Crime; Its Causes, Character and Cure* (J. F. Hope, London, 1858), p. 208.

[9] Janet Reno, 'Law Enforcement in CyberSpace', Presentation to the Commonwealth Club of California, 14 June, 1996.

[10] Stanley Cohen, *Folk Devils and Moral Panics* (Paladin, St Albans, 1973), p. 9; see also this volume's Introduction.

[11] John Springhall, *Youth, Popular Culture and Moral Panics* (Macmillan Press, London, 1998), p. 146.

Moral panics surrounding the alleged negative effect upon children of new media have a long history, indeed they can be traced back almost as far as civilisation itself:

> Since the Greek philosopher Plato first expressed concern about the influence of the dramatic poets on the 'impressionable minds' of young people, a succession of new media – the novel, music hall, the cinema, comics, television, video and computer games – have each in turn become the focus of recurrent waves of public anxiety.[12]

Victorian concerns about popular, cheap fiction to which children had access and 1990s worries over access to internet pornography by children merely followed a pattern of moral panic throughout the ages: it was a wise man who once said 'there is nothing new under the sun'.[13]

Penny Dreadfuls: Victorian Moral Panic

The term 'penny dreadful' is widely used to describe the cheap, serialised literature available in the Victorian period, and at the centre of moral panic in that time. The concept of serialised literature had its genesis in France in the 1830s, when one of the leading newspapers began to print novels specifically designed for serialisation in a daily newspaper. The format was soon imported to England, where, from the 1840s onwards, a number of weekly titles such as *The London Journal* and *The Family Herald* printed stories in the French mould, if not translations of the French originals.[14] Falling costs of printing such journals made them ever more viable as cheap periodicals which could be turned out in large numbers to sell at a profit to the growing literate population. The quality of such works was low – poor plot and characterisation were accompanied by poor grammar and composition. However, this cheap fiction, sold in weekly instalments typically costing a penny each, was popular amongst the English working classes, and by the 1860s, the most successful such publications sold in the region of 30,000 to 40,000 copies weekly.[15]

The early mass-market serial publications were not specifically aimed at children; rather they were the preserve of the working classes more generally. However, by the 1860s, change was afoot. Population figures

---

[12] David Buckingham, 'Child's Play? Beyond Moral Panics', in David Buckingham (ed.), *Moving Images – Understanding children's emotional responses to television* (Manchester University Press, Manchester, 1996), pp. 19-56.

[13] *Ecclesiastes*, I, ix.

[14] Springhall, *Youth*, pp. 39-40.

[15] *Ibid*, p. 43.

returned in the 1861 census of England and Wales indicated that 45 per cent of the population were under 20 years of age.[16] Even prior to the arrival of compulsory education for all (introduced by the Education Act 1870), literacy was rapidly becoming widespread, particularly among the young. There was thus a clear market for cheap fiction aimed directly at the young: publishers noted this, and thus was born what is now recognised as the 'true' penny dreadful.[17] The 1860s and 1870s saw a whole slew of mass-market titles marketed deliberately at the young of the working and lower middle classes. As one detractor put it, 'The titles of those publications speak for themselves' [18] The subject matter covered in the penny dreadfuls included lurid crimes, gothic romance and horror (such as the vampire related titles), historical epics, school stories – and much else besides. Particularly popular themes included such figures as pirates and highwaymen – the concept of the professional gentleman criminal was a strong one, along with, it would appear, the triumph of the underdog. The fact that in these stories the underdog was often a lawbreaker, or at least a rogue, was bound up in much of the criticism the genre began to attract.

The penny dreadful was at its peak in the 1860s, and remained a mass format for the remainder of the nineteenth century. Criticism of the genre is, however, almost as old as the revolution in cheap publishing itself. The growth of literacy in the latter half of the nineteenth century was cast in a mainly positive light by commentators from the middle classes, a belief in the power of literature to shape the minds of the poor for their benefit being generally held. However, there were those who also saw shadows in what they feared as the equal capacity of the popular press to do much harm. Early critics, such as the Rev. Samuel G. Green, expressed fears for the moral well-being of the working classes at the hands of cheap and plentiful popular literature:

> The working classes of England are becoming essentially a reading people [but]... there are still multitudes who read without discernment or intelligence... those who do not read are invariably influenced by those of their companions who do... The whole of this portion of the community may therefore be regarded as, in a great measure, subject to the power of the press. But what literature have they to guide them? The country is now flooded with cheap books and newspapers, but the

---

[16] *Ibid*, p. 45.

[17] See, for instance, *ibid*, pp. 39-44.

[18] John Parker, 'On the Literature of the Working Classes. Prize Essay', in Viscount Ingestre (ed.), *Meliora: or, Better Times to Come. Being the Contribution of Many Men touching the Present State and Prospects of Society* (John W. Parker & Son, London, 1853), 2nd Series, p. 183.

answer to this question is startling and sad. The Christian public will not soon forget the facts disclosed in 1847 by Mr. Oakey in his tractate on 'the Power of the Press, is it rightly employed?'.... The grand total issue of publications whose influence is all upon the side of moral corruption is thus 28,862,000. And on the other side, adding together... we have but 24,418,620. So that the balance in favour of the former is beyond four millions! To which it may be added, that the religious literature referred to circulates chiefly among professing Christians of the middle classes; while that of a demoralising character finds its way, in a very large proportion, to the homes and haunts of the poor.[19]

It is interesting to note the good Reverend's reliance upon secondary sources and emotive claims, bordering on the hysterical, based upon supposed statistical evidence: both are a familiar theme from our modern moral panics. Of course, there were those voices of reason that offered hope of a remedy to the perceived social problem: 'The conviction is fast spreading that, to create an intelligent people, books must be used as the chief instrument', and since 'cheap blasphemous books' were the main threat to the working classes, the remedy was to put 'better books within the reach of the people'.[20]

Lord Brougham, in an 1858 public address to the National Association for the Promotion of Social Science, made reference to the 'circulation of the most abominable matter' in weekly newspapers, adding, though, 'it would be a great mistake to suppose that the benefits of the Popular press are negative only'.[21] As the 1860s and 1870s saw the decline of adult titles and the reorganisation of the cheap periodicals, with the emergence of titles such as those described above, aimed explicitly at the rapidly growing number of literate minors, the doomsayers began to claim a strong link between publications of that ilk and corruption of the young, particularly in the working classes. One critic thundered:

> There is a great amount of trash connected with penny weekly literature.... The subscribers to this... literature of extravagant and horrible fiction... are not to be found among the adult working classes of London.... The purchasers are to be found among boys and girls, who, not having rightly-educated parents to direct them in their

---

[19] Rev Samuel G. Green, *The Working Classes of Great Britain: Their Present Condition, and the means of their Improvement and Elevation. Prize Essay* (John Snow, London, 1849), pp. 115-6.

[20] James Augustus St. John, *The Education of the People* (Chapman and Hall, London, 1858, republished, Woburn Books, 1970), pp. 140-5.

[21] Lord Brougham, *Addresses on Popular Literature. An Address Delivered at the Meeting of the National Association for the Promotion of Social Science, at Liverpool. October 12 1858* (Edward Law, London, 1858), pp. 22-3.

reading, from the love of the marvellous and adventurous inherent in their natures, greedily devour the wretched literary garbage which unprincipled publishers offer with stimulating pictorial garnishings, to tempt and gratify their morbid appetites.[22]

A perceived link between juvenile crime and cheap literature had been drawn as early as January 1856, when the *Daily Telegraph* reported the following case:

> a boy whose head scarcely reached the dock, [who was] charged by his mother... with stealing 10s. It appeared that the prisoner was a most incorrigible lad, and notwithstanding all the attempts of his mother to reform him, he still continued the practice of thieving.... The [boy] had previously robbed her of 5s, but she then forgave him. He had been away from home for a week since he had taken the money, and she was afraid he had been led away by bad companions *and low books*.[23]

Once identified, the perceived threat posed to children of previously good character by penny dreadfuls was seized upon by the press and commentators; the following extract is far from atypical:

> Our criminal population (and especially the juvenile portion thereof) has for some time been seriously engaging public attention.... A further cause of juvenile delinquency arises from demoralising publications, the number of which, from the immense circulation they obtain, it is difficult to compute. One thing is certain, that they are fraught with a great evil to the community.... The young and ardent mind is naturally prone to take pleasure in works of an exciting character.... Hence we find that many of our juvenile criminals possess little or no education beyond that of being able to read, or being otherwise familiar with those disreputable and demoralising memoirs.... A taste having once been formed for, and the mind once addicted to this vile and vapid stuff, books of a healthy character can never be relished, even should they be perused, which is very seldom the case.[24]

No convincing evidence that the penny dreadfuls, a term itself coined by those who campaigned against the continued publication of these titles in the 1870s, bore any causal relationship with the growing problem of juvenile delinquency in the cities of the Victorian era was ever adduced. Yet as is ever the case with moral panic, the fact that the perceived threat was based on little more than hearsay and gossip did nothing to stem the rising tide of concern. An editorial which appeared in a new weekly

---

[22] Parker, 'Literature', p. 183.

[23] *Daily Telegraph*, 1 January 1856, emphasis added.

[24] Samuel Day, *Juvenile Crime; Its Causes, Character and Cure* (J. F. Hope, London, 1858), pp. 203-6.

publication of the apparently more respectable kind reflected what became common-place beliefs surrounding the dreadfuls at this time:

> The police-court reports in the newspapers are alone sufficient proof of the harm done by the 'penny-dreadfuls'.... It is almost a daily occurrence with magistrates to have before them boys who, having read a number of 'dreadfuls', followed the examples set forth in such publications, robbed their employers.... This and many other evils the penny dreadful is responsible for. It makes thieves of the coming generation, and so helps fill our gaols.[25]

A particular panic of the late nineteenth century surrounded the highwayman genre of dreadfuls, which celebrated the exploits of Dick Turpin, and others. Victorian court records show many cases where penny dreadfuls of this genre received the blame for crimes committed by children. In 1872, Joseph Bennett, 17, and his accomplice, a younger boy, appeared at Bow Street Petty Sessions Court to answer charges of breaking and entering. In his testimony to the court, the police constable responsible for apprehending the boys made much of their reading matter of choice: highwayman-related penny dreadfuls. This appears to have been regarded as a clear indication of criminal intent. Certainly the fact that one of the boys, no doubt in an attempt at mitigation, reportedly claimed to have been tempted to commit the theft 'by reading these tales' received much attention.[26] In another case, a 19-year-old house painter, Purdee, was found guilty of daylight armed robbery, executed in the manner of a highwayman. Again much was made of Purdee's choice of reading material – penny dreadfuls of the highwayman genre. Particularly damning was the fact that during the commission of his crime, he had referred to himself as 'Captain Hawk', one of the popular highwayman characters in the dreadfuls. Evidence suggesting possible motivations from sources other than his reading material was excluded both by the police and the judiciary.[27]

Such reports served only to galvanise the determination of moral campaigners, such as the Pure Literature Society, who throughout the period called for penny dreadfuls to be banned. The majority of the (working-class) general public may never have been active in these middle-class, censorious movements, however, they were certainly

---

[25] Alfred Harmsworth, Editorial, *The Halfpenny Marvel*, 1893 (first issue). Cited in Springhall, *Youth*, p. 75.

[26] Cited in Jno. P. Harrison, 'Cheap Literature Past and Present', *Companion to the Almanac of the Society for the Diffusion of Useful Knowledge or Year Book of General Information for 1873* (London, 1872), pp. 75-6.

[27] Harrison, 'Cheap Literature', cited Springhall, *Youth*, p. 80, note 17.

affected by the ensuing moral panic generated by these campaigns and press reports of cases in which dreadfuls were, however tenuously, linked to the commission of crimes. Extensive press coverage was given to the case of Alfred Saunders, a 13-year-old errand boy who, in early 1876, appeared in a petty sessions court to answer the relatively minor charge of theft of £7 4s from his father. Saunders not only admitted the theft, but also that he had spent some of the money on highwayman-themed papers. Testimony was given to the effect that the boy was in the habit of reading such material, and examples were produced for the edification of the court. Also produced in evidence were other items that the boy had purchased with the stolen money: a toy pistol, a lantern and a cigar holder – all readily identifiable with the popular image of a highwayman.[28]

While the highwayman titles were at the centre of most moral panic during the 1860s and 1870s, following, it seems, a quiet period in the 1880s, the moral panic returned with renewed fervour in relation to dreadfuls more generally. The 1892 suicide of George William Seymour was reported in the *Pall Mall Gazette* under the title 'A Victim of the Penny Dreadful'. The boy was reportedly 'addicted to reading penny novels'. The coroner's verdict referred to 'a lad with an active brain, who was fond of exciting reading, and no doubt had a predisposition to suicide' The *Pall Mall Gazette* reported that the boy 'committed suicide while temporarily insane, the insanity being caused by reading trashy novels'.[29] In 1895, 13-year-old Robert Allen Coombes was found 'guilty but insane' on charges of matricide, a verdict which owed much to evidence, given by a doctor acting for the defence, that Coombes, who had a history of mental illness, may well have been motivated by 'pernicious literature'.[30] The extensive press coverage which the case received served only to firmly establish once again in the public mind the link between juvenile crime and cheap literature; and so the moral panic was propagated for some time yet.

Perverse Domains: 1990s Cyberporn Panic

It is a symptom of moral panic that new media will often be its centre. As this happened in relation to the arrival of the nineteenth century mass printing industry, so too the internet was the cause of much (unwarranted)

[28] Petty Sessions, *Hampstead and Highgate Express*, 1 January 1876; 6 January 1876, p. 6; see also Springhall, *Youth*, p. 85.

[29] 'A Victim of the Penny Dreadful', *Pall Mall Gazette*, 17 November 1892, p. 7; see also Springhall, *Youth*, p. 90.

[30] Springhall, *ibid*, pp. 90-2.

concern during the last decade of the twentieth century. Again, moral panic took the form of the dangers of a perceived threat to children: cybersex. More specifically, fears abounded not only that children could easily gain access to all manner of filth online, but that also minors exploring cyberspace were easy prey for paedophiles. The moral panic surrounding the availability of 'cyberporn' effectively began in the USA during 1995. On 3 July that year, *Time* magazine ran an article entitled 'On a screen near you: Cyberporn' as its cover story. This article gave the casual reader otherwise uninformed about the issue the impression that the internet is rife with pornography.

The piece was based upon a research paper written by one Marty Rimm at Carnegie Mellon University in Pittsburgh, Pennsylvania.[31] Rimm claimed that

> pedophilic [sic] and paraphilic (including urination, voyeurism, transgenderism, S&M and bestiality) pornography are widely available [on]... Usenet, World Wide Web, and commercial 'adult' BBS [bulletin board services].[32]

Such images were claimed to be in greater demand than supply, and accounted for half of those downloaded from private adult bulletin board services.[33] The *Time* article caused some outrage and much concern, especially amongst parents, throughout the USA, yet it was not completely factual.[34] A myriad of frightening statistics were thrown at the reader, such as that 'on those Usenet newsgroups where digitised images are stored, 83.5 per cent of the pictures were pornographic'[35] In fact the actual proportion of pornographic material available online was much smaller than claimed. Independent analysis of the figures collated by the Rimm study suggested that

> fewer than one half of one per cent of the messages on the internet are 'associated with' newsgroups that contain pornographic imagery; since some... of those messages are, presumably, not themselves porno- graphic, the actual proportion of pornographic messages is even smaller than that.[36]

---

[31] P. Elmer-Dewitt, 'On a Screen Near You: Cyberporn', *Time*, 146, 1, 3 July 1995.

[32] Marty Rimm, 'Marketing Pornography on the Information Superhighway', *Time*, March 1995.

[33] Rimm, 'Marketing Pornography'

[34] M. Barr, 'Why Did Time Do It?', *Time Magazine*, 3 July 1995.

[35] Elmer-Dewitt, 'Cyberporn'

[36] David G. Post, *A Preliminary Discussion of Methodological Peculiarities in the Rimm Study of Pornography on the 'Information Superhighway'*, (1995), http://www2000.ogsm.vanderbilt.edu/novak/david.post.html.

It should be noted that Usenet newsgroups, while potentially accessible by children, are distinct from the world wide web, by far the more popular end of the internet by this time and certainly the more common online haunt of the vast majority of children. The whole tone of the *Time* article was very reminiscent of the words of Reverend Samuel G. Green, with its uncritical reliance upon spurious sources. Rimm, whose paper was used as the basis of the story, was, in fact an undergraduate student reading electrical engineering, not believed to have any particular expertise in this area of research.[37] The rhetorical style of the *Time* piece echoes much Victorian castigation against the penny dreadful: 'When the kids are plugged in, will they be exposed to the seamiest sides of human sexuality? Will they fall prey to child molesters hanging out in electronic chat rooms?'.[38]

On this side of the Atlantic, the issue of computer pornography first came to light in the early part of 1993, when John Major, then Conservative Prime Minister, issued instructions to the Home Office to the effect that the 'young and vulnerable' required protection from the looming threat of computer porn. Home Secretary Michael Howard included measures in his Criminal Justice and Public Order Bill which reflected Major's call. During the first quarter of 1994, the Parliamentary Select Committee for Home Affairs published a report which argued that new legislation specifically tailored to deal with computer pornography was necessary. Meanwhile, James Ferman, the Director of the BBFC, drew comparisons between computer pornography and 'the international trade in drugs'. Opposition MP Frank Cook (Labour) went so far as to claim 'computer pornography is tantamount to the injection of heroin into a child's school milk'.[39] Again this modern rhetoric strongly echoes the words of self-appointed moral crusaders against penny dreadfuls, such as James Greenwood.[40] At around this time the British press began to print articles asking – as did the *Daily Telegraph* – are your children watching porn behind the bedroom door?'.[41] On television, ITV's (in)famous *Cook Report* told 'a story which will frighten any parent, or, indeed, any partner of a home computer addict'.[42] Once more, moral panic, just as in the nineteenth century, was whipped up by the press.

---

[37] D. L. Hoffman and T. P. Novack, *A Detailed Analysis of the Conceptual, Logical and Methodological Flaws in the Article: 'Marketing Pornography on the Information Superhighway'*, 1995, http://www2000.ogsm.vanderbilt.edu/novak/rimm.review.html.

[38] Elmer-Dewitt, 'Cyberporn'

[39] A Calcutt, 'Exposed: Computer Porn Scandal in Commons', *Living Marxism*, April 1994.

[40] James Greenwood, 'Penny Packets of Poison (1874)' in Peter Haining (ed.), *The Penny Dreadful, or Strange, Horrid and Sensational Tales!* (London, 1975), pp. 357-71.

[41] Cited Calcutt, 'Exposed', *ibid.*

[42] Cited, *ibid.*

A pro-censorship lobby arose to demand new, restrictive laws to control this threat to children; many making such demands pointed to a February 1994 Parliamentary Select Committee report as clear evidence of the problem, yet this report was characterised by the acceptance of hearsay and what, in the last instance, amounted to no more than gossip. The report made a number of claims relating both to children's access to porn and internet stalking by paedophiles, yet lacked hard evidence to support them. Particularly telling was the report's conclusion that 'although we do not have hard evidence, I think instinctively one would think that it is likely to increase as a problem'.[43] Various claims were made as to the spread of pornographic computer disks in UK schools – these too remained uncorroborated by hard evidence.[44] Also seized upon by the press were statements made to the Committee by Vicki Merchant, a harassment officer at the University of Central Lancashire, and collator of the first survey of computer pornography in UK schools. Merchant's own preliminary findings proved only that rumours of cyberporn had spread rapidly from school to school. However, no less than the *Sunday Times* reported this as fact, claiming 'explicit computer porn plagues 50 per cent of schools'.[45] These disks were not the internet. However, the net was effectively found guilty by association by moral campaigners, rarely the sort to let the facts stand in the way of a good panic. The Select Committee expressed concerns that minors are able to access material from specialist 'adult' bulletin board services online. Yet memoranda submitted to the committee suggested that such cases were rare, if they happened at all, went unpublished.

The internet remains far from the uncontrolled den of iniquity that self-appointed moral guardians portrayed at this time; a plethora of laws applied to online pornography. In the main, the Obscene Publications Acts 1959 and 1964 apply to the control of pornography.[46] Specific child pornography falls under the ambit of the Protection of Children Act 1978.[47] By the early 1990s, advances in technology had created a lacuna in

---

[43] Cited, *ibid.*

[44] The report as published made reference to an 'apparently quite significant case... in the Bedfordshire area' In actuality, while Luton police did indeed seize a total of 754 computer disks in a much publicised swoop at a Dunstable school, claiming to have broken up a 'porn ring', it later came to light that on analysis *all* of the disks seized were shown to be entirely lacking in pornographic content. The document revealing this received no citation in the final report; it remains in the House of Lords public records office where it may be viewed by appointment only. Calcutt, 'Exposed'.

[45] Cited in Calcutt, 'Exposed'

[46] As amended by the Criminal Justice and Public Order Act 1994, which expanded the meaning of 'obscene article to incorporate information in transit across the internet'

[47] Again, as amended by the Criminal Justice and Public Order Act 1994.

the Protection of Children Act 1978 which until that time covered actual photographs of children. Paedophilic images could now be created without need of an actual child: breasts could be reduced and pubic hair removed from a picture of an adult in order to make it look child like – a child's head could even be superimposed. The 1994 Act closed the loophole, creating the concept of a 'pseudo-photograph' for the first time in UK law.[48] Several other statutes, among them the Criminal Justice Act 1988, which renders mere possession of paedophilic material a serious arrestable offence in the UK, are also applicable here. Yet despite these laws covering the internet within their ambit, the moral panic, boosted by such stories as 'The launch of the first cyber-brothel' in December 1994, continued to grow.[49] Much as the apprehensions about juvenile delinquents in the Victorian era, rather than convincing the public that crime was being dealt with, served only to highlight and exaggerate the perceived problem, so too successful police operations against internet paedophiles, such as Operation Starburst during July 1995 (which resulted in the apprehension of 37 international paedophiles and numerous convictions), only worsened public panic.

In August 1996, Chief Inspector Stephen French, of the Clubs and Vice unit of the Metropolitan Police, sent an open letter to the Internet Service Providers' Association (ISPA), requesting that they ban access to 134 Usenet newsgroups, many of which were deemed to contain pornographic images or explicit text.[50] Approximately 55 per cent of the newsgroups which the Clubs and Vice Unit sought to ban were primarily sites for the distribution and exchange of pictures. Following this letter, a tabloid-style exposé of ISP Demon Internet appeared in the *Observer*. The same paper published a self-congratulatory follow-up story in which it claimed to have prompted a Demon policy change involving the adopting of a system permitting parental control over net access. Demon countered this article saying that it had announced the 'porn policy' earlier. Whatever the rights

---

[48] Significantly, moves to introduce a similar provision in the US by means of the Child Pornography Protection Act 1996 were thrown out as being unconstitutional; the court noted in particular that no actual children could be considered to suffer harm directly enough as a result of such images in order to justify limiting adult free speech in this way. See *Free Speech Coalition –v– Reno* US 9th Circuit Court of Appeals (Latest: http://www.aclu.org).

[49] 'Brothel is Launched on Internet', *Daily Telegraph*, 9 December 1994.

[50] The ISPA was established in 1995 to act as a representative body for ISPs in the UK. ISPAuk has a membership of over 80 companies and claimed to represent 'around 90 per cent of the UK dial-up market' by March 1998. ISPA members are subject to a strict code of conduct, and further they co-operate with the Internet Watch Foundation (see below). See also http://www.ispa.org.uk.

and wrongs of these cases, such news stories served only to further
entrench the image of the internet as being rife with all sorts of
pornography.

The Internet Watch Foundation (IWF), then known as 'Safety Net',
came into being in late 1996.[51] This initiative, supported by the police,
government and industry, operates on the basis of a hotline to which
members of the public can report any obscene or otherwise illegal material
which they come across; details will then be passed to the relevant ISP in
order that the offending content can be removed. The IWF has made clear
that its first priority is child pornography, a clear reflection of priorities set
in the wake of the moral panic over the alleged dangers of 'net-savvy'
paedophiles. By the late 1990s, the IWF was able to claim a fair measure
of success in its annual reports on its website, however, this made little
impact upon the moral panic. In November 1997, Gary Glitter was arrested
and later (5 May 1998) charged under the Protection of Children Act 1978
with 50 counts of 'making indecent pseudo photographs' and 50
alternative offences in respect of the possession of indecent photographs
of children under the age of 16. This story generated much press coverage,
coinciding with other well-covered police seizures of illegal pornographic
material, mostly child pornography, much of it not of internet origin.
Through news reportage, especially that of the tabloid outrage variety, an
impression was created in the public mind that the spread of computerised
pornography, especially child pornography, was easily available to
children using the internet, and reaching epidemic proportions.

Still the shock stories continued: the 'convicted British child molester...
jailed after flying to the United States to meet a 15-year-old girl he had met
over the internet'.[52] There was the former Tory mayor convicted of
possession of paedophilic images[53] and the 'UK internet porn king...
[whose] sites featured extreme pornography, including bestiality and
torture... [one of which] took in up to £30,000 a week'.[54] A computer game
designer – 'One of the masterminds behind sexy... heroine Lara Croft' –
was 'charged with trying to procure a nine-year-old girl for sex'.[55] A slew
of lurid tabloid stories raked over the sordid details of the Gary Glitter case
upon his conviction in November 1999, his early release from prison in
January 2000, when he apparently left Britain to 'begin a new life in

---

[51] See http://www.internetwatch.org.uk.

[52] BBC News Online, 6 February 1999.

[53] *Metro* (London edition), 13 July 1999.

[54] BBC News Online, 30 July 1999.

[55] BBC News Online, 8 November 1999.

Cuba',[56] and his return to the UK, when a 'mob of vigilantes threatened to attack [him]'.[57] Never far from the headlines was a reminder that the supposed source of the paedophilic images in respect of which the former celebrity was convicted was the internet.

In 1999 and 2000, just as the twentieth century began to draw to a close, a new element to internet panic began to surface. In a similar way in which the internet had come to be blamed for all manner of sexual depravity, a few high profile cases emerged in which, it was claimed, the internet was responsible for extreme violence. In April 1999, two American teenage pupils at Columbine High School 'killed as many as 23 people and injured 22' during a killing spree with guns and home-made bombs, before turning their guns on themselves.[58] Although the massacre occurred in the USA, it was widely covered by the UK press; several 'explanations' were expressed in these reports, including the boys' reported fixation with Hitler and their 'fandom' of 'shock-rocker' Marilyn Manson.[59] Most strikingly, much was made of the fact that the pair had run a website espousing their pro-Hitler beliefs (much implication that these beliefs too were developed online), and which 'carried a chilling forewarning of the massacre... "Preparin' for the big April 20!! You'll all be sorry that day!"'.[60] The normally sedate *Evening Standard* editorial screamed:

> The... group also turned to the internet to spread its poison. This unique method of communication enables extremists to advertise, to recruit and to fuel the madness of others, and also to acquire easy access to information about means of inflicting destruction.[61]

This theme of the internet as source of the means of destruction was furthered by media reports following the trial of 24-year-old David Copeland in June 2000. A self-confessed neo-Nazi, Copeland carried out three nail bomb attacks in public areas of London during 1999, the first two targeting black and Asian communities, the third, which killed three and maimed another four, targeted London's gay community in Soho. Typical of reports of the case was that in *The Sun*, headed 'Soho Killer used the Internet to build his bombs – he downloaded his plans in cyber café'.[62]

---

[56] *Metro* (London edition), 12 January 2000.
[57] *Metro* (London edition), 7 August 2000.
[58] *Evening Standard*, 21 April 1999.
[59] See, for instance, 'Outcasts who were obsessed with Hitler', *Metro* (London edition), 22 April 1999.
[60] *Metro* (London edition), 22 April 1999.
[61] *Evening Standard*, 21 April 1999.
[62] *The Sun*, 6 June 2000.

Other lesser reports during 2000 made connections between the internet and, for instance, the 1999 murder of TV presenter Jill Dando.[63] While there clearly needs to be action taken where bomb-making instructions appear online, suggestions that Copeland carried out his attacks as a direct result of contact with the internet, or blaming the internet directly for the Dando murder, mirror directly the beliefs of the Victorian moral campaigners that the direct cause of juvenile crime was exposure to the trashy fiction of the penny dreadful: *Plus ça change, plus la même chose.*

The End of a Panic

The last stage of a moral panic, as identified above, is that it simply disappears: this may be because it simply fades out, because public interest has waned, or it may be that something else has emerged which has caught public fears, and a new moral panic has begun. Often it is a mixture of both. The penny dreadful panic of the Victorian age seems simply to have faded away as the popularity of the publications themselves waned, and publishers either ceased trading or altered tack.[64] Moral panic surrounding the internet quietened considerably, if not actually disappeared altogether, during 2001, however, the internet remains a hugely popular mass media for information and entertainment; it is a possibility that a single, horrific case could revive the same hysteria, much as the dormant panic over film violence of the mid 1980s 'video nasty' scare bubbled to the surface once more in the wake of the Bulger murder in the early 1990s. Some brief mentions of the internet were made in relation to the 11 September 2001 attacks in New York. However these failed to catch the public imagination. Perhaps a new panic will emerge – at the time of writing, mobile-phone muggings involving teenagers as both perpetrators and victims are receiving much coverage – whether this will provide a fresh moral panic, only time will tell.

---

[63] '"Stalker" used Net to trace Dando address', *Metro* (London edition) 19 January 2000.
[64] Springhall, *Youth*, pp. 94-7.

Chapter 11

Discourses of Denial and Moral Panics: The Pornographisation of the Child in Art, the Written Word, Film and Photograph

Susan Edwards

Introduction

This chapter explores the pornographisation of the child in art, the written word, film and photograph, considering those artistic representations which have been argued to inhabit the boundaries of art and pornography in the works of the nineteenth century photographers including Julia Margaret Cameron, Clementia Harwarden, and in the twentieth century, Tierney Gearon. In both eras, the dominant discourse, in contemporary culture and legal thought, denies and disavows the existence of child pornography preferring to interpret nude 'texts' at least as the artistic depiction of innocence or harmless child 'erotica' thus positioning the issue of child pornographisation in the wider context of the realisation of child sexual abuse and its representation. The role played by particular events, notably the nineteenth century trial of W. T. Stead and the twentieth century trial of Gary Glitter in igniting a social panic with much expressed moral outrage, became defining moments in shaping new interpretations in terms of the understandings of sexual abuses against children. The chapter examines the statutory and judicial discourse which in both periods has eschewed child pornography, culminating in an analysis of the way in which the most recent panic has resulted in increasing sentences for making and distributing child pornography.

A Discourse of Silence

Child pornography, in law (although not in fact), is a very recent phenomenon. If the knowledge of the battered child emerged in social work practice discourse in the 1960s and the realisation of child prostitution in the 1980s, then, child pornography emerged in the 1990s out of the discourse of feminism on the one hand and work with sex offenders on the other. Possibly the single most influential factor which imprinted the reality of child pornography in the public and legal mind was Gary Glitter's conviction. His celebrity status ensured the issue became a long-lasting headline story. Up until that defining moment governments had largely eschewed the problem of child pornography, regarding it as peripheral to child protection.

To the nineteenth century public mind, even the *idea* of child pornography was officially remote. Although children enjoyed no legal status or protection from physical abuse or exploitation, child pornography was nevertheless unthinkable as a reality. Victorian images of childhood were often contradictory, children being either extolled as virtuous or else portrayed as victims of poverty. In child portraiture, art or photograph, there was the child nude, but representing not the longings of paedophiles, or child pornographers, but metaphorised purity, innocence and grace, an ephemeral state before original sin.[1] Nude and semi-nude children in the photography of Julia Margaret Cameron and Clementine Hawarden were allegorically represented with the child becoming the iconoclastic projection of truth and beauty.[2] Winged children of both classical and angelic varieties were a recurrent feature in Cameron's representations of childhood.[3] Child nudes, however portrayed, were supposedly simply sublime representations of cherubism and sweet innocence.

Yet, there was a darker side of the representation of the child in these nineteenth century 'texts'. Child pornography and sexual abuse may have been hidden from history but were by no means absent from it. If child pornography in its grossest form was said not to exist, in its ambiguous form it was legitimated – by its potential for an acceptable alternate encoding or reading – as a projection of innocence. Even before the Victorian age, the eroticisation and pornographisation of the child was an acceptable feature in artistic representation, as for example in the 'golden age' of eroticism during the Renaissance and in Hogarth's works.

There is overwhelming evidence of Victorian child pornography in both painting and drawing. Thomas Rowlandson included in his collection

---

[1] R. Von Krafft-Ebing, *Psychopathia Sexualis* (Rebman, London, 1901) (1899, 10th German edn.), p. 522.

[2] A. Hopkinson, *Julia Margaret Cameron* (Virago, London, 1986).

[3] J. Howard, *Whisper of the Muse. The World of Julia Margaret Cameron* (Colnaghi, London, 1990). See in particular the following photographs: 'Annie'; 'Venus Chiding Cupid'; 'I Wait'

many works which could be described as pornographic, including 'Inquest of Matrons or Trial for Rape', showing an old woman examining a young girl, and a young girl being eyed by two men.[4] Wayland Young noted that 'Dirty old men figure a great deal, paying to peer up a whore gawping at a nude model'.[5] Other artists were preoccupied with child nudes. In 1847, J. T. Withe produced an album of erotic/pornographic photographs of children. George Cruikshank, and his father Isaac, were also renowned for producing pornographic drawings, many of children.[6] Graham Oveden has commented that Victorian postcards featured five times as many nude studies of children as of adults.[7] Of Philip Wilson Steer, Fraser Harrison noted 'He was by no means exceptional in his preoccupation with pubescent girls, but he did differ from his more morbid contemporaries... in portraying his nymphets in their gayest mood'.[8] Written child pornography was also rife, perhaps best epitomised by the anonymous *My Secret Life*. The author described sexual liaisons with both children and adult women:

> I passed a little girl dressed like a ballet girl, and looked at the girl who seemed about ten years old, then at the woman who winked. I stopped, she came up and said 'Is she not a nice little girl?' 'Yes, a nice little girl', I replied. 'Would you like to see her undressed?'.[9]

Real Child Sexual Abuse or Fantastic Inventions?

Efforts to expose the child pornography trade were strenuously resisted, although there was a growing awareness of the sexual abuse of children including prostitution and abuse within the family. Evidence in the *Chadwick Papers* 1838-40 described how girls were regularly seduced by their masters and turned out into the streets.[10] On 11 January 1868, the *Illustrated Police News* carried a story of a mill manager who had allegedly committed an outrage on a 12-year-old-girl. Such reports,

---

[4] Rowlandson's work is available in the British Museum.

[5] W. Young, *Eros Denied* (Corgi, London, 1969) p. 70.

[6] I. Bloch, *Sexual Life in England* (Corgi, London, 1965) p. 529.

[7] C. Townsend, 'A Picture of Innocence: attitudes about nude pictures of children', *History Today*, 1986 46, p. 5; p. 8; Young, *Eros Denied*, p. 95.

[8] F. Harrison, *The Dark Angel* (Fontana, London, 1977), p. 140. See, for example, Steer's 'A Summer's Evening'

[9] Cited, H. Montgomery Hyde, *A History of Pornography* (Four Square Books, London, 1966), p. 123. Recently, the noted collector of pornography, Henry Ashbee, has been identified as the anonymous author.

[10] S. Edwards, *Female Sexuality and the Law* (Martin Robertson, Oxford, 1981), p. 138.

though, were the commonplace fare of most newspapers.[11] It was not until 1884 that any real attempt was made to protect women and young girls from rape and seduction by masters and employers when, in the debate on the Criminal Law Amendment Bill, the Bishop of Lichfield said that no offence was more frequent. Yet, when the bill became law in 1885, the very clause intended to protect young women was considerably diluted in its effect. Section 7 stated that a guardian or master was to be charged with only misdemeanour or assault, and further that 'it shall be a defence to any charge under this section to show that such a girl had been unchaste previously to the time of the offence charged'.

The work of Tardieu, his successor in Paris, Paul Brouardel, and Paul Bernard all meticulously documented the problem of child physical and sexual abuse.[12] Tardieu's figures for 1858-1869 in France recorded 9,125 accusations of rape or attempted rape on children. In a paper published in 1860 he reported one case of child sexual abuse on a 17-year-old girl which had been committed over a period of years, including graphic medical reports of the abused and infected body which had been kept locked in a coffin, and subjected to horrifying abuse.[13] Such findings were, especially in Britain, eschewed in preference for denial or else condemnation of the child victim as liar, evil, or later in psychoanalysis, hysteric. Tardieu, recognising this ongoing conspiracy of silence wrote later 'This study, undertaken eighteen years ago, is the first to have been attempted on this subject, about which writers in the field of legal medicine have subsequently remained completely silent'.[14] However, the silence was not complete. Krafft-Ebing in *Psychopathia Sexualis* detailed extensively what he calls *'paedophilia erotica'*.[15] Freud before his 'U-Turn', had written,

> In some cases, no doubt, we are concerned with experiences, which must be regarded as severe traumas — an attempted rape... I therefore put forward the thesis that at the bottom of every case of hysteria there are one or more occurrences of premature sexual

---

[11] See Kim Stevenson, 'Ingenuities of the Female Mind: Legal and Public Perceptions of Sexual Violence in Victorian England 1850-1890' in Shani D'Cruze (ed.) *Everyday Violence in Britain c1850-1950: Class and Gender* (Longmans, London, 2000).

[12] J. Masson, *The Assault on Truth* (Faber and Faber, London, 1984), p. 199, highlighting Tardieu's most important contribution, his 1857 work *Etude medico-legale sur les attentats aux moeurs (A Medico-legal Study of Assaults on Decency)*. Tardieu's treatise on sexual assaults on children went through seven editions and one German edition and was much referred to by Krafft-Ebing.

[13] *Ibid*, p. 22.

[14] *Ibid*.

[15] Krafft-Ebing, *Psychopathia*, pp. 521-9.

experience, occurrences which belong to the earliest years of childhood.[16]

Such dangerous continental perspectives did not find ready hearers in Britain.

For the most part, children who were the objects of male desire or inappropriate sexual interest were portrayed not as victims but as the instigators of the 'seduction'. The prevailing trend was to evade the issue of the origins of abuse in real events. Many eminent members of the medical profession gave credence to the 'false allegation' hypothesis. Eminent Victorian medical men, including Drs. Flint, Smith, Dixon Mann, Norman and Tait, seemed united in their belief that child abuse was the invention of children. In 1886, Dr. Routh, addressing the British Gynecological Society, announced that women and young girls were 'the most decided liars in creation':

> One lady once confided to me a story that her own father, when she was a girl of 17, had taken her down to Brighton and there they had lived as man and wife. This of course I did not believe for an instant.... Another told me that her own brother had come into her bedroom at night and tried to ravish her, an equally untrue delusion. As medical jurists we should never forget the mendacity of these women.[17]

The 'eminent' gynaecologist, Lawson Tait, appointed as police surgeon to Birmingham City Police, similarly doubted that real events were at the basis of rape allegations. He wrote, for instance, of 'Two dirty little wretches of ten and twelve, who had been thrashed by their father for stealing, promptly turned round on him with a charge of having seduced them'.[18] Belief in the sexual voracity of young girls was well-established. In 1897, C. D. Colby, writing in the *Medical Record*, removed the clitoris of a six-year-old girl because of this:

> the parts had been kept thoroughly cleansed; she had been made to sleep in sheepskin pants and jacket made into one garment, with her hands tied to the footboard and, by a strap about her waist, she was fastened to the headboard, so that she couldn't slide down in bed and use her heels; she had been reasoned with, scolded, and whipped, and in spite of it all she managed to keep up the habit.[19]

---

[16] Cited Masson, *Assault*, pp. 261-3.

[17] Edwards, *Female Sexuality*, p. 138.

[18] *Ibid*, pp. 126, 128.

[19] *Medical Record*, 7 August 1897. See also S. Edwards, 'The medical control of female sexuality in the nineteenth century', *British Journal of Sexual Medicine*, 1981, January, pp. 46-9.

Such authorities concluded that if men had consorted with children, then, quite simply, it was the children who had corrupted them, not *vice versa*. As Deborah Gorham commented, opponents of the 'natural' innocence of all children

> insisted that the young girls who became prostitutes or who became sexually active at an early age belonged to a social class that could not possibly preserve the moral or the sexual innocence of its members. Therefore, any attempt to protect such girls was seen as futile and as leading to the entrapment of middle and upper class male youths, who were usually portrayed as more innocent than the girls they seduced or whose services they purchased.[20]

She added that 'the two familiar images of adult women, the angel-in-the-house and the fallen woman, have their counterparts in the opposing images of the child redeemer and the wayward evil girl'. While the 'child redeemer' (nearly always female) was a popular Victorian fictional trope is a familiar figure in Victorian fiction, it contrasted with a perspective where 'The child prostitute was seen at one moment as an innocent flower and at the next moment as irretrievably and dangerously corrupt'.[21] Such images of evil, wayward and hysterical children remained current even in the face of compelling evidence of their victimisation.

Moral Outrage – Moral Panics

The nineteenth century defining moment which contributed most to contemporary realisation of the extent and nature of sexual abuse of the children was undoubtedly the *Pall Mall Gazette*'s sensational series, 'The Maiden Tribute of Modern Babylon'. Stead's revelations provoked high levels of moral outrage which resulted in a re-reading of the evidence concerning the reality of child sexual abuse, child nudity and other representations of children. Detailing the extent of the social evil of child prostitution in London and on the Continent, Stead insisted that 'he only struck the match that fired a charged mine of enthusiasm'.[22] Ellice Hopkins the noted Victorian purity campaigner, wrote at length about the

---

[20] D. Gorham, '"The Maiden Tribute of Modern Babylon" Re-Examined. Child Prostitution and the Idea of Childhood in Late-Victorian England', *Victorian Studies*, 1978, Spring, p. 370.

[21] *Ibid*, pp. 370-2. One of the ugliest sexual superstitions of the period was the belief that if a man had venereal disease, he could be cured by having intercourse with a virgin – which has a curious echo in the current situation in parts of Africa, where, reportedly, virgin intercourse cures AIDS.

[22] *Pall Mall Gazette*, 4 July 1885, p. 1.

horrors of child prostitution, in what she called 'a ruthless exposure of a certain class of offences against young children'.[23]

The denial and disavowal of child pornography persisted into the twentieth century. While child sexual abuse was gradually recognised as an unfortunate social reality, child pornography remained a discrete and quite separate sphere of consideration, and those who were absorbed by it were considered harmless. Child pornography continued to be largely untrammelled by the law. When child pornographers were punished sentences were derisory, since as judges declared their preoccupation was no more than pedagogic fantasy. Any consideration of the contemporary discourse on child pornography prior to the conviction of Gary Glitter soon reveals its marginality and irrelevance to the discourse on child protection. Child pornography is marked by its absence and exclusion from any mainstream discourse. Little, if any, discussion is be found within criminal law texts with the exception of specialist books on sexual offences.[24] With rare exceptions, there are no publications on the problem to be found in the major UK law journals, and the issue has, by commission or omission, been displaced outside the major concerns of both family and criminal law.

Foucault has provided an analysis of the process of censure and the determination of what passes for 'knowledge'. The ecliption of child pornography can be explored using his construct of 'erasure', describing the processes and procedures by which competing perspectives are removed. Foucault asserted that 'in any society the production of discourse is at once controlled, selected, organised and redistributed according to a number of procedures'.[25] The silence of discourse, the absence of knowledge and informed debate in this area is responsible for the confusion in this area of law that has remained manifest in recent police investigations and overly-hasty revisions in sentencing practice. For example, sentences of imprisonment for the offence of possession have been increased to five years and 'making' and 'taking' indecent photographs etc., to ten years. Child pornography, as a former Solicitor General of the US concluded, is 'incendiary'.[26] The emerging discourse has been controlled, selected and

[23] E. Hopkins, 'The Apocalypse of Evil', *The Contemporary Review*, 1885, p. 334. See also F. Harrison, *The Dark Angel* (Fontana Collins, London, 1977), p. 226, surveying the Victorian evidence for child prostitution, and the brothels catering to paedophiles.

[24] P. Rook and R. Ward, *Rook and Ward on Sexual Offences* (Sweet and Maxwell, London, 1997).

[25] See Michel Foucault, *The Will to Truth* trans. A. Sheriden (Tavistock, London, 1981), p. 121.

[26] A. Adler, 'Inverting the First Amendment', *University of Pennsylvania Law Review*, 2001, 149, 4, p. 935.

organised largely by a judiciary whose 'world view' on the problem has forged fallacious distinctions between 'types' of child pornographers, giving authority to these misconceived stereotypes.

Contemporary Panics and Policing Perverse Desire

It is in the wake of such misunderstandings that social panic ensues, expressing itself through moral outrage, as in the aftermath of the arrest of Gary Glitter. On 13 November 2001, Glitter's trial for 'making' child pornography commenced. Overnight, government ministers and childrens' organisations flocked to give comment. Charged with 54 specimen offences, John Royce QC, described images in Glitter's possession including adult males ejaculating on children, children in bondage, children apparently being tortured and children being sexually abused, 'some not out of nappies'. Glitter pleaded guilty to 'making' indecent photographs following the Court of Appeal judgment in *R v Bowden* (Lord Justice Otton, Mrs. Justice Smith and Mr. Justice Collins).[27] This held that the downloading and/or the printing of computer data of indecent images of children from the internet was capable of amounting to an offence of 'making' contrary to Section 1 of the Protection of Children Act 1978. The Court ruled that the Act was not only concerned with the original creation of images, but also their proliferation, and that to download or print was to create new material which hitherto might not have existed. Following the *Bowden* ruling, Glitter pleaded guilty and was sentenced to four months imprisonment for downloading onto his personal computer in excess of 4,000 images of 'child pornography'.[28]

Public fury followed what was regarded as a derisory prison sentence. The court was, however, somewhat bound by the sentence handed down in *Bowden* where the Court of Appeal had quashed a four month prison sentence and substituted a conditional discharge for a similar offence. But moral outrage erupted and overnight, the paedophilic 'witch-hunt' and panic had embraced another constituency — that of the child pornographer. The result was that child pornography law emerged with unprecedented

---

[27] *Bowden* [2000] 2 All ER 418.

[28] In summing up, Mr. Justice Butterfield said to Glitter: 'You had over 4,000 images of children. The nature of the pornographic material in this case was in my judgment of the very, very worst possible type... The images are not simply of pre-pubescent children being sexually abused in every possible way. This would be bad enough. But they were of pre-pubescent children being tortured.... One image showed a little girl who was seven or eight years old with her legs tied together, gagged, with her hands tied behind her back, bearing the marks, real or artificial, of a savage beating. It was entitled "The Lover's Guide to Better Child Sexual Abuse"'

doctrinal expansion, characterised by a growth in child pornography prosecutions, together with a feverish and misconceived sentencing revision.[29] A new sentencing maximum of ten years has been imposed on the judiciary by the government in the absence of any proper consultation. Such draconian sentences may satisfy the public sense of moral outrage and disgust, but it is doubted whether there will be any significant shift in judicial attitude.

Child Nudity and Ambiguity

By the 1980s, while the vilest forms of child pornography were considered rare, there was a growing concern with regard to nude images of children. Indeed, such was the concern that all photographs of naked children became saturated in ambiguity or something much more sinister — sexual abuse and adult predatory paedophilic desire. This 'drift' of the law towards the prohibition of the depiction of child nudity is part of a legal expansionist trend fed by a growing fear and xenophobia, both in the US and in the UK. Ron Oliver was arrested in 1992 and had his portfolio containing photographs of nude children impounded. As part of that same police operation, Graham Ovenden's house was searched. In 2001, Jenni Blythe attracted a similar repressive zeal, when she refused to remove three photographs from the Saatchi Gallery in London, which the police had pronounced indecent under the Protection of Children Act 1978. Two of the photographs were taken by the photographer Tierney Gearon, one showing Gearon's children standing on a golden beach clad only in masks. In the US, photographs taken by artists like Sally Mann, Alice Sims and Jock Sturges have similarly straddled the boundaries of what is currently considered the threshold of child pornography. Sally Mann's 'Venus after School' (a composition depicting a naked child in a position of Manet's portrait of a prostitute) and the composition 'Popsicle Drips' (of a boy's naked torso) both resulted in police investigation.[30]

During the last decade or so, parents have found themselves being policed as part of this ascription of pornography to, and encoding of, the canon of family photographs, with paedophilic intention being identified in what had hitherto been identified as 'harmless' pictures. In 1989, Lawrence Chard was charged after taking photographs of his family swimming naked. The jury subsequently acquitted him. In 1995, Julia Somerville and her partner were questioned after a photographic

---

[29] Adler, 'Inverting', p. 933.

[30] See also the photography of Alice Sims, David Hamilton and Jock Sturges in the US.

processing assistant told police that a film left for processing contained 28 photographs of Somerville's seven-year-old girl in the bath. After four weeks the Crown Prosecution Service discontinued proceedings.[31] When 'naked' means 'indecent' and when family photographs depicting nudity amounts to 'child pornography', the question arises – are police overreacting? Or is there a real problem in the comfortable presumption that a nude photograph of a child taken or possessed by a family member renders the taker and the photograph benign?

Similar concerns of where to draw the line have dominated discussion on whether the film industry is exploiting children. Films, such as 'Taxi Driver', with the characterisation of the 13-year-old child prostitute played by Jodie Foster, and the 1998 film production of 'Lolita', have caused considerable consternation, both here and in Australia. Both the British and the Australian Boards of Film Classification sought advice with regard to whether 'Lolita', for instance, was pornographic or not in reaching a decision to certificate.[32] Thomas Mann's 'Death in Venice', filmed with the highly-respected Dirk Bogarde in the title role, claimed to represent the purest form of the love of a man for a young boy. However, it seems to the twenty-first century mind merely a legitimation of paedophilic desire.

The Legal Response to Child Pornography

In the nineteenth century there was no separate law to regulate child pornography, as Tom Lewis discusses in his chapter. Like adult pornography, child pornography was prosecuted under the obscenity laws.[33] By 1857, the Obscene Publications Act was in force. In 1868, in the celebrated case of *R v Hicklin*, the test of obscenity was established as that which depraved and corrupted the minds into whose hands such a publication falls.[34] On 31 March 1874, the police raided the studio of Henry Hayler confiscating 130,248 obscene photographs and 5,000 plates, the worst of which represented Hayler with his wife and two sons. Hayler is reported to have left the country to evade prosecution.[35] It was not until

---

[31] *The Guardian*, 13 January 1996.

[32] S. Edwards, 'Why Lolita should be Banned', *The Age*, 25 February 1999.

[33] See also for a discussion on adult pornography P. Wagner, 'The pornographer in the courtroom: trial reports about cases of sexual crimes and delinquencies as a genre of eighteenth-century erotica' in P. Bouce (ed.), *Sexuality in Eighteenth-century Britain* (Manchester University Press, Manchester, 1982).

[34] G. Robertson, *Freedom, the Individual and the Law* (Penguin, London, 1989). See also chapters by Tom Lewis and Gavin Sutter in this volume.

[35] See Bloch, *Sexual Life*, p. 538.

a century later in the 1970s that the growing social evil of child pornography was specifically provided for in statute. Until section 1(1) Protection of Children Act 1978 (as amended by sections 84(1) and (2) Criminal Justice and Public Order Act 1994) the making, taking or distribution of child pornography was not a specific offence.

Triable either way, and following the Criminal Justice and Courts Sentencing Act 2000, this offence, of taking, permitting to be taken or making an indecent photograph or pseudo-photograph of a child, including publication, distribution and possession with a view to being distributed, carries a maximum sentence of ten years imprisonment. Indecency was not defined in statute, although the Court of Appeal held that it is whatever right-thinking people understand the term to mean 'by applying the recognised standards of propriety'.[36] The exclusive concern of the criminal law in Britain and North America is with film and photograph. The image itself must be indecent, and creation, possession and distribution of the indecent image comprise the offences under the criminal law. 'Making' in *Bowden* has been extended to include downloading from the internet or computer, an interesting amplification of points raised in Gavin Sutter's chapter.[37] 'Taking' means the physical taking of the picture. The Criminal Justice Act 1988 section 160 (CJA) sought to strengthen and extend the law regulating child pornography creating an offence of 'possession'. Originally a summary only offence, the offence is now triable either way and under the Criminal Justice and Courts Sentencing Act 2000, a maximum sentence of six months has now been extended to a term of imprisonment not exceeding five years or a fine, or both.

The law is restricted to child pornography in a 'photograph', a definition which has been expanded as new technologies have developed. Photograph means positive or negative, pseudo-photographs, or manipulated photographs and encrypted data 'stored on a computer disc capable of conversion into a photograph'.[38] Given that manipulated images now comprise child pornography, the definition of child has also been extended. 'Child' no longer means 'a person under the age of 16', and liability is provided 'where the predominant impression conveyed is that the person

---

[36] See *Drew* [1999] Crim LR 581; *Caley* [1999] 2 Cr App R (S) 154; *Archer* [1999] 2 Cr App R (S) 92; *Grigg* [1999] 1 Cr App R (S) 443, *R v Mould* Court of Appeal, Criminal Division, Transcript: Smith Bernal 6 November 2000; *Graham-Kerr* [1988] 1 WLR 1098.

[37] [2000] 2 All ER 418. Followed in *Hopkinson* where police officers executed a warrant issued under the Protection of Children Act 1978 at the appellant's home in Scarborough and seized a quantity of images of males in indecent poses, which had been received via the internet and by e-mail.

[38] Section 84(7) CJPOA following *R v Fellows and Arnold* [1997] 2 All ER 549.

shown is a child notwithstanding that some of the physical characteristics shown are those of an adult'. Whether a photograph is 'indecent' is wholly a matter for the jury and such a finding of fact must be derived from the photograph alone. In a lengthy summing up, in the only contested case in a study conducted in 2000 by the author, the judge said:

> You've been told correctly by counsel that the test of indecency according to previously considered cases is whether or not a picture in this instance offends against recognised standards of propriety. It means this, and mark these words: are you sure that there is indecency to be found in the film or video that you have watched?[39]

This is considered, by some, to be an obvious limitation of the Act, since a photograph which a jury may not consider inherently indecent may have been taken in indecent circumstances or for a wholly indecent motive. Unlike the OPA which criminalises any article, indeed anything at all which is considered likely to 'deprave and corrupt', the law regulating child pornography is restricted to photograph or film. Excluded from the law's domain are other representations. The written word, cartoon comic strips of the abuse of children, sculptures, paintings are all beyond the arm of the law, however graphic or gratuitous.[40] Child pornography 'literature' remains an untrammelled and protected discourse under current law.

Confusion in Law – Criminalising the Product, the Conduct or the Desire

The problem with the legal response to child pornography is that it lacks coherence and the object of the legislation is somewhat muddled. The law claims to police indecent representation, a position which (as both Lewis and Sutter also comment) is ambiguous and uncertain enough. However, the prosecution of those who secretly film photographs of children which under other circumstances would fail the indecent threshold suggest that the application of the law is concerned with regulating potential predatory conduct, regardless of the photographic product of the predators' accomplishment. At the same time, the law claims not to be interested in circumstances or more specifically secret motive, quashing a conviction where that secret motive had been admitted in evidence. Yet if motive is irrelevant in arriving at a definition of 'indecent', it is hugely significant in decisions to prosecute.

---

[39] S. Edwards, 2000, Case No. 27.
[40] S. Edwards, 'A Plea for Censorship', *New Law Journal*, 1 November 1991.

There is also the issue of the defence of 'legitimate reason'. Under section 1(4) Protection of Children Act 1978 this operates where an accused can prove that he had a legitimate reason for distributing or showing photographs, such as police photography and clinical psychiatry. Examples of what might constitute 'legitimate reason' were provided during the debate on the Protection of Children Bill 1977.[41] Unfortunately, legitimate reason defence betrays a fundamental misunderstanding of persons likely to be involved in child pornography, potentially protecting the guilty parent.[42] After all, child sexual abuse in the majority of cases is perpetrated by those adults with legitimate access to children.[43] The list is comprehensive, from family members, via teachers and priests to doctors.[44] Considerable misgivings were expressed in 1977 that a 'legitimate reason' defence could be so couched as to undermine the intention of the Bill, but no solution was found.[45]

In short, the law regulating child pornography is contradictory, ambiguous and confused. It allows so-called 'literature' to go unchallenged. It leaves unresolved the issue of the image which, under certain circumstances might be either deemed indecent because taken by a paedophile, or not indecent because taken by a parent, or under suspicion because exhibited in an art gallery. This has coloured prosecutorial and sentencing practice. Criticism of the derisory sentencing of child pornographers has also contributed to the high levels of moral outrage necessary to such panic. Judges passing sentence in cases involving child pornography have all too frequently misunderstood the child pornographer. Lord Lane, when reducing Oliver Brooke's one year sentence to six months, said of this paediatrician collector and distributor, who had amassed a huge collection of child pornography:

> The circumstances of the case are truly extraordinary... because the appellant is a man of the highest reputation in the medical world as a Consultant Paediatrician... An investigation carried out by the police... revealed that in his professional office was contained a large quantity of pornographic indecent photographs of young girls. It emerged that for reasons which it is hard to gauge this man over the years had amassed a huge and minutely documented and indexed

---

[41] *Hansard*, Lords, 1977, 392, cols 539-55.

[42] See *R v J* [1997] Crim LR 297.

[43] See J. Renvoize, *Incest* (Routledge, London, 1985); S. Edwards, *Sex and Gender in the Legal Process*, Blackstone Press, London, 1996).

[44] Reuters North European Service, 19 December 1986; T. Tate, *Child Pornography* (Methuen, London, 1990), p. 249.

[45] *Hansard*, Lords, 1977, 392, cols 539; 547.

collection of this type of photograph. The distribution was on a very limited scale. It is not inappropriate, perhaps, in view of the puerility of this type of behaviour, to compare it rather to a schoolboy collecting cigarette cards in olden times, because the duplicates were handed to other adults – three or four of them only – who were likewise minded to indulge in this sort of puerility.[46]

Reinforcing this, consider the position of Justice Owen in *Fellows and Arnold*, a case involving about 11,650 pictures stored in numerous computer sub-directories and where one of the sub-directories was entitled 'Young/Minors', and contained 1,875 pictures of children engaged in various sexual acts or poses. In passing a two year sentence on the first defendant, for possessing indecent photographs of a child (upheld on appeal), and six months on the second for distributing indecent photographs of a child, Owen accepted the defence submission that 'neither of them was a danger to children in the future'.[47] Again, Justice Owen, in a case involving a schoolmaster, commented:

> We have been provided with photographs of that which was recovered, and certainly some of them show children in a sexual and seductive manner. But the charges were based on five magazines, all of them showing photographs and naked children. They did not show any sexual activity. They did not include adults. Some of the photographs were posed and some were not. Indeed some of them were wholly innocent, merely being photographs of a pretty young child. Some of the photographs were accompanied by a text, which could be said to be indecent in a pathetic sort of way... there was no corruption, and it is hard to see how the photographs which we have seen could, of themselves, have led to corruption.[48]

Even where judges regard the offence of some seriousness, they have nevertheless frequently continued to take the view that pornographers are men who merely fantasise.

In another case, the judge described the defendant as no more than a pathetic man: 'in this particular case there is an element of the pathetic as well; an adult looking at five indecent pictures of children, briefly obtaining some lonely sexual gratification from them and now facing a very bleak future'.[49] The work of Sykes and Matza, and later Taylor, has amply demonstrated the way in which defendants neutralise their normative attachment to the principles of the criminal laws. Judges in

---

[46] Tate, *Child Pornography*, p. 249.

[47] *Ibid.*

[48] *Holt* (1995) 16 Cr App R (S) 510.

[49] *Owens* [2001] EWCA Crim 1370.

giving their reasons for sentence similarly engage in such neutralisation narratives.[50] The presentation of such men is that they are not dangerous, but pathetic; not likely to commit sexual abuse but merely fantasise. Judicial understanding or misunderstanding of the child pornographer has led in the past to derisory sentencing practices and to the forging of artificial distinctions between types of defendants.[51]

Conclusion

The parallels between nineteenth and twentieth century denial of child pornography in visual and written texts are striking. The gross sexual abuse of children, which is fuelled by and in return fuels child pornography, continues whilst art and literature continue to claim a higher, deeper and more intellectual moral ground and objective when dealing with childhood nudity and or sexuality. Krafft-Ebing referred to child abuse and pornography as perversions. To the twentieth and twenty-first century mind, the power of film, media and mass communication to sell the unthinkable and dress it up as the acceptable is hegemonic.

True the child now has *locus standi* and legal rights, unlike her nineteenth century counterparts, and the family and the state have legal as well as moral duties to protect children. Yet rights in the abstract have become the contemporary force to be reckoned with, where the right to freedom of speech (which includes pornography), and the right to privacy (which includes possession of child pornography), wage war against the right of the child to be protected. In Britain, the Human Rights Act 1998, which embraces freedom of speech, is pitted against the United Nations Convention on the Rights of the Child, which includes the right to be free from exploitation in pornography. This war will wage on in a society of relative values where there are no longer absolutes. Many of us will remain incandescent that the right of children to be free from the harm of child pornography is still not absolute.

---

[50] G. Sykes and D. Matza, 'Techniques of Neutralisation', *American Sociological Review*, 1957, XX pp. 664-70; L. Taylor, 'The Significance and Interpretation of Replies to Motivational Questions: the case of Sex Offenders', *Sociology*, 1972, 6, pp. 23-39.

[51] *R v Dash* (1994) 15 Cr App R (S) 76, nine-month upheld. *R v McGuigan* [1996] 2 Cr App R (S) 253. The defendant pleaded guilty to six counts of possessing indecent photographs of a child with intent to distribute. On appeal, a sentence of 18 months was reduced to 12 months. Reid, a research scientist in Glasgow stored 1,871 pictures of child pornography on his computer for possession and was given a three month prison sentence, *Times Higher Education Supplement*, 17 October 1997, p. 60.

Chapter 12

Why Can't a Woman Be More Like a Man? Attitudes to Husband-Murder 1889-1989[1]

Judith Knelman

In the nineteenth century and into the twentieth, wife-murder was taken less seriously than any other kind of murder in the English justice system. Indeed, wife-murder was so prevalent as to be regarded as 'normal', possibly because it was accepted by both sexes that women were in the power of men. Husband-murder, by the same token, was considered monstrous, second in degree only to treason. Well into the nineteenth century the charge of petty treason was still on the statute book, and women convicted of husband-murder were still being dragged to the scaffold in a hurdle.

The justice system, established and largely maintained by men for men, accepts that murder can be the unintended result of a fit of ungovernable passion and tends to make allowances for such losses of control – in men. Women, weaker and calmer than men, are much less likely to kill their spouses without premeditation. As the 1889 case of Florence Maybrick shows, Victorian law did not even give the same leeway to wives accused of having murdered their husbands as it did to husbands accused of having murdered their wives. Recently, though, there has been a tendency in this country to accept mitigation in examples of husband-murder by victims of domestic abuse. The high-profile appeals in the 1990s of Kiranjit Ahluwalia, Sara Thornton and Emma Humphreys suggest that the English justice system now recognises, at least in the abstract, that husband-murder should not be punished more severely than wife-murder. However, it is still more comfortable for the system to accept weak-mindedness rather than

[1] The research for this chapter was funded by a grant from the Social Sciences and Humanities Council of Canada, to whom I am grateful.

provocation as an excuse for husband-murder. The accepted pattern has
been that wives provoke and husbands react.

Abused Wives and Accused Wives

In the latter half of the nineteenth century and into the twentieth, women
accused of husband-murder aroused spirited indignation in court and in the
press, particularly if they stepped outside their gender stereotypes. Cases
of wife-murder, by contrast, were greeted with complacency. Every so
often the more liberal newspapers would point to a cluster of cases that
suggested that men who killed their wives were under-punished. Harriet
Taylor and John Stuart Mill demanded: 'Is it because juries are composed
of husbands in a low rank of life, that men who kill their wives almost
invariably escape – wives who kill their husbands, never?'[2]

In 1846, the *Daily News* drew attention to 'the recently-introduced, but
very prevalent practice of wife-killing', which juries tended to dismiss as
justifiable homicide or manslaughter in order to spare the perpetrator the
noose.[3] A few days later, the *Examiner* observed, 'It seems to be
considered one of the marital rights to kick and beat a wife to death, or to
break her neck by flinging her down stairs, without incurring the capital
penalty'.[4] The following year, *The Times* remarked on the peculiar
disparity of two sentences, transportation and ten years for the theft of half
a guinea from a letter and nine months hard labour for wife-murder.[5] In
1851, Taylor and Mill were prompted to write a leading article for the
Morning Chronicle by a comment in a judge's charge to the jury that
though there were no murder cases to be heard there were several cases of
manslaughter and many more of personal violence committed by men
upon their wives. They pointed out that many women were being subjected
to 'prolonged death' at the hands of husbands 'who have enough of caution
just to stop short of the point which terminates the existence of their
victims'.[6]

In 1869 *The Times* remarked on the incongruity of sentences handed out
to three different men by the same judge (Justice Mellor) on the same day
in August: five years for wife-murder, 18 months for a botched attempt at
wife-murder; and 15 years for a beating given with clenched fists to a

---

[2] *Morning Chronicle*, 29 March 1850, p. 4.
[3] *Daily News*, 24 August 1846, p. 3.
[4] *Examiner*, 29 August 1846, p. 547.
[5] *The Times*, 5 February 1847, p. 5.
[6] *Morning Chronicle*, 28 August 1851, p. 4.

neighbour who had earlier given evidence in court against the perpetrator. The successful wife-murderer had, in an unprovoked drunken rage, pushed his wife downstairs and expressed satisfaction when told she was dying. The wife in the second case had escaped death only because her husband had been too drunk to properly sharpen the knife with which he tried to cut her throat after hitting her on the head. But it was the attack by the angry neighbour that the judge singled out as a brutal and atrocious outrage. 'Really we have no wish to be unfair', said *The Times*,

> but it would almost seem a justifiable inference that murdering or half-murdering a wife is in judicial eyes less 'brutal and atrocious' than in the eyes of ordinary men because it has no novelty about it. If Justice Mellor had never before tried such cases as the first two we have described, he might possibly have thought them deserving of as severe a sentence as that which he passed upon the third. But murderous assaults upon wives are so common that he has probably tried scores of them, and unconsciously growing callous, has come gradually to look upon them as everyday events.[7]

It is important to recognise that this sympathy for *abused* wives did not extend to sympathy for *accused* wives. It was one thing to speak up for a powerless victim but quite another to defend a woman who might have murdered her husband. A wife who behaved immodestly, even if it could not be proved that she was guilty of murder, was a threat to all men.

After a reprieve was announced for Fanny Oliver, convicted on highly circumstantial evidence of having poisoned her husband, *The Times* reprinted, on the same day as it criticised Justice Mellor, a misogynistic editorial from the *Medical Times and Gazette* cautioning that she should not be freed. 'A married woman who dictates love-letters to a former lover, purchases arsenic, giving the lover's as her own name, who nurses her husband through an illness, and in whose husband's body arsenic is found after death', said the article authoritatively, 'cannot be surprised if society considers her a dangerous person, and disposes of her accordingly'.[8] By its decision to reprint this extract from a 'professional' source, *The Times* presumably agreed with its perspective. Fanny Oliver, frail and unbalanced to begin with, grew physically and mentally weaker in prison until she was finally released on medical grounds in 1886.

By the 1870s, the law was still harder on wife-killers than it had been. Even men who murdered in a fit of misguided passion while drunk were routinely executed – unless it could be established that they had been

---

[7] *The Times*, 6 August 1869, p. 7.
[8] *Ibid*, p. 10.

legitimately provoked by their wives' bad behaviour. In 1873, William Lace, who had bashed his wife against a dresser, chased her out of the house and then kicked her to death, all because some of his drinking mates had mischievously suggested that she had been unfaithful to him, was tried before Justice Mellor. He was found guilty of murder and hung.[9] Michael Kennedy was hung at the end of December 1871 for shooting his wife in the head when she refused him a kiss because he was drunk, and in early January 1872 Edward Hancock, a butcher, was hung after he stabbed his wife to death for imagined infidelities.[10] Still, there were notable exceptions favouring men who had killed their wives. In July 1871 Justice Mellor found Matthew Cook, who had, in a state of *delirium tremens*, cut his wife's throat over an imagined infidelity, not guilty by reason of insanity.[11] In another courtroom in the same session, George Ellis, whose wife came tumbling onto the pavement after a neighbour heard her call out, 'Oh, George, don't put me through the window', was found guilty and sentenced to death but later reprieved because no one witnessed the crime.[12]

Following the trend set in the 1870s, there were several cases of wife-murder tried in the 1880s in which decent men who had been provoked by profligate spouses were respited and released after ten or 15 years. The Matrimonial Causes Act 1857 had made secular divorce possible for a husband who could prove his wife's adultery, but this was an expensive option that was not realistically open to the lower classes, and perhaps the justice system recognised this difficulty. Alfred Moon, who strangled his wife in 1881 after she taunted him about another man with whom she had taken up, was released on licence in 1891. Henry John Billing shot his wife in 1884 after she spent their rent money and pawned the furniture; he was released on licence in 1894. Robert Plampton stabbed his wife, who had pawned the blankets off their bed, while both were drunk; and though he was found guilty of murder the jury recommended mercy and he was subsequently respited. Imprisoned in 1884, he was released on licence in 1896. James Ash, a sailor, was found guilty of having stabbed his wife to death in 1881 for having taken up her old habit of prostitution. But he was respited because the jury recommended mercy, and later released on licence in 1896. A Home Office clerk noted on Ash's file, '15 years in

---

[9] *The Times*, 11 August 1873, p. 11; 28 August 1873, p. 11.

[10] *The Times*, 12 December 1871, p. 10; *The Times*, 8 January 1872, p. 10.

[11] *The Times*, 31 July 1871, p. 11.

[12] *The Times*, 31 July 1871, p. 11; 9 August 1871, p. 7.

prison seems quite enough for this offence. There is no reason to disbelieve his account of the provocation he received'.[13]

The Case of Florence Maybrick

By the 1880s, middle-class morality was being tested by divorce court journalism, which made it obvious that not all wives were happy, or even faithful. Indeed, once the newspapers began covering divorce cases, there was a general fear in England, argues Barbara Leckie, 'that women's sexuality could not be controlled and that women's sexual transgression would not be adequately punished'.[14] The perceived extreme deviance of Florence Maybrick, an admitted adulteress whose husband had died in suspicious circumstances, stoked that fear, and the justice system was used to send a message to all discontented wives. From the outside, the Maybrick marriage seemed like any other. But it was a shell. James was supporting another woman, one with whom he had lived in common law and who had borne him five children before he married Florence. Florence was an American whom he had wed in 1881 for her money. When she discovered his infidelity, Florence apparently felt free to loosen her own bonds. As a consequence, on at least one occasion, James beat her up and threw her out. She wrote him a cringing letter and they were reconciled. Not long afterward he became ill and died in May 1889.

The Maybrick case had all the elements of a sensation novel and was presented as such in the press. What made it especially gripping was the utter unexpectedness of the accused perpetrator, with her fragile good looks and demure Southern accent. Their house in Liverpool was filled with lurking servants and relatives who later testified about what they described as Florence's 'suspicious' behaviour. The story proved to be one of the most sensational of the nineteenth century, stirring up fears and myths about female poisoners, passive-aggressive wives and liberated women. By this time, it was not out of the question that a sane and privileged woman could be a criminal. More and more ordinary middle-class women were engaged in volunteer or paid work outside the home and were therefore visible in the wider world. Furthermore, in agitating for better treatment of criminal women and prostitutes, feminists, by emphasising their sisterhood with this class, had blurred the line that had up to then more or less protected women of their own class against

---

[13] PRO/HO144/84/A7101.

[14] Barbara Leckie, *Culture and Adultery: The Novel, the Newspaper, and the Law 1857-1914* (University of Pennsylvania Press, Philadelphia, 1999), p. 77.

accusations of criminality. This effect, coupled with the growing conviction that women's emancipation was increasing the rate of female crime in the late nineteenth century, undermined the position of Florence Maybrick in 1889.[15]

There were more than a dozen articles about Florence in *The Times* in the two and a half months between her husband's death and her trial. At first it looked as though she was guilty. The inquest, on 5 and 6 June 1889, brought in a verdict of wilful murder against her. On 8 June the *Illustrated Police News* filled three-quarters of its broadsheet front page with a collection of sketches depicting her arguing with her husband, soaking arsenic out of flypapers (an action which she said she did for her complexion), tampering with his medicine, and coaxing him to swallow a preparation that would make him sick. At the end of the first day of the police court hearing before the magistrate, held on 13 June, she was loudly hissed by a number of women.[16] The next day the case was remanded for trial. During her trial, she insisted on making a statement in court acknowledging her adultery, which prompted the judge, the misogynistic Sir James Fitzjames Stephen, to point out to the jury that this established her motive. She maintained that any arsenic she had given her husband was on his instructions, for his regular medicinal purposes. By the end of the trial she had gained the sympathy of the public. In a backlash against his hostility to her the judge was hissed in the street, while the prisoner he had just condemned was cheered on her way back to jail.

Unfortunately for her, the question of whether Florence Maybrick had deliberately poisoned her husband somehow got lost in the larger issue of how far wives could be trusted. Her directness had set people against her who saw her as having corrupted the Victorian domestic ideal. At one level the trial was a battleground between the supporters of established gender roles and the challengers. People sympathetic to her flocked to rallies and meetings and collected signatures on petitions pressing for a reprieve. But there was a strong conservative element that did not flinch at the idea of hanging her. After the trial the Home Office reviewed 'pressing' newspaper cuttings from medical and scientific journals and newspapers and petitions from medical men, many of whom argued that James Maybrick's death was due to natural causes.[17] At the eleventh hour a reprieve was announced because there was some doubt that arsenic had

[15] For a discussion of connections between women's politics and attitudes to female criminality at the end of the nineteenth century, see Lucia Zedner, *Women, Crime, and Custody in Victorian England* (Clarendon Press, Oxford, 1991), pp. 68-76.

[16] H. B. Irving, 'Mrs. Florence Maybrick', *Famous Trials III*, James H. Hodge (ed.), (Penguin, London, 1950), p. 108.

[17] PRO/HO144/539/A50678F.

caused the death even if she *had* given it to him. Not everyone was relieved: Queen Victoria sent a note to the Home Secretary regretting 'that so wicked a woman should escape by a mere legal quibble' and expressing the wish that Maybrick's sentence should never be further commuted.[18]

For 15 years, Maybrick fought to get out of prison while five successive Home Secretaries (Henry Matthews, H. H. Asquith, Sir Matthew White Ridley, C. T. Ritchie, and A. Akers-Douglas) fended off consistent and high-level appeals for her release. Just as consistently, the Home Office insisted, without specifying exactly how it had reached this conclusion, that since the trial her guilt had been proved beyond doubt. Once the possibility of hanging her was removed, the Home Office seems to have embarked on a determined campaign to keep her in prison. There was never any proof provided at the time of these replies to its critics and the unsealed files have not since then yielded any. It was hard to see why, if there had *not* been a murder, Mrs. Maybrick could legitimately be punished for it; nor how she could be imprisoned for attempted murder when she had not been tried for that crime. Implicit in the memoranda on the case is the argument that she deserved to be punished for giving her husband poison even if it could not be proven that poisoning was the cause of death. The Home Office seems not to have paid much attention to the other, less easily pinned-down problem, which was the error of the judge in putting together some clues for the jury that did not necessarily add up. Roger Chadwick, in a modern analysis of the case, concludes that if the judge had not interfered 'to supply motive and coherence to an otherwise shaky and circumstantial case' the jury would probably have acquitted her.[19]

In 1900, in response to yet another application of pressure for the release of their countrywoman by the American government, Charles Murdoch, Assistant Undersecretary at the Home Office, noted in an internal memorandum that

> three S.S. [Secretaries of State] who have specifically examined the facts of the case believe in the prisoner's guilt – and if guilty, her crime is of the first magnitude, viz. in having endeavoured to poison

---

[18] Victoria to Sir Henry Ponsonby, Memo, 22 August 1889. Cited G. E. Buckle (ed.), *The Letters of Queen Victoria, Third Series: A Selection from Her Majesty's Correspondence and Journals between the Years 1886 and 1901* (John Murray, London, 1930), pp. 527-8. The legal quibble, spelled out in the Home Secretary's announcement in the House of Commons, was that although she had administered poison to her husband with intent to murder there was reasonable doubt whether the arsenic was the cause of his death.

[19] Roger Chadwick, *Bureaucratic Mercy: The Home Office and the Treatment of Capital Cases in Victorian Britain* (Garland, New York, 1992), pp. 306-7.

her husband by slow and painful degrees in order to escape from the ties of marriage and associate with a lover with whom she had committed adultery.[20]

Of course, these three Secretaries of State had been taking the advice of senior civil servants, chief among them Murdoch, who was Principal Clerk of the Criminal Department at the Home Office from 1884 until his promotion in 1896, when he was succeeded by H. B. Simpson. The initials of these men appear on many of the minutes in the Maybrick files. Were they acting on Queen Victoria's instructions? A few months after her death in 1901, the Home Office decided to release Mrs. Maybrick on licence.[21] This would not be until 1904, after the standard 20 years minus five years for good behaviour. In other words, she was treated like any other convicted murderess. A pardon was out of the question.

Less than six months before the Maybrick trial, William Rigg was convicted at Durham of the murder of his wife. At the time of the murder he had just emerged from two months in prison for an assault on her. He expressed his anger at her for having turned him in earlier by punching her, cutting her throat, and then bludgeoning her. Unlike the Maybrick case, this one was obvious. The judge remarked just before sentencing him to death that he had never heard of 'a more clearly proved case of murder and a more brutal case of murder'.[22] Rigg was then examined in case there were grounds for a reprieve but was found to be healthy and sane. On hearing this, the Home Secretary nevertheless commuted his sentence to life imprisonment on the assumption that 'when he murdered his wife he was not responsible for his actions'.[23] Rigg was released on licence in 1909, after serving 20 years, five years more than Maybrick.[24]

Murder or Manslaughter?

This sort of bias did not die with Queen Victoria. Indeed, Victorian attitudes carried over into the inter-war period and were compounded by the accumulation of evidence in 1914-18 that women were as capable as men in the socio-economic sphere. The execution in 1923 of Edith Thompson and Frederick Bywaters for the murder of her husband brought out again society's worst fears about the havoc that could ensue if women

---

[20] PRO/HO144/1638/A50678/709.

[21] *Ibid.*

[22] *Newcastle Daily Chronicle*, 1 March 1889.

[23] PRO/HO144/539/A49944/12.

[24] PRO/HO144/539/A49944/32.

were as free as men were to give in to sexual temptation. Thompson's bold and blatant sexuality inspired a general fear that too much modernity would unravel the fabric of society. Her counsel, Sir Henry Curtis-Bennett, said flatly: 'They hung her for her immorality'.[25] The head of the English penal system from 1865 to 1898, C. G. L. Du Cann, believed that

> the disgust of the trial Judge, Justice [Montague] Shearman, for marital infidelity and his unimaginative, literal mind hung this unhappy creature. Strongly prejudiced as he was against immorality, he over-emphasised and over-simplified this aspect of the case, instead of warning the jury against letting mere indignation prejudice them.[26]

The beginning of women's suffrage in 1918 and the Sex Disqualification Removal Act 1919 had brought women close to nominal legal parity with men, but they were still expected to be passive, compliant, and emotionally fragile.

Two other women found guilty in murder trials presided over in the same December 1922 session by Justice Shearman were sentenced to death, but with a recommendation to mercy and almost immediately reprieved: Daisy Wright, a penniless charwoman who had thrown her two-year-old daughter off a bridge, and Ellen Jones, who had stabbed the other woman in her husband's life. Both women were perceived as down-trodden, depressed and highly emotional. They had acted in a way that men, prone to be carried away by strong passions, could understand. Thompson, on the other hand, had wallowed in her immorality and taken pleasure in imagining ways of getting rid of her husband. Notwithstanding the certainty of her contemporaries that Thompson got the punishment that she deserved, there has been some doubt in the years since that she should have been convicted at all and general agreement that she should not have been hung. Eight women were hung in England after Thompson, the last one, Ruth Ellis, being the most controversial. Ellis had endured physical and mental abuse from her partner, who drank heavily, but she was by no means a stereotypical victim. Shortly after he beat her up, causing her to have a miscarriage, she thought she caught him being unfaithful and shot him. In 1955, when her case was tried, the judge refused to entertain her counsel's submission that the murder charge be reduced to manslaughter by provocation, and she was executed. Later the Homicide Act 1957

---

[25] Quoted by Lewis Broad, *Sunday Dispatch*, 30 November 1952, p. 4.

[26] C. G. L. Du Cann, *Miscarriage of Justice* (London: Frederick Muller, 1960), p. 206; cited Jean Graham Hall and Gordon D. Smith, *R v Bywaters and Thompson* (Barry Rose Law Publishers, Chichester, 1997).

extended the scope of provocation, and recently judges have allowed a blurring of the line between extended provocation and diminished responsibility. Ruth Ellis might have been found guilty only of manslaughter today, as her sister recognised in a recent effort to get her conviction overturned.

From the mid-1970s, the press began remarking on cases in which husband-killers in England were allowed to plead manslaughter and were let off lightly. In the 1990s, three appeals by women jailed for spousal murder in the late 1980s brought out public opinion on the issue of whether this was justice or expediency. Feminists had been arguing that women accused of the murder of their partners had a harder time than men did in getting the charge reduced to manslaughter. Men who killed nagging wives were being let off lightly on grounds of provocation or diminished responsibility while women who killed brutal husbands were being denied these grounds. Today the justice system will consider that domestic abuse can be cumulative, and that a response that appears unreasonable or out of proportion may be a desperate woman's way of coming to terms with a chronically threatening situation. The Homicide Act 1957 leaves it to the jury to decide whether the provocation that prompted the loss of self-control leading to a murder was reasonable. But the loss of self-control that caused a murder must be a sudden and temporary unbalancing. This may explain why a violent man has killed, but not a battered woman.

In 1989, Sara Thornton stabbed her abusive, alcoholic husband, Malcolm, for hurling insults at her while he lay in a drunken heap on the sofa. In 1990 she was found guilty of murder and jailed for life. On appeal in 1991 she attempted to have the charge reduced to manslaughter. Her lawyers argued that a build-up of provocation can push the weaker partner to kill without a sudden loss of self-control – that a battered woman may have lost control long before she acts against her oppressor. But this example of provocation did not fit the definition above. The appeal court found that there was a cooling-off period in her argument with her husband when she went looking for a knife and then sharpened it. 'If the woman conforms to the image of the "good and loving" wife', says Jennifer Nadel in a study of the Thornton case, 'she is more likely to find herself dealt with sympathetically, with the compassion she deserves'.[27] This was the scenario in the case of Kiranjit Ahluwalia, who in 1989, after enduring ten years of brutality, threw a bucket of petrol over her sleeping husband, Deepak, and lit it. 'I gave him a fire bath to wash his sins', she said later.

[27] Jennifer Nadel, *Sara Thornton: The Story of a Woman Who Killed* (Victor Gollancz, London, 1993), p. 219.

His ill-treatment included hitting her with screwdrivers or a telephone, beating her if she spoke without his consent, threatening to burn her face with an iron, and carrying on with a girlfriend. At her trial the same year she was found guilty of murder and given the mandatory sentence of life in prison, but in 1992, at a retrial ordered by the Court of Appeal, she was allowed to plead guilty to manslaughter on grounds of diminished responsibility and sentenced to time she had already served – three years and four months. The defence argued successfully that severe depression brought on by the strain of living with a physically and psychologically abusive man constituted an abnormality of mind that affected her self-control. However, an attempt to get the court to accept that prolonged provocation mitigated the intention to kill was not successful. 'Provocation is basically a masculine idea that... ought to be abolished as a plea but retained for assessing mitigating circumstances', Sue Bandalli, a solicitor campaigning for legal changes for female killers, told *The Times* in an interview in 1992. She added, 'It assumes a man who murders his unfaithful wife is behaving reasonably if he is provoked, but if you are a reasonable man you do not kill your adulterous wife, you leave home'.[28]

More conservative observers were alarmed that any easing of the legal definition on provocation would simply legalise revenge killing. Commenting in *The Times* after the freeing of Ahluwalia, Janet Daly protested: 'We are still in the business of trying to prevent the taking of life rather than inventing new ways to sanction it, aren't we?' She argued that it was ridiculous to excuse women's violence against their husbands just to even things out judicially. 'Perhaps it is as much the final triumph of liberalism that we find nothing absurd in the idea that all groups in society should have an equal right to commit the ultimate crime, or to be let off once they have committed it'.[29] In 1995 came a landmark ruling on provocation. Emma Humphreys, a former teenage prostitute who had stabbed her brutal and possessive partner, Trevor Armitage, and been found guilty of murder in 1985, was freed when the Court of Appeal agreed to substitute for the murder verdict one of manslaughter. The court took into account the extended and extreme provocation behind the attack. The decision made clear that a defence of provocation could succeed in a case where a string of incidents had built up over time to drive the woman to murder. The defendant had been subjected over a period of months to verbal abuse, beatings, imprisonment and rapes. The jury was instructed to take account of her history in considering whether or not a reasonable

---

[28] *The Times*, 1 April 1992, Law Times section, p. 5.
[29] *The Times*, 29 September 1992, p. 14.

woman with a similar background of abuse and neglect would have been provoked to lose control in similar circumstances. Research on battered women, argues Sheila Noonan, suggests that self-preservation rather than provocation is the root cause. 'The difficulty is that judicial categories have an either/or quality. Although the English courts have been unprepared to countenance self-preservation, it would seem that some of the analysis of contextualising violence has now been sanctioned by virtue of the Humphreys case'.[30]

Sara Thornton appealed again against her conviction in 1996. In commenting on her prospects in the light of the Humphreys decision, a *Times* leader argued that Emma Humphreys had acted under provocation in the legal sense as Thornton had not. '"Slow burn" cannot be a mitigating factor where the person who kills does so with premeditation', said *The Times*. 'To hold otherwise would rob both provocation and revenge of their respective meanings'.[31] In 1996, Thornton's conviction was reduced to manslaughter on the ground of diminished responsibility, but not provocation, though the court found that the abnormality of mind that she demonstrated was due to sustained provocation. This seems as far as the justice system is prepared to go in assisting women murderers. As Simon Jenkins, a columnist for *The Times*, wrote after the verdict was announced: 'A person cannot be provoked to justifiable homicide, at least in the view of the law, by a man who is lying supine and insensible with drink'. He added, 'That a woman may find it harder to murder a man may seem unfair on women, although plenty seem to manage it'.[32] The issue, surely, is not equal opportunity but a single standard that does not privilege either sex. Elizabeth Mytton, a teacher of criminal law, argues that the conceptual framework of the law is simply too male-oriented to be useful in conveying the behaviour of a woman on trial for the murder of an abusive partner.[33] Susan Edwards points out that the 'considerable stretching' of appeals procedures and legal categories behind these successful appeals implies 'a concern amongst appeal court judges and the Lord Chief Justice that in doing law, the law may not be doing justice'.[34]

---

[30] Sheila Noonan, 'Battered Woman Syndrome: Shifting the Parameters of Criminal Law Defences (Or (Re)Inscribing the Familar?)', in Anne Bottomley (ed.), *Feminist Perspectives on the Foundational Subjects of Law* (Cavendish, London, 1996), pp. 59-60.

[31] *The Times*, 8 July 1995, p. 19.

[32] *The Times*, 1 June 1996, p. 20.

[33] Elizabeth Mytton, 'The Radical Potentialities of Biographical Methods for Making Difference(s) Visible' (Bournemouth University, Poole, Dorset, School of Finance and Law Working Paper Series, 1997).

[34] S. Edwards, *Sex and Gender in the Legal Process* (Blackstone, London, 1996), p. 373.

Conclusion

Even in the nineteenth century critics of the justice system called attention to its male bias and forced some adjustments. In an age when marriage is no more advantageous to one sex than the other, the law still puts women on the defensive. It more easily excuses spousal murder by women who fit the role of victim, thus perpetuating the power dynamic that privileges men. 'In the context of victim precipitation in homicide it is women as a class who are regarded as naggers, taunters, adulterers', says Edwards; 'men, frequently, have good sound moral reasons for being provoked, reasons which earn a status within the very fabric of defences and mitigation'.[35] Feminist legal scholars are therefore calling for a revamping of the language and the assumed norms behind the law on provocation to make it gender-neutral. That would change the letter of the law, but not necessarily the spirit.

---

[35] *Ibid*, p. 400.

Chapter 13

Gendered Assumptions – Madness, Pregnancy and Childbirth

M. E. Rodgers

Introduction

The stereotypical image of women is often one of high emotion and hysteria, although today this would not lead to an easy assumption of insanity. From a gendered perspective past and present, emotional outbursts, however defined, partake of the flavour of an essentially feminine form of 'bad', or socially unacceptable, behaviour. It has been claimed, notably by Elaine Showalter, that during the Victorian period, madness itself was defined as a 'female malady', though this has been challenged by Joan Busfield, arguing this to be a false premise.[1] Today, we are proud to believe, such assumptions are no longer made. But how well-founded is this complacency? This chapter seeks to go beyond the mechanics of simple stereotyping to explore the nuances involved in gendered labels, past and present.

An evaluation of the insanity statistics in 1845 illustrated that generally men outnumbered women in both private and pauper madhouses, highlighting the insubstantial nature of the evidence for Showalter's claim.[2] However, while it may indeed be the case that women were no

---

[1] See E. Showalter, *The Female Malady: Women, Madness and English Culture, 1830-1980* (Virago, London, 1987); J. Busfield, 'The Female Malady? Men, Women and Madness in Nineteenth Century Britain', *Sociology*, 1994, 28, 1, p. 259.

[2] J. Thurnam, *Observations and Essays on the Statistics of Insanity* (1845) pp. 145-55, cited, W. L. Parry-Jones, *The Trade in Lunacy* (Routledge and Kegan Paul, London, 1972). Thurman had surveyed the statistics for both private licensed houses and pauper madhouses and found that in the former, women were outnumbered by men by approximately 30%, and that in pauper madhouses, the women were generally outnumbered by men, with the exception of London houses. Parry adds that the balance shifted towards the end of the nineteenth century, although this 'came to be attributed, in part, to the lower mortality rate among women than among men', p. 49. It is also worth noting that Burrows, who wrote widely on madness, included figures on confinement in his work. See George Man Burrows, *Commentaries, on the causes, forms, symptoms, and treatment, moral and medical, of insanity* (Underwood, London, 1828).

more pre-disposed to madness than men in the Victorian period, it is true to say that for what were (indeed still are) considered irrefutably biological reasons, women were more pre-disposed to *certain types* of diagnosis of madness linked to different sexual function. In particular, puerperal insanity and madness alleged to arise from pregnancy and the consequences of childbirth were women's 'diseases'. The cavalier approach of Victorian alienists to diagnosis and explanation of the causes of female insanity may seem untenable in today's society.[3] Yet it would appear that many of the assumptions that underpinned medical diagnosis and treatment in Victorian times have resonance with the approach taken by modern medical men when dealing with 'bad' or 'unreasonable' feminine behaviour.

These approaches have become so entrenched within medical discourse that it is difficult to escape them, the more so since they have been influential in the development and operation of the legal regime since Victorian times. This chapter will explore the medical theories in relation to women and madness in the mid to late Victorian period and illustrate how this medical discourse remains valid today, both through the practices of medics and the application of the law. This continuity, arguably based more on moral judgments about women's behaviour than science, relates to the enduring nature of stereotypes about the wider social significance of so-called 'unwomanly' behaviour. Because of the importance of women to the future of society, through their role as child-bearers, manifestations of what is culturally constructed as 'unwomanliness' are still, today, as they were in a Victorian past, subjected to particular scrutiny.

The Victorian Alienist – Madness in Women and its Causation

To modern eyes, medical tracts dating from the mid-eighteenth century onwards, appear highly unscientific in terms of the approach to causation of mental illness and women's madness. Yet for their time, the fact that mental illness was viewed as a physical condition by most alienists, is still enlightened, given modern methods of diagnosis and treatment of mental health problems. However, despite the fact that these tracts were in one respect 'cutting edge', difficulties arise in relation to the breadth of assumptions asserted by Victorian medics, and the causal links made between observable physical changes and presumed insanity. As early as

---

[3] 'Alienist was an earlier name for psychiatrist', see N. Theriot, 'Women's Voices in the Nineteenth Century Medical Discourse: a step toward deconstructing science', *Journal of Women in Culture and Society*, 1993, 19, 1, p. 3.

1758 William Battie, a leading alienist of the eighteenth century stated 'it is a repeated observation that Madness frequently succeeds or accompanies fever, Epilepsy, *Childbirth* and the like muscular disorders'.[4]

Throughout the nineteenth century, this link between pregnancy, childbirth and insanity was made by numerous practitioners, in terms of causation. The concentration was on both the 'exciting' nature of pregnancy, in that pregnancy was said to excite the brain and its functions, and the perceived link between the uterus and the brain creating not just an image of an over-emotional woman, but one of a mad woman. Popular Victorian literature frequently referred to visibly pregnant women as 'ill', for instance.[5] Writing in the early part of the nineteenth century, Dr. Butler stated that, 'Pregnancy seems to add greatly to the natural sensibility of the female constitution... this very weak and mobile state of the nervous system is very much increased in childbirth'.[6] The weakness of a woman's nervous system hence led to a greater impact from 'exciting causes' whether these be 'gestation, parturition and all its consequences' or 'education or occupation'.[7] As Burrows further explained:

> Gestation itself is a source of excitement in most women and sometimes provokes mental derangement.... The accession of mental disturbance may be coincident with conception... or it may come on at any time in pregnancy, continue through it... or persevere through all the circumstances consequent on parturition.[8]

The physiological nature of a woman's reproductive organs were also thought to be causative of madness.

There appears to have been little medical support for the theory that the development of insanity in women can be put down to 'the influence the genital system exercises on the brain' amongst the alienists writing in England then, or those in other states.[9] However, there does appear to be more consensus on the link with the uterus as an exciting cause – George

---

[4] W. Battie, *A Treatise on Madness* (J. Whiston and B. White, London, 1758), pp. 52-3 (emphasis added).

[5] See, for instance, Evelyn Everett Green, *Olive Roscoe, or, the New Sister* (Religious Tract Society, London, 1898).

[6] Dr Butler, 'Puerperal Fever', in *Essays on the puerperal fever and other diseases peculiar to women. Selected from the writings of British authors previous to the close of the eighteenth century*, Fleetwood Churchill (ed.), (Sydenham Society, London, 1849).

[7] Burrows, *Commentaries*, p. 240.

[8] *Ibid*, pp. 363-4.

[9] Georget, cited in G. M. Burrows, *Commentaries*, p. 383. Burrows comments that 'in no instance, this author adds, has he discovered any genital affection'; see also N. Theriot, 'Nineteenth-century Physicians and "Puerperal Insanity"', *American Studies* 1989, 30, 2, pp. 69-88, where a review of the disease and its diagnosis is conducted.

Man Burrows commented that 'The connection and reciprocal influence between the uterus must not be overlooked... irritation of the uterus will, during pregnancy or the progress of labour, provide convulsions, apoplexy and mania'.[10] He further asserted that, 'The condition of the uterine system in gestation and afterwards in the puerperal state, is very different... and like any other irritative process, may elicit the latent hereditary orgasm, or give birth to the maniacal action'.[11] Likewise John Connolly, MD, was of the opinion that 'During pregnancy, partly perhaps from an undue circulation in the brain, and partly from a morbid state of the brain itself, explained by its sympathy with the states of the uterus, the mental facilities and moral feelings sometimes undergo singular modifications'.[12]

These theories did not lose currency in subsequent years. Maudsley, writing in 1873, referred to the influence of the generative organs in the production of insanity.[13] The extent of the wider social acceptance of this medical connection can be seen in its adoption by the legal system. This operated both in relation to the diagnosis criteria for female admission to a lunatic asylum, but also in the development of other laws affecting women's experience. However, before any consideration of the legal acceptance of puerperal insanity is undertaken, it is important to reflect briefly on the symptoms exhibited by these women that led to a diagnosis of insanity and hence were seen as an integral part of that insanity. The nature of the type of symptoms that gave rise to the label of puerperal insanity, regardless of the source of information, are striking in their homogeneity during the period.

Medical texts throughout the nineteenth century refer to a range of acts on the part of the woman that would support such diagnosis (other of course than the fact of pregnancy or recent confinement for childbirth). For example, in 1814 John Armstrong MD referred to his cases as follows:

> the patients began to talk incoherently, they frequently made attempts to get out of bed, and occasionally having lain still a short time, suddenly started, and spread out their hands, which were then very tremulous, as if to ward something off that was approaching them.[14]

---

[10] Burrows, *Commentaries*, p. 378.

[11] *Ibid*, p. 379.

[12] J. Connolly, *An Inquiry Concerning the Indications of Insanity with suggestions for the better protection and care of the insane* (first published, London, 1830, reprinted Dawsons, London, 1964).

[13] H. Maudsley, 'The Female Life Cycle', quoted, V Skultans, *Madness and Morals Ideas on Insanity in the Nineteenth Century* (Routledge and Kegan Paul, London, 1875).

[14] J. Armstrong, *Facts and Observations, relative to the fever commonly called puerperal* (Longman, Hurst, Rees, Orme and Brown, London, 1814), pp. 8-9.

Sixteen years later, John Connolly spoke of the woman patient being 'restless, irritable, loquacious', adding that she 'becomes unable to exercise her attention or memory; or experiences emotions of unhappiness without external cause'.[15] In the mid-nineteenth century this 'incessant talking' was echoed in Bucknill and Tuke's *Manual of Psychological Medicine*. They also commented on the number of cases where the pregnant woman manifested

> a total negligence of, and often very strong aversion, to her child and her husband... and, although the patient may have been remarkable previously for her correct, modest, demeanour, and attention to her religious duties, most awful oaths and imprecations are now uttered, and language used which astonishes her friends.[16]

The fact that much of this babbling or incoherent rambling was of a coarse, and hence unnatural female language, is illustrative of the cultural stereotypes underpinning Victorian medical assumptions. 'Good' women could not be readily assumed to be guilty of such inappropriate or 'bad' behaviour, therefore such conduct could only be indicative of madness.

Examination of the casebooks from asylums in the Nottingham area verifies the importance of these symptoms to the diagnosis, and consequently to the admission of the women to such institutions. Nottingham had several asylums, and practice there can be taken to be generally representative of how insanity was being diagnosed. For example, in 1886, Sarah, an 18-year-old, was admitted to Mapperley Hospital with puerperal mania – the recorded cause being her confinement approximately two weeks earlier. The Female Casebook states that, 'on admission [the] patient was in an acutely maniacal state, [talking] incoherently and using most filthy and disgusting language without intermission and even when spoken to or eating her meals she continued the same filthy talk'. Several days later, she was still 'in the same state of excitement and very troublesome tearing her clothing, dirty in her habits and up to all sorts of mischief'. A partial recovery occurred when she 'became almost suddenly herself, left off talking incoherently and using filthy language' but this was short-lived. Sarah was eventually discharged seven months after admission.[17] Elizabeth, who was also admitted to Mapperley Hospital, was said to be 'excited and restless, moving about

---

[15] Connolly, *Inquiry*, p. 425.

[16] J. C. Bucknill and D. H. Tuke, *A Manual of Psychological Medicine* (London, 1858, reprinted Hafner Publishing, New York, 1968), p. 238.

[17] Nottingham Record Office, SO/HO/6/2/1/1, Mapperley Hospital Female Casebook, 2 August 1883-March 1888.

constantly unless restrained. She kept up a constant incoherent rambling talk crying at one moment laughing the next'. She remained in Mapperley for nearly one year, having made no progress for many months. Again, as with Sarah, her disorder of acute mania was caused, according to the records, by her confinement two weeks prior to admission and four days before her symptoms manifested themselves.[18] Records from the County of Nottingham Asylum in Sneinton, albeit less descriptive, support the nature of symptoms and frequent diagnosis of puerperal insanity for women patients, witness the case of Annie. The medical records noted that she had a

> loss of natural expression, constant restlessness, persistently deranging her bedclothes leaving her body in a half-naked condition. Refuses to answer questions or does so in a senseless manner, laughs, cries, swears, whistles and sings for hours together... articulation generally so hurried and imperfect that only a few words she says can be understood.[19]

In addition, she 'will not take any notice of her children'.[20]

The fact that the behaviour exhibited by these women was considered to be 'unnatural' and not conforming to stereotypical expectations of female conduct is evident from the manner of its presentation, as Bucknill and Tuke clearly demonstrate. Women's 'bad behaviour', when taken in the context of pregnancy or childbirth would often trigger the diagnosis of insanity, albeit one recognised by the medical profession to be a condition that was likely to be cured. Theriot, in the context of US physicians and their patients, appears to reflect a similar theme in that it was primarily the behaviour of the woman, coupled with the fact of childbirth *per se*, that triggered the diagnosis of madness. She concludes that, 'It would seem that nineteenth-century physicians' views of proper womanly behaviour along with their ideas about the power of the uterus to disrupt women's mental balance influenced their perception and definition of puerperal insanity'.

However, by contrast she doubts the extent to which assumptions about behaviour labelled as being un-typical influenced the medical reaction:

> Focusing too closely on the obvious ideological content of physicians' account... one might overlook that physicians' guesses were very much in keeping with... ideas on insanity in general.... Indeed, much of the medical discourse on puerperal insanity seems

---

[18] *Ibid.*

[19] Nottingham Record Office, SO/HO/1/9/3, Medical Superintendence Record 1888-1890. Within this casebook, approximately ten per cent of admissions were mainly due to puerperal causes.

[20] *Ibid.*

to have been influenced very little by male doctors' concepts of femininity.[21]

While it may be tempting to agree with this latter argument, and concur that this ill-founded link between reproductive organs and the brain resulted in the diagnosis of insanity, the fact that women's behaviour was highlighted so frequently by the alienists such as Battie, Tuke and Maudsley, together with her contradictory approach, casts doubt on her hypothesis. In addition, today, when mental health diagnosis is more 'scientific', behaviour is still being used to demonstrate 'madness'. This emphasises the continuing deeply-rooted connections between medical discourse and cultural assumptions, something which has also implications for the conclusions reached by the legal profession since that, too, is affected by such cultural stereotyping.

Legal Acceptance of Puerperal Insanity

The fact that medical theory has an impact upon legal regulation is one that is tacitly recognised, although rarely investigated and evaluated. Insofar as women are concerned, both in Victorian England and today, popular and legal acceptance of the medical view-point can be a double-edged sword. For any individual to be admitted into an asylum in the nineteenth century, there was a clear legal process that had to be undergone, and this legal process can be seen to accept the authority of the medical discourse in relation to women and their particular forms of madness. The development of that legal intervention has been traced by many authors, such as Kathleen Jones.[22] By the late Victorian period, before acceptance by an asylum of a patient, there needed to be medical certification in relation to the medical condition. For private patients the law required two medical certificates 'each signed by a Registered Medical Practitioner stating that he has separately examined the patient and on such examination found him to be of unsound mind'.[23] Pauper patients also enjoyed such protection. They were not admitted to a County Asylum without the production of a medical certificate declaring that they were insane.[24]

---

[21] Theriot, 'Women's Voices', p. 76.

[22] K. Jones, *A History of the Mental Health Services* (Routledge and Kegan Paul, London, 1972); see also D. Wright, 'The certification of insanity in nineteenth-century England and Wales', *History of Psychiatry*, 1998, 9, p. 267.

[23] PRO/MH/51/237/143, Lunacy Commission, Book No. 2. See also the Treatment of Insane Persons Act, 9 Geo. IV, c 41 (otherwise known as The Madhouse Act 1828).

[24] County Asylums (Amendment) Act 1819, 59 Geo.III, c 127, also the County Asylums Act 1828.

The need for medical certificates was designed to prevent illegal detention, since public concern existed throughout the period that individuals were being incarcerated whilst perfectly sane.[25] In relation to pauper patients, the need for a certificate, and authorisation from the magistrates, ensured that rate-payers' funds were not being spent unwisely! The need for certification (which still remains in place today) provided a legal validity to the medical practitioner's knowledge and diagnosis of puerperal insanity. In keeping records of admissions, asylums were required to note the nature of insanity and the causes thereof, again supporting the medical theories of the day. The Lunacy Commission (1876) 'were desirous of being in a position to publish certain information with regard to insane Patients... showing (*inter alia*) the causes of the insanity'. In the Schedule they listed as some of the physical causes of insanity, including 'Pregnancy, Puerperal, Lactation, Uterine Disorders'.[26] The acceptance of these causes by the Commissioners demonstrates the extent to which the medical discourse was entrenched in popular understanding.

Further evidence to support the connection between reproduction and insanity can be gained from consideration of the criminal law, and in particular the development of the offence of infanticide, which was first introduced to the statute book in 1922 and still remains as an alternative charge in relation to child/infant death. Infanticide, as dealt with in the Infanticide Act 1922 occurred when a woman caused the death of her new-born child due to any wilful act or omission, 'but at the time of the act or omission she had not fully recovered from the effect of giving birth to such child, but by reason thereof the balance of her mind was then disturbed'.[27] This offence was subsequently amended in the Infanticide Act 1938; section 1(1) provided that 'Where a women by any wilful act or omission causes the death of her child being a child under the age of 12 months, but at the time of the act or omission the balance of her mind was disturbed by reason of her not having fully recovered from the effect of giving birth... or by reason of the effect of lactation consequent upon the birth... she shall be guilty of felony, to wit of infanticide' This amendment, to include the age of the child, was included as a result of a restrictive interpretation of the 1922 Act in the case of *R v O'Donoghue* (1927) where argument concentrated on whether a four-week-old child could be said to be 'new-

---

[25] Jones, *History*; Parry-Jones, *Trade in Lunacy*.

[26] PRO/MH/51/237/156, Lunacy Commission circulars, 18 February 1876. The Commission was initially established by the Lunatics Act 1845, 8 and 9 Vict., c 100.

[27] Infanticide Act 1922 s.1(1).

born'.[28] It would, however, be wrong to conclude that a 'lessening' of the impact on mothers who killed their infants was a twentieth century issue. Repeated attempts had been made in the mid and late nineteenth century to ameliorate the affects of the death penalty, or rather the imposition thereof, with commutation shortly after sentence.[29] Subsequent debate on infanticide has frequently focused on the issue of medicalisation of the offence. It has been suggested on the one hand that the legislation 'was the product, not of nineteenth century medical theory about child-birth, but of judicial effort to avoid passing death sentences' [30] On the other, the contrasting perspective is that 'the psychiatric principles from which the legal classification of infanticide is derived are well-supported'.[31]

It is understandable that arguments exist both for the development of the law being simply to reduce an unpopular and over-draconian remedy *and* for the law being based on the medical links between childbirth and the woman's state of mind, given that at the time of the original debates on infanticide medical theory was 'less refined' on the effects of childbirth, and that the death penalty still existed. It is suggested that it is clear that the medical discourse has influenced the operation of law, and that the medical view prevailed. In 1865 when reform of the criminal law was being discussed by the Capital Punishment Committee the language and approach of Victorian alienists was clearly reflected. For example, Sir George Grey stated, 'I think that in almost all cases the murder would be murder in the first degree, except in a case, which may easily be conceived, in which a woman immediately after the birth, in a state of weakness *and great excitement*, might take away life' [32] Fitzjames Stephen, applying his commanding legal knowledge concluded that, 'a woman just after childbirth is so upset, and is in such a hysterical state altogether, that it seems to me that you cannot deal with her in the same manner as if she was in a regular state... I believe also (*though that is more a medical than a legal question*) that women in that condition do get the strongest symptoms of what amounts... to a temporary madness'.[33] In the debates leading up to the 1922 Act, the medical elements were questioned by parliament. As

---

[28] (1927) 20 Cr App R 132.

[29] For an explanation of the various attempts to introduce Infanticide clauses in the nineteenth century legislation see D. Seaborne Davies, 'Child Killing in English Law', *Modern Law Review*, 1937, p. 203; *Modern Law Review*, 1938, p. 269.

[30] K. O'Donovan, 'The Medicalisation of Infanticide', *Criminal Law Review*, 1984, p. 259.

[31] D. Maier-Katkin and R. Ogle, 'A Rationale for Infanticide Laws', *Criminal Law Review*, 1993, p. 903.

[32] *Parliamentary Papers*, 1865, xxi, p. 197.

[33] *Ibid*, p. 291, emphasis added.

highlighted by Tony Ward, 'Lord Parmoor was unhappy with the use of terminology which "would necessitate consideration of medical evidence"', but 'the wording was strongly defended'.[34] The fact that the legislation reflected upon the state of the woman's mind ensured it retained the link with the medical theory of childbirth affecting the balance of the mind and hence underpinning the Act. Again, when the repeal of the 1922 Act and re-enactment in the 1938 Act was debated in the Lords, the fact that such women were mentally ill was accepted. As Lord Atkin stated,

> the effect of the Bill... is to preserve all the conditions of the present Act. The condition will still be there that the woman has not recovered from the effects of child-birth, as well as the condition that the balance of her mind is disturbed; and... where it can be said that those conditions extend beyond the month then the verdict can still be returned of infanticide.[35]

Given the consistency of approach, and the emphasis throughout on the causes of an insanity which 'are well know and can easily be recognised' it is difficult to agree with O'Donovan that it is the Infanticide Act 1938 which 'makes explicit the medicalisation of the crime'.[36] The medical discourse within the crime had been evident in the nineteenth century, many decades before this legislation was on the statute book.

Infanticide remains on the statute book today, with modern psychiatric evidence supporting the claim that women do suffer mental illness just before and immediately after childbirth: 'Women are 25 times more likely to become psychotic in the month immediately after childbirth. The relative risk declines thereafter but, even so, in the twelfth month after delivery the risk is still double that of pre-childbearing months'.[37] If women are, today, less likely to be condemned to asylums on grounds which, today, would count as 'bad' behaviour by the medical and legal professions, the impact of the Victorian alienists, and the behaviour/madness hypothesis continues in medical interventions which extend beyond the infanticide legislation.

---

[34] T. Ward, 'Legislating for human nature: legal responses to infanticide, 1860-1938', in M. Jackson (ed.), *Historical Perspectives on Child Murders and Concealment, 1500-2000* (Ashgate, Aldershot, 2002).

[35] *Hansard*, Lords, 22 March 1938, col. 300.

[36] *Ibid*, Speech, Archbishop of Canterbury, col. 302; O'Donovan, 'Infanticide', p. 262.

[37] M. N. Marks, 'Characteristics and causes of infanticide in Britain', *International Review of Psychiatry* 1996, 9, pp. 99-106.

Modern Resonances – Irrational Women and Childbirth

The debate on women's insanity has lessened somewhat in the late twentieth century, with improved diagnostic and treatment tools, and a more coherent legal regime underpinning compulsory intervention by way of detention and treatment. Despite these alleged advances, the assumptions of the Victorian alienists, and the link between pregnancy, childbirth, behaviour and madness can still be identified. This is particularly so when the question of compulsory caesarian sections comes before the courts. Different opinions between women and doctors about this form of medical intervention resulted in a flurry of legal cases in the 1990s. The context of these cases, in terms of legal discussion, is that of women's ability to consent to treatment – the caesarian – under the special conditions of advanced pregnancy, and reasons why the women were deemed incapable, mentally, of consenting, thereby enabling the courts to authorise treatment. In medical law, the autonomy of the patient has become the principle guiding medical interventions.[38] However, common law provides legal justification for doctors to treat where a patient cannot exercise their own autonomy.[39] In cases where there is doubt about capacity to consent the courts can be asked to grant a declaration, which thereby enables the medical treatment to proceed. In this scenario the court will normally rule on the capacity point, having had regard to the evidence of the medical experts.

It is arguable that the courts, in dealing with these matters rely heavily on the forensic experts. Hence, if agreeing with them, the courts are simply endorsing a line of professional thinking that has, in reality, changed little over the centuries in that women throughout pregnancy and in childbirth lose the ability to reason and make so-called rational decisions, and by virtue of this lack of rationality, are in reality mad (if temporarily so). To highlight this, two cases will be explored: *Re S (adult: refusal of medical treatment)* (1992) and *St George's Healthcare NHS Trust v S, R v Collins and others, ex parte S* (1998).[40]

In *Re S*, the Family Division of the High Court was faced with an emergency application to declare that it would be lawful for the medical practitioners to carry out a caesarian section despite the woman's refusal of such treatment. Given that the whole process before the court took less than one hour, the judgment and the court's reasoning is somewhat lacking. However, distilling the essentials of the case, the mother-to-be

---

[38] See *Schloendorff v The Society of New York Hospital* [1914] 105 NE 92.
[39] *Re F (Mental Patient: Sterilisation)* [1990] 2 AC 1.
[40] [1992] 4 All ER 671, [1998] 3 All ER 673.

had refused her consent to the caesarian due to her religious beliefs. She was in a 'desperately serious' condition as was 'the situation of the as yet unborn child'.[41] The medical consultant 'has done his best, as have other surgeons and doctors at the hospital, to persuade the mother that the only means of saving her life, and also I emphasise the life of her unborn child, is to carry out a Caesarian section operation'.[42] The issues, therefore, were simply that the mother's refusal endangered her life and that of the foetus and that she could not be persuaded to change her mind. Capacity to consent, or refuse, the treatment was not specifically focused on, although the assumption must have been that she did not have such capacity, otherwise, why would she refuse the treatment and behave in such an irrational fashion? This lack of mental capacity suggests, in the terminology of the Victorian alienists, a temporary insanity due to her situation of childbirth. Her wishes, since they were 'patently unreasonable and irrational', must therefore be ignored by both the medical practitioners and the courts. The simplistic logic of Victorian 'pregnancy results in insanity' is clearly reflected.

In the second case, *St George's*, the logic suggested above is again implicit within the actions of the medical profession, although the case is interesting also for the fact that the court did not accede to the medical viewpoint. The patient, S, was 36 weeks pregnant when she first sought medical advice. She was advised that due to pre-eclampsia she would need to have the labour induced and be admitted to hospital. However, S did not wish to undergo induced labour, and 'recorded in writing her "extreme objection to any medical or surgical intervention" and made it "absolutely clear that it is against my wishes and I shall consider it an assault on my person"'.[43] This refusal of medical attention did not accord with the views of the medical practitioners – they believed that she had a 'profound indifference to the consequences of refusing treatment for her serious physical condition. She is pregnant and *her behaviour is putting her own life and the life of her unborn baby at risk*'.[44] As a result of her refusal of treatment, S was detained in hospital under the Mental Health Act 1983 and then transferred to a normal delivery unit. The doctors also sought permission from the court to conduct an emergency caesarian on the basis of her detention under the 1983 Act, with the justificatory claim that without the intervention 'both she and the foetus would probably die'. At

---

[41] [1998] 3 All ER, per Stephen Brown, p. 672.

[42] *Ibid.*

[43] [1998] 3 All ER 673, per Judge LJ, p. 680.

[44] *Ibid*, p. 679, emphasis added.

the initial court hearing, a declaration was granted enabling the caesarian to take place. Subsequently S appealed, claiming that the hospital acted contrary to the law.

The Court of Appeal upheld S's claim. She should not have had a caesarian section, since the court found she was not mentally incapable, although this was a matter that the doctors did not agree on, or decided was not an issue, since the foetus was at risk and S was not behaving appropriately. The court, in the context of the Mental Health Act 1983, stated:

> The Act cannot be deployed to achieve the detention of an individual against her will merely because her thinking process is unusual, even apparently bizarre and irrational, and contrary to the views of the overwhelming majority of the community at large. The prohibited reasoning is readily identified and easily understood. Here is an intelligent woman. She knows perfectly well that if she persists with this course against medical advice she is likely to cause serious harm, and possibly death, to her baby and to herself. *No normal mother-to-be could possibly think like that.* Although this mother would not dream of taking any positive steps to cause injury to herself or her baby, her refusal is likely to lead to such a result. *Her bizarre thinking represents a danger to their safety and health. It therefore follows that she must be mentally disordered* and detained in hospital in her own interests and those of her baby.[45]

This speech by Lord Justice Judge clearly demonstrates both the modern medical approach and the reality that it mirrors the assumptions of the Victorian alienists that bizarre, irrational, or in other words, unwomanly, behaviour when coupled with pregnancy or childbirth indicates madness. Madness should thus be diagnosed and used as the basis for decisions on medical and legal treatment of the patient. Little has changed, in reality, since the times of George Man Burrows and his ilk except perhaps for the fact that the legal system, through the courts, is more willing to question the medical discourse as being inappropriate today.

Conclusion

Despite the changes in approach to mental health problems that have been achieved both in medical and legal practice in the twentieth century, assumptions, founded on nothing more than observation, have gained such validity and truth that they continue to play a role today as they did in Victorian times. The male medical discourse of the Victorian alienists

---

[45] *Ibid*, p. 692, emphasis added.

connecting female madness with a woman's immature reproductive organs and her reproductive functions, can be seen to hold true today. Modern medical theory may play down the resonance with medical history, but the behaviour of St George's Health Care Trust flies in the face of such denial. The legal regime, while now being prepared to decry this approach, albeit unintentionally, in caesarian cases, itself maintains the link through infanticide legislation, with its singling-out of reproduction as a means to reduce the impact of child-death at the hands of the mother. Medicine and law are inextricable linked by acceptance of Victorian discourse, and it is unlikely that these ties will ever be broken.

Chapter 14

From Unlawful Assembly to Aggravated Trespass: The Control of Protest in the 1880s and 1990s

Richard Stone

Introduction

This chapter is concerned with a particular form of public 'bad behaviour', that is the disorder which can arise from, or be provoked by, an otherwise lawful activity, as a result of others objecting to it. Its focus is therefore 'public order', particularly the legal controls available to the authorities to try to maintain such order in the face of public pressure. A comparison will be drawn between the approach to such issues in the late Victorian period, and at the end of the twentieth century. The basis will be an examination of two sequences of events which, while not being identical, have a sufficient degree of similarity to make it worthwhile to consider them together.

The sequence of events chosen from the nineteenth century is that surrounding the 'Salvation Army riots' of the 1880s, leading to what became the key case on what constituted an 'unlawful assembly' – *Beatty v Gillbanks*.[1] From the twentieth century the focus is the anti-hunting protests of the 1990s which led to the creation of additional offences and police powers enacted in the Criminal Justice and Public Order Act 1994. In both cases there was a lawful public activity – the processions of the Salvation Army, and the actions of the hunts – which was disrupted by protesters. In the case of the Salvation Army the most frequent protests came from the 'Skeleton Army', in the case of hunting from anti-field-sports protesters (some in organised groups, some rather more *ad hoc*). After examination of these incidents, attempt will be made to draw some

---

[1] (1882) 15 Cox CC 138. This report is preferred to the 'official' report in 9 QBD 138 because the Cox report records the arguments of counsel more fully, giving the judgment of Cave J in full (the QBD report simply records that he concurred). *The Times*, 14 June 1882, gives even more detail of exchanges between judges and counsel.

conclusions about the similarities and differences in the reaction to the two cases by the Home Office, the courts, and, to a limited extent, the media (in the form of newspaper reporting).

The Salvation Army

The Salvation Army, described by Bailey as a 'variant of late Methodist revivalism', was based on an intensely personal Christianity, and a vigorous promotion of total abstinence from alcohol.[2] Formed in 1878 by the self-styled General William Booth, it fairly quickly became active across the country.[3] Targeted at, and primarily recruited from, the working classes, the particular aspect of its activities of interest here is the holding of processions through towns, together with open-air meetings. These could be noisy affairs, involving singing, and the banging of drums. From an early stage (at least from 1879) there was strong opposition, which led to widespread riots.[4] Bailey estimates that such riots affected some 60 towns and cities between 1878 and 1891. From 1880 opposition to the Salvationists in the south tended to come from the 'Skeleton Army' or 'Skeleton Armies'. As Bailey explains, 'The Skeletons often wore elaborate costumes, and their processions were executed with care, incorporating parodied elements of the Salvationist parades'[5] Their disruption took the form of playing music, beating old kettles, trays, etc, alongside the Salvationist procession.[6] It also could involve physical assaults, such as pelting them with lime dust, turnips, refuse, cow-dung and liquid manure.[7]

A combination of factors lay behind this hostility. Despite the religious focus of the Salvation Army, there is little evidence that the hostility was primarily the work of other religious groups who saw the Army as a threat, though it is true that on occasion Anglican clergy can be found in the

---

[2] Victor Bailey, 'Salvation Army Riots, the "Skeleton Army" and Legal Authority in the Provincial Town', in A. P. Donajdgrodzki (ed.), *Social Control in Nineteenth Century Britain* (Croom Helm, London, 1977), p. 235. This provides a good outline of the social context to the riots.

[3] Prior to 1878 the organisation had taken the form of a 'Christian Mission' It was only in 1878 that the military trappings were adopted, together with the name 'Salvation Army'

[4] See Bailey, 'Salvation Army', p. 233. Horridge points out that the activities of the Christian Mission were also the subject of disruption, G. K. Horridge, *The Salvation Army, Origins and Early Days: 1865-1900* (Ammonite Books, Godalming 1993), pp. 95-6.

[5] *Ibid.*

[6] Horridge, *Salvation Army*, p. 92, identifying this as part of an 'ancient tradition' of 'rough music'

[7] Bailey, 'Salvation Army', p. 234.

forefront of peaceful protest.[8] The basis of the criticism from other religious groups seems not to have been related to doctrinal conflict, though Sandall does note that the *Church Times* had queried how any good could 'be expected to come of a movement which systemically takes the opposite line to St Paul's injunction that women should keep silence in the churches'.[9] More generally the criticism is directed at the perceived 'vulgarity' of the Army's approach to worship, which was thought to 'coarsen religion' and thereby offended 'respectable' people.[10] Thus the religious press is reported as describing Army meetings as 'like a rowdy company in a public-house making a game of religion', as involving 'vulgar, senseless noise', and as entering on 'the downward path of pandering to the lowest tastes of the most degraded classes'.[11] This type of reaction indicates that to certain sections of 'respectable' society, the noisy Salvation Army marches through the streets would be seen as 'behaving badly', because of the inappropriate behaviour utilised in the name of evangelising Christianity.[12] As one *Times* leader asserted, 'The worship they conduct... is not quite of the sober and monotonous character that finds most favour with English respectability'.[13] Similarly, the Lord Chancellor, responding to a question about the Salvation Army riots, noted that, while the Army was 'sincere and well-intended', nevertheless 'it is the duty of religious persons to avoid the prosecution of their objects in a manner which may give any unnecessary occasion for disorderly proceedings on the part of those who are opposed to them'.[14]

Such criticisms do not, however, explain the violent opposition which the Army aroused in the 1880s. This seems to stem from other sources, though it probably found some legitimacy in the fact that Army's activities were not approved by the older religious bodies. The Army felt it had a clear mission to bring the Christian religion to those whom existing

---

[8] Horridge, *Salvation Army*, pp. 114-5. This refers to high-level discussions in 1882 about a possible union between the Army and the Church of England. See also PRO/HO/45/9607/A2886/16, with the petition submitted to the Home Secretary by the Mayor of Basingstoke in August 188: the first four signatories are the Vicar and three other clergyman. This file also contains a 'counter-petition' sent a few days later, on which the first signature is that of the Congregational minister.

[9] *Church Times*, 25 November 1881, quoted by R. Sandall, *The History of the Salvation Army* (Thomas Nelson and Sons Ltd, London, 1950), vol. 2, p. 161.

[10] Bailey, 'Salvation Army', p. 241.

[11] See Sandall, *Salvation Army*, pp. 162-3.

[12] For the growth of the concept of 'respectable' society, see F. M. L. Thompson, *The Rise of the Respectable Society* (Fontana, London, 1988).

[13] *The Times*, 13 October 1881.

[14] *The Times*, 5 May 1882, p. 10.

religious organisations failed to reach – what William Booth himself referred to as the 'submerged tenth'.[15] This was, in effect, the poor and the working class. It seems likely that there would have been some working class hostility to such intrusion, including its threat to aspects of established working class culture.[16] This hostility could then be used by local tradespeople, and in particular brewers and publicans who objected to the Salvationists' promotion of teetotalism. Interestingly, the Skeleton Army seems to have been the result of a middle-class channelling of natural working class hostility to the Salvationist movement. This background to the attempts to disrupt the Salvation Army's processions by violence may be seen as being reflected in the unsympathetic attitude of the magistracy towards the Salvation Army, at least in some areas.[17]

Beatty v Gillbanks – The Salvation Army versus the Skeleton Army

The case of *Beatty v Gillbanks* arose out of a clash between the Salvation Army and the Skeleton Army in the Somerset town of Weston-Super-Mare where there had been several 'run-ins' during the first couple of months of 1882.[18] On 23 March a Salvation Army procession of over 100 was accompanied by a 'disorderly and riotous mob of over 2,000 persons'.[19] The police lost control of the situation for a time and there was much fighting, though it seems that no one was charged with any offence.[20] These events led to the publication of a notice in the name of two of the local magistrates which, in the light of the recent disturbances, required, ordered and directed 'all persons to abstain from assembling to the

---

[15] See Bailey, 'Salvation Army', p. 235.

[16] *Ibid*, pp. 240-1.

[17] See also Sandall, *Salvation Army*, chapter 30, in which he alleges an 'unholy alliance' between brewers and magistrates.

[18] The West Country seems to have been one of the main areas in which opposition to the Salvation Army manifested itself in counter-marches, very often involving some degree of violence. See Bailey, 'Salvation Army'; Horridge, *Salvation Army*.

[19] This information is taken from the case stated by the magistrates: (1882) 15 Cox CC 138, p. 140. Nevertheless, the figure of 2,000 protesters must be viewed as a possible exaggeration, given that the 1881 census records the total population of Weston-Super-Mare as only just over 6,000. On the other hand, there is some evidence of Skeleton Army providing 'mutual support' between towns in the West Country in late 1882, so it is possible that even in March 1882 the numbers were swollen by 'outsiders' See Horridge, *Salvation Army*, p. 102.

[20] The case stated particularly notes that neither Beatty, leading the procession, nor either of the others later arrested with him, were seen to commit any act of violence on 23 March: *Beatty v Gillbanks* (1882) 15 Cox CC 138, p. 140.

disturbance of the public peace within the said parish'.[21] The notice was displayed around the town, and a copy was served on Beatty. This notice did not specifically refer to the Salvation Army. Some issued in other towns were more explicit as to their intended target. For example, a notice issued by the Basingstoke Magistrates in February 1882 specifically related to Salvation Army processions, while at the same time requiring people from assembling to protest at such processions (thus maintaining at least a semblance of even-handedness).[22]

The use of notices of this kind was encouraged by the Home Office. There was in effect a 'standard letter' used in response to questions from magistrates or mayors as to how they should deal with problems arising from Salvation Army processions.[23] An example is the letter sent to the Town Clerk of Stamford on 4 October 1881, which contained the following advice: 'Such processions not being illegal in themselves cannot in the absence of other circumstance be legally prevented; but where they provoke antagonism, and lead to riotous collisions... the magistrates should by every means in their power endeavour to prevent them'. They should therefore 'cause' a sworn information to be laid by the Chief Constable, showing why a breach of the peace, and probably a riot, will follow from further processions. The magistrates should then 'issue notices and promulgate them to the effect that such information having been laid... they give notice to all persons who intend to take part in such processions that the processions cannot be permitted to take place'.[24] The 'leaders of the movement' should be called upon to prevent any processions. If it is necessary, nevertheless, to prevent processions, then the police should be reinforced by assistance from the county police and the swearing-in of special constables.

> The forming of the procession should be stopped, each person being told the reason why it will not be allowed, and they should be urged

---

[21] *Ibid.*

[22] PRO/HO45/9607/A2886/29.

[23] In a parliamentary answer to a question on the issue, Home Secretary Sir William Harcourt defended his use of the letter by stating that it had been drawn up on the advice of the Law Officers and had been used 'for several years', *Hansard*, 1882, 267, col 990. The MP for Scarborough, Mr. W. S. Caine, a leading figure in several temperance organisations, appears to have been a regular questioner on the issue, see, *Hansard*, 268, 1882, col. 544; 1882, col. 1271; 1882, col. 1826; 1882, col. 1941.

[24] PRO/HO45/9607/A2886/18B. Similar letters were sent to Basingstoke on 1 April 1881, and to Exeter on 14 October 1881. No evidence remains that a letter was sent to Weston-Super-Mare, but it seems likely that by the spring of 1882 the advice of the Home Office would have become widely known amongst local authorities. The letter to Stamford was reproduced in *The Times*, 11 October 1881, p. 6.

to disperse quietly before force is used.... If, however, in spite of every effort to prevent it, the attempt to form a procession is persevered in, force may be used to prevent it, and care should be taken that sufficient force for that purpose is at hand.[25]

It will be seen that this letter contains clear and specific advice, and that the actions of the Weston-Super-Mare magistrates followed the Home Office recommendations.

Despite this, on the following Sunday (26 March 1882) Beatty again led a Salvation Army procession through Weston-Super-Mare, consisting of '100 or more persons'.[26] The accompanying mob started with only about 100 persons, but numbers rapidly increased as the procession passed on. Eventually Beatty was stopped by a police sergeant and asked if he had received the magistrates' notice. When he admitted that he had, he was then told to stop leading the procession and disperse, or he would be arrested. Beatty refused and was arrested. Two other Salvation Army officers, William Mullins and Thomas Bowden took over the leadership of the procession and were also arrested. At the subsequent hearing, all three were found to have been engaged in an 'unlawful assembly... to the disturbance of the public peace'. They were bound over to keep the peace, in their own recognisances, with two sureties, for twelve months.[27] In default they were to be imprisoned for three months. The defendants, as seems to have been commonly the case with Salvationists in this situation, refused to be bound over and were therefore committed to Shepton Mallet gaol.[28] Although the defendants indicated their objection to the magistrates' ruling, the magistrates initially refused to state a case for the High Court.[29] An order was obtained requiring them to do so, and to release the defendants from gaol pending the hearing.[30]

---

[25] *Ibid.* The reason was 'fear of a collision and a breach of the peace'

[26] (1882) 15 Cox CC 138, p. 140.

[27] *The Times*, 5 April 1882. The amounts were, respectively, £100 for Beatty, £50 each for Bowden and Mullins; £50 each for Beatty, £25 for the others.

[28] See, for example, *The Times*, 9 September 1879. Note also the reports of Captain Maycock apparently using revelations of his experiences in Warwick Gaol to attract people to his preaching in Leamington, *The Times*, 21 October 1879, p. 8; 28 October 1879, p. 6. See also Sandall, *Salvation Army*, p. 186; *The Times*, 5 April 1882.

[29] 'Stating a case' for the High Court was (and in many circumstances still is) the standard route of appeal from the magistrates where a point of law was in issue. See David Bentley's chapter in this volume.

[30] Sandall, *Salvation Army*, p. 186; Horridge, *Salvation Army*, p. 108. The Home Secretary had already been asked to ensure that the defendants received certain privileges while in prison, particularly on account of Beatty's alleged 'delicate' health: PRO/HO45/9619/A15220, documents 3 and 4.

Beatty v Gillbanks – the Queen's Bench hearing

The Queen's Bench hearing was seen as a test case for the way in which local councils and magistrates had been dealing with problems arising from the Salvation Army processions. The hearing took place on 13 June 1882 before two judges, Justice Field and Justice Cave. It is clear from the report of the exchanges between judges and counsel that the judges were hostile to the prosecution arguments, and sympathetic to the Salvation Army. To the allegation that the Army paraded the streets intending to collect a mob, Justice Field replied:

> Surely not a 'mob' in the evil sense of the word. Their object is to awaken some sense of religion in the lower classes, and with that view they go through the streets singing hymns in order to induce people to follow them to their meeting-house and join in their religious services. Can this fairly be called 'collecting a mob'?[31]

Neither judgment makes any reference at all to the magistrates' notice distributed following the events of the 23 March, nor indeed to the problems that had arisen on previous occasions. The focus was simply on what the Salvation Army were doing on the day of the arrests. On that basis, both judges found that its members were acting perfectly lawfully. They had no intention to commit any riotous or other unlawful act, which the court saw as being essential to the offence of unlawful assembly. There was therefore no basis for binding them over to keep the peace. Justice Field stated that it was the *members of the Skeleton Army* who ought to be dealt with by the magistrates and the police. In not respecting the rights of the Salvation Army to march:

> there is no doubt that the magistrates and police... will understand their duty and not fail to do it efficiently, or hesitate, should the need arise, to deal with the Skeleton Army and other disturbers of the public peace as they did in the present case with the appellants.[32]

---

[31] (1882) 15 Cox CC 138, p. 143. It is possible that the approach of the Queen's Bench judges was influenced by the views expressed in parliament on 16 May 1882 by the Lord Chief Justice, when, during a debate on the Salvation Army, he had strongly supported the view that processing down the street singing hymns was a lawful act which deserved the protection of the law. His support for the Army was not unequivocal. He also noted that 'there was hardly any act which could not be so done as to become a nuisance to the public peace', and that local authorities might then have to 'determine that such acts, though lawful in themselves, should not be done, because the public peace was thereby endangered', *Hansard*, 1882, 269, cols 821-2; Horridge, *Salvation Army*, p. 107.

[32] (1882) 15 Cox CC 138, p. 146.

The case resulted, therefore, in a victory for the Salvation Army (judgment being given for the appellants with costs), and a defeat for their opponents.

The Aftermath

One effect of the decision in *Beatty v Gillbanks* was to cast doubt on the advice which had been given to local authorities by the Home Office. The judgment made no reference to this, but immediately afterwards the Home Office sought advice from the Law Officers on the contents of the letter which the Home Office had been using. The advice was that, in the light of *Beatty v Gillbanks* (assuming that the Home Secretary was not proposing to challenge the view of the law expressed in that decision), the letter would require 'considerable modification'.[33] The advice should be that Salvation Army marches were not unlawful even though they might induce others to commit a breach of the peace. Persuasion only should be used to prevent the Army from forming a procession, and while processing peaceably they were entitled to protection.

In fact there is little evidence of subsequent direct Home Office intervention, even though problems with Salvation Army processions continued through the 1880s.[34] Local authorities at times tried to resort to local legislation (i.e. bye-laws) to deal with the situation, but it was unclear whether this was an appropriate use of local authority powers, and they were challenged both in the courts and in parliament.[35] There was no suggestion of national legislation being used to address the problem, though there were petitions for a general power to be used against the Salvation Army.[36] Indeed in 1888 there is a letter on file indicating that the Home Secretary 'did not at present see his way to promoting legislation on the area'.[37] It was not until some 50 years later, with the enactment of the Public Order Act 1936, passed in the light of problems arising from fascist processions and meetings, that national legislation addressed the matter.

---

[33] PRO/HO45/9613/A9275/19.

[34] Horridge, *Salvation Army*, p. 108, suggesting most relevant correspondence has been destroyed.

[35] See Horridge, *Salvation Army*, pp. 110-3; Bailey, 'Salvation Army', pp. 245-6.

[36] Horridge, *Salvation Army*, p. 110.

[37] PRO/HO/45/9613/A9275/38.

The Hunting Protests

From the end of the 1980s there has been increasingly strong opposition to hunting, particularly hunting with dogs. In 1993 *The Times* contains some 75 entries dealing with the issue – that is, more than one a week. Opposition included attempts to disrupt the activities of the hunts, by distracting the hounds, getting in the way of riders, or in any respect making it more difficult for the hunt to take place. Inevitably, this type of protest led to clashes between hunters and protesters. Some were violent, and there has been at least one fatality.[38] Most of the serious injuries seem to have been suffered by the protesters rather than the hunters.

In contrast to the response to the Salvation Army riots, the initial reaction of the police appears to have been generally to arrest protesters.[39] Protesters, in turn, had some success in seeking compensation for wrongful arrest. Actions for false imprisonment against the Hampshire police and the Lincolnshire police were settled out-of-court, with the police paying compensation.[40] The local authority elections of May 1993, however, produced a new dimension. In several relevant areas, Labour or Liberal Democrat councils supportive of the views of the hunt protesters were elected. This led to the prospect of the introduction of bans on hunting on council land, first imposed in Somerset (August 1993) and Leicestershire (September 1993).[41] Nevertheless, the hunting community was reported in November 1993 to be 'optimistic that the sport is under less threat than for some time'.[42] This may be in part because of what was in the wind from the Home Office.

On 6 November 1993 the Home Secretary, Michael Howard, announced a proposal to introduce a criminal offence of 'disrupting a country sport' as part of its drive to curb the activities of demonstrators who obstructed

---

[38] See *The Times*, 5 April 1993, p. 7. A 15 year-old boy protester was caught under a horse-box. A verdict of accidental death was recorded, *The Times*, 8 September 1993, p. 7.

[39] The arrests would seem to have been based generally on offences under the Public Order Act 1986 – for example, s.4 (threatening, abusive or insulting behaviour likely to provoke or cause fear of violence) – or under the common law power to arrest in order to prevent a 'breach of the peace' (see R. Stone, Breach of the Peace: the Case for Abolition, *Web Journal of Current Legal Issues*, 2001, 2. See also *Steel v UK* (1999) 28 EHRR 603.

[40] Hampshire police paid £16,200 to 28 protesters, *The Times*, 6 February 1993, p. 2; Lincolnshire police paid £8000 to an unspecified number of protesters, *The Times*, 11 November 1993, p. 11. Arrests continued. In 1999 a protester was awarded £3500 damages in an action against the police, following arrest in 1995 for 'breach of the peace' on his way to a hunt, *The Times*, 16 November 1999, Law Section, p. 3.

[41] See *The Times*, 7 August 1993, p. 7; 30 September 1993, p. 30.

[42] *The Times*, 1 November 1993, p. 2.

'traditional' country pursuits.[43] This was a marked contrast to the response
to the Salvation Army 'riots'. The Home Office acted largely 'behind the
scenes' to support the actions of local authorities, actions primarily
directed against the Salvation Army. There was a clear reluctance to
introduce national legislation to tackle the problem. In 1993, however, the
immediate reaction was to introduce national legislation, and create new
criminal offences. Moreover, the point of attack was not the modern
equivalent of the Salvation Army, the participants in the hunt, but the
protesters, that is the equivalent of the Skeleton Army. The Home
Secretary's proposals were eventually given effect in the Criminal Justice
and Public Order Act 1994 (considered in more detail below).

In contrast to the central government position, an increasing number of
local authorities started to ban hunting on their land. Surrey, Oxfordshire
and Northamptonshire did so in November 1993, with the British Field
Sports Society claiming that it was a 'purely political and anti-
establishment move'.[44] Devon followed suit in January 1994.[45] In
February, however, the legality of these bans was challenged in the
High Court. The Quantock Staghounds had sought judicial review of
Somerset's decision. On 9 February 1994, Justice Laws held that the ban
was unlawful.[46] The case was based on the proper interpretation of powers
under the Local Government Act 1972, and whether the phrase in section
120 (1)(b), granting powers for 'the benefit, improvement or development
of their area', could be interpreted to cover a ban on hunting based on
'ethical' or 'moral' objections to the practice.

Laws held that a prohibition on hunting could only be justified if the
relevant council 'reasonably concluded that the prohibition was objectively
necessary as the best means of managing the deer-herd, or was otherwise
required, on objective grounds, for the preservation or enhancement of the
amenity of their area'.[47] Where an activity was permissible under the general
law, then objections based on distaste or ethical views were insufficient to
give a local authority power to ban it. Whereas parliament could legislate
against activities on moral grounds, a subordinate body would be presumed
not to have that power 'unless the empowering statute positively required it
to bring its moral views to bear'.[48] The Liberal Democrat leader of Somerset

---

[43] *The Times*, 6 November 1993, p. 5.

[44] *The Times*, 17 November 1993, p. 2; 19 November 1993, p. 12.

[45] *The Times*, 15 January 1994, p. 6.

[46] *R v Somerset County Council, ex parte Fewings* [1995] 1 All ER 513.

[47] *Ibid*, p. 529.

[48] *Ibid*, p. 530.

Council described the ruling as 'extraordinary', and talked about seeking support from the '34 other county councils' that had introduced bans for an appeal.[49] The appeal was not heard until March 1995, when the Court of Appeal upheld the decision of Justice Laws, albeit on slightly narrower grounds.[50] In the meantime, in July 1994 Northamptonshire had overturned its ban in the face of legal action from the British Field Sports Society.[51] The challenge to hunting from local council bans was effectively stopped in its tracks.

It is tempting to see the High Court decision in *R v Somerset County Council, ex parte Fewings*, as parallel to the High Court decision in *Beatty v Gillbanks* as regards the Salvation Army.[52] In both cases the decision had the effect of confirming the right to engage in a lawful activity, emphasising that the law should be applied in a way which would allow it to continue. The resonance must not be pressed too far, however. In *Beatty v Gillbanks* the focus was on a common law criminal offence (unlawful assembly) and what was necessary to be proved to establish that offence; in *ex parte Fewings*, the focus was the exercise of local authority powers under a statutory provision – a question of administrative rather than criminal law. The judges in the two cases were therefore engaged in rather different tasks, and although the impact of both decisions was significant, they operated in rather different ways. *Beatty v Gillbanks*, while indicating that the magistrates had acted inappropriately on the facts of the case, inevitably left it open that other magistrates, faced with different facts, could find the Salvationists guilty.[53] *Ex parte Fewings*, at least on the basis on which the decision was reached at first instance, effectively prevented *all* local authorities from using their powers in the way Somerset County Council had done. On the other hand, it was only indirectly concerned with legal issues of 'public order', which were, of course the main focus of *Beatty v Gillbanks*.

---

[49] *The Times*, 10 February 1994, p. 4.

[50] [1995] 3 All ER 20. The majority took the view that the local authority had simply not addressed the section 120 criteria in reaching its decision; it left open the question of whether the 'cruelty' of hunting could be a relevant matter under those criteria. Simon Brown LJ, on the other hand, would have allowed the appeal.

[51] *The Times*, 15 July 1994, p. 10. The Council also agreed to pay the BFSS's legal costs of £10,750.

[52] [1995] 1 All ER 513.

[53] Prosecutions and convictions did continue (though not without further controversy) through the 1880s.

The Criminal Justice and Public Order Act 1994

The next important event was the passing of the Criminal Justice and
Public Order Act 1994, containing a provision, Section 68, designed to
fulfil Michael Howard's promise. But the eventual provision was more
general in its scope, bringing the offence under the general heading of
'aggravated trespass'. The offence is wide enough to cover any trespasser
who disrupts a lawful activity taking place on land in the open air. The
actus reus needed to commit the offence involves trespass on land other
than a road or highway.[54] It would not, therefore, have covered the
activities of the Skeleton Army in its attempts to disrupt the Salvation
Army processions, since these activities nearly all took place on the public
highway. The intention (or *mens rea*) of the trespasser must be to
intimidate, obstruct or disrupt those engaged in the lawful activity. A
person reasonably suspected of committing an offence may be arrested by
a uniformed constable. In addition there is a power in section 69 for a
police officer to direct trespassers reasonably believed to be about to
commit or to have been involved in the commission of an offence under
section 68 to leave the land. It may also be used where two or more people
are suspected of trespassing with the common purpose of intimidation,
obstruction or disruption. A person failing to comply with such a direction
commits an offence, and may be arrested.

The enactment of this offence was unsurprisingly welcomed by the
hunting community. It was used for the first time in November 1994 to
arrest five hunt saboteurs who had been blowing horns near a hunt in
Northamptonshire, and has been regularly used since then.[55] As a
postscript it should, of course, be noted that following the election of
the Labour government in 1997, the attitude of central government has
changed. The government has allowed free votes on whether hunting
should be banned which have shown a clear majority in the House of
Commons in favour of banning hunting with dogs; though this is not
supported in the House of Lords. It seems likely, however, that at some
point in the next few years a ban, or licensing system, of some sort will be
imposed.

---

[54] That is, the physical acts required for the offence, ignoring the mental state (or *mens rea*)
of the person performing them.

[55] *The Times*, 7 November 1994, p. 2.

Comparisons and Conclusions

In both cases we have an example of a lawful activity being disrupted by protesters. In the end, in both cases the law eventually operates to protect the lawful activity. What comparisons and conclusions can be drawn between these two sequences of events? The major difference lies in the role of the Home Office, rather than in popular attitudes. In the nineteenth century the Home Office initially appeared to be more favourable to the anti-Salvation Army protesters, whereas in the twentieth century the sympathies appeared to lie with the hunt. Thus in the 1880s the approach was to control the behaviour of the group who, while acting lawfully, was thought to be 'provoking' a violent response; in the 1990s the control was targeted at those actually taking part in the disruptive activity. These approaches were translated into practice in different ways, however.

The possible role of 'class conflict' in both situations might be considered at first sight as providing a possible explanation for the difference in the Home Office's attitude. In relation to the Salvation Army, the aim of the Army was to involve 'working class' people in its activities. This may well have been seen as some sort of threat by the middle classes, and therefore by the Home Office. In contrast, hunting is seen as predominantly an upper class or upper-middle class activity, so it is not surprising that a Conservative Home Secretary would act to protect it. In truth, however, both situations are more complex. Not only were there divisions in attitudes amongst the Victorian working class itself towards the Army's evangelistic and teetotal approaches, but also, there is evidence that to some extent both sides were being 'manipulated' by the 'middle class'. This includes the senior officers of the Army on the one hand, and the local business people (in particular the brewers) on the other. Turning to the twentieth century example, although hunting is seen as a middle/upper class activity, it actually involves a wide range across the country classes. Nor can it be said that the protesters were drawn from any particular class. In the end, therefore, attempts to analyse either situation on the basis of class conflict require more detailed and sophisticated analysis than is currently possible on present information. The suspicion must be, however, that even further investigation might well come to the conclusion that there is no simple 'class' analysis of either situation.

As regards the position of the press, supposedly reflecting 'public' opinion, as the columns of *The Times*[56] and other newspapers including the

---

[56] Which as a 'newspaper of record' for both periods, provides a reasonable basis for comparison of attitudes.

radical press, such as *Reynolds News*, indicate, attitudes towards the Army varied. There are some sympathetic articles.[57] The Army was also clearly seen as to some extent the authors of their own misfortune, by the manner in which they chose to evangelise.[58] In relation to hunting, press reaction has been similarly varied. *The Times* seems to have remained largely neutral, with no leading articles on the issue during 1993 or 1994. The only feature dealing directly with the arguments for and against hunting was an article by Simon Jenkins arguing that the National Trust should not impose a ban on hunting on its land, while at the same time indicating his own distaste for the sport.[59] The reporting of both sides appears to have been largely objective. In neither period does the press appear as a significant influence on the legal and political processes which took place, an interesting reflection on wider public attitudes about the levels of 'bad' behaviour involved, especially in the light of Rowbotham and Stevenson's chapter.

In both cases a High Court decision has been an important part of the course of events. The decision in *Beatty v Gillbanks* was, legally, more directly relevant to public order issues, but *R v Somerset County Council, ex parte Fewings* was also important in that it probably gave impetus to the pro-hunting lobby, and may have discouraged some protesters. The two cases do not, however, indicate any significant difference in the role of the courts in the two periods under consideration. This leaves the approach of the government as indicating the main discontinuity between the 1880s and the 1990s. This is shown not only in which 'side' was taken in the dispute (i.e. the 'lawful actors' or the 'protesters'), but perhaps more significantly, in the methods used to deal with the problem.

In the 1880s the public order issue was seen as a matter for the local authorities, to be dealt with by existing powers. It was assumed that there were sufficient powers already available to the police and magistrates under the common law to deal with any problems. The only issue was how, and in what direction, those powers were to be employed. The Home Office could give a lead, but ultimately could not direct what should be done. Any movement for local or national legislation specific to the problem was resisted. By contrast, in the 1990s, the almost immediate response was to propose enactment of national legislation, despite the fact that there were already extensive relevant police powers both at common

---

[57] For example, *The Times*, 13 October 1881, p. 9.

[58] For example, *The Times*, 26 January 1882, p. 9; 26 June 1882, p. 9. See also 10 October 1883, p. 9, on the problems the Army had encountered in Switzerland.

[59] *The Times*, 23 October 1993, p. 18.

law, or under statute.[60] The reason for this is probably a shift as regards the accepted view of the balance of responsibilities as regards maintaining public order. In the 1880s this was still regarded primarily as a matter for magistrates, as it had traditionally been, rather than for central government. In other words it was a local, rather than a national, issue. By the 1990s, however, the role of the justices had changed. The police, rather than the local magistracy, is regarded as bearing the main responsibility for public order, and, despite the fact that the police force is organised in regions rather than nationally, the Home Office is treated as answerable for the way in which the police operate, and whether they have sufficient powers to carry out their responsibilities. It is thus the move from local to centralised control that is the main reason why the common law offence of 'unlawful assembly' is thought to be adequate to deal with the situation in 1882, whereas in 1993 a special offence of 'aggravated trespass' is felt to be necessary to deal with this particular kind of 'bad behaviour'. A conclusion is difficult on which approach might in the long run be better designed to maintaining the appropriate balance between the various interests involved. The modern rush to legislation, however, does run the risk of over-regulating, and creating powers to deal with particular issues rather than establishing principles as to the amount of disorder which is tolerable in a civilised society. The case of *Beatty v Gillbanks* is almost certainly still a more significant contribution to that issue than is the Criminal Justice and Public Order Act 1994.

---

[60] Respectively, particularly including powers to control 'breaches of the peace', see R. Stone, 'Breach of the Peace: the Case for Abolition', p. 2; the Public Order Act 1986, and the Police and Criminal Evidence Act 1984.

Further Reading

J. Ashton, *The History of Gambling in England* (Duckworth, London, 1898).

V Bailey (ed.), *Policing and Punishment in Nineteenth Century Britain* (Croom Helm, London, 1981).

D. Bentley, *English Criminal Justice in the Nineteenth Century* (Hambledon, London, 1998).

L. Blom-Cooper, *Blasphemy: An ancient wrong or a modern right?* (Essex Hall Bookshop, 1971).

E. Bristow, *Vice and Vigilance: Purity movements in Britain since 1700* (Gill and Macmillan, Dublin, 1977).

J. Busfield, 'The Female Malady? Men, women and madness in nineteenth century Britain', *Sociology*, 1994, 28, 1.

A. Calder-Marshall, *Lewd, Blasphemous and Obscene* (Hutchinson, London, 1972).

K. Chesney, *The Victorian Underworld* (Readers Union, Newton Abbott, 1970).

S. Chibnall, *Law and Order News: An analysis of crime reporting in the British press* (Tavistock, London, 1977).

D. B. Cornish, *Gambling: A review of the literature* (Home Office Research Study No 42, HMSO, London, 1978).

S. Cohen, *Folk Devils and Moral Panics* (Paladin, St Albans, 1973).

S. D'Cruze (ed.), *Everyday Violence in Britain, c1850-1950: Gender and class* (Longman, London, 2000).

H. Dean (ed.), *Begging and Street Level Economic Activity* (The Social Policy Press, Bristol, 1999).

D. M. Downes, B. P Davies, M. E. David and P. Stone, *Gambling, Work and Leisure* (Routledge and Kegan Paul, London, 1976).

L. Elliott and D. Atkinson, *The Age of Insecurity* (Verso, London, 1998).

C. Emsley, *Crime and Society in England 1750-1900* (Longman, London, 1996).

M. Foucault, *The History of Sexuality* (Vintage, New York, 1980), especially vol. 1.

D. Garland, *Punishment and Welfare* (Gower, Aldershot, 1985).

A. E. Graham and C. Emmas, *The Last Victim: The extraordinary life of Florence Maybrick, the wife of Jack the Ripper* (Headline, London, 1999).

J. Harris, *Private Lives, Public Spirit: Britain 1870–1914* (Penguin, London, 1993).

B. Harrison, 'State Intervention and Moral Reform in the Nineteenth Century' in P. Hollis (ed.) *Pressure from Without* (Edward Arnold, London, 1974).

G. Himmelfarb, *The Idea of Poverty. England in the early industrial age* (Faber and Faber, London, 1984).

R. Hopkins Burke, (ed.), *Zero Tolerance Policing* (Perpetuity Press, Leicester, 1998).

K. A. Jones, *A History of the Mental Health Services* (Routledge and Kegan Paul, London, 1972).

M. Jones, *Justice and Journalism* (Barry Rose, Chichester, 1974).

G. Kelling and C. Coles, *Fixing Broken Windows: Restoring order and reducing crime in our communities* (The Free Press, New York City, 1996).

C. Kenny, 'The Evolution of the Law of Blasphemy', *Cambridge Law Journal* 1922, 1.

D. Kidd-Hewitt and R. Osborn (eds), *Crime and the Media: The post-modern spectacle* (Pluto Press, London, 1995).

J. Knelman, *Twisting in the Wind: The murderess and the English press* (University of Toronto Press, Toronto, 1998).

L. W. Levy, *Blasphemy: Verbal offense against the sacred from Moses to Salman Rushdie* (Knopf, New York, 1993).

L. J. Ludovici, *The Itch for Play: Gamblers in high and low life* (Jarrolds, London, 1962).

M. Maguire, *et al* (eds), *The Oxford Handbook of Criminology* (Oxford University Press, Oxford, 1994).

S. Marcus, *The Other Victorian: A study of sexuality and pornography in mid-nineteenth century England* (Meridian, New York 1974).

M. N. Marks, 'Characteristics and causes of infanticide in Britain', *International Review of Psychiatry* 1996, 9.

J. S Mill, *On Liberty* (ed. S. Collini) (Cambridge University Press, Cambridge, 1989).

R. Munting, *An Economic and Social History of Gambling in Britain and the USA* (Manchester University Press, Manchester, 1996).

D. Nash, *Blasphemy in Modern Britain: 1789 to the present* (Ashgate, Aldershot, 1999).

D. Nash, 'Blasphemy in Victorian Britain? Foote and the freethinker', *History Today* 1995, 45, 10.

L. Nead, *Victorian Babylon: People, streets and images in nineteenth century London* (Yale, New Haven, 2000).

W. L. Parry-Jones, *The Trade in Lunacy: A study of private madhouses in England in the eighteenth and nineteenth centuries* (Routledge and Kegan Paul, London, 1971).

G. Pearson, *Hooligan. A history of respectable fears* (Macmillan, London, 1983).

H. Perkin, *The Rise of Professional Society. England since 1880* (Routledge, London, 1989).

G. Robertson, *Obscenity* (Weidenfeld and Nicolson, London, 1979).

N. Rogers, 'Policing the Poor in Eighteenth-Century London: The Vagrancy Laws and their Administration', *Histoire Sociale – Social History*, 24, 1991, pp. 127-47.

J. Rowbotham, '"All Our Past Proclaims Our Future": Popular biography and masculine identity during the Golden Age, 1850–1870', in I. Inkster (ed.), *The Golden Age. Essays in British economic and social history, 1850-1870* (Ashgate Publishing, Aldershot, 2000).

P. Schlesinger and H. Tumber, *Reporting Crime: The media politics of criminal justice* (Oxford University Press, Oxford, 1994).

R. Sindall, *Street Violence in the Nineteenth Century: Media panic or real danger?* (Leicester University Press, Leicester, 1990).

V. Skultans, *Madness and Morals: Ideas on insanity in the nineteenth century* (Routledge and Kegan Paul, London, 1975).

J. Springhall, *Youth, Popular Culture and Moral Panics* (Macmillan Press, London, 1998).

G. Stedman Jones, *Outcast London* (Oxford University Press, Oxford, 1971).

J. F Stephen, *Liberty Equality Fraternity* (ed. R. J. White) (Cambridge University Press, Cambridge, 1967).

K. Stevenson, 'The Respectability Imperative: A golden rule in cases of sexual assault?' in I. Inkster (ed.), *The Golden Age. Essays in British economic and social history, 1850-1870* (Ashgate Publishing, Aldershot, 2000).

D. Taylor, *Crime, Policing and Punishment in England 1750-1914* (Macmillan, Basingstoke, 1998).

H. Taylor, 'Rationing Crime: The political economy of criminal statistics since the 1850s', *The Economic History Review*, 1998, LI, 3.

N. Theriot, 'Women's Voices in the Nineteenth Century Medical Discourse: a step toward deconstructing science', *Journal of Women in Culture and Society*, 1993, 19, 1.

F M. L. Thompson, *The Rise of Respectable Society: A social history of Victorian Britain 1830-1900* (Fontana, London, 1988).

J. Tosh, *A Man's Place: Masculinity and the middle class home in Victorian England* (Yale, New Haven, 1999).

E. Trudgill, *Madonnas and Magdalens: The origins and development of Victorian sexual attitudes* (Heinemann, London, 1976).

J. Walkowitz, *City of Dreadful Delight: Narratives of sexual danger in late Victorian London* (Virago Press, London, 1992).

N. Walter, *Blasphemy Ancient and Modern* (Rationalist Press Association, London, 1990).

T. Ward, 'Legislating for human nature: legal responses to infanticide, 1860-1938', in M. Jackson (ed.), *Historical Perspectives on Child Murders and Concealment, 1500-2000* (Ashgate, Aldershot, 2002).

R. Webster, *A Brief History of Blasphemy: Liberalism, censorship and the satanic verses* (Southwold, 1990).

J. Weeks, *Sex, Politics and Society: The regulation of sexuality since 1800* (Longman, London, 1989), 2nd edn.

R. Weis, *Criminal Justice: The true story of Edith Thompson* (Hamish Hamilton, London, 1988, reprint, Penguin, London, 2001).

D. Wilson and J. Ashton, *What Everyone in Britain Should Know About Crime and Punishment* (Blackstone, London, 1999).

Index